In the SHADOW of the FALLEN TOWERS

The Seconds, Minutes, Hours, Days, Weeks, Months, and Years after the 9/11 Attacks

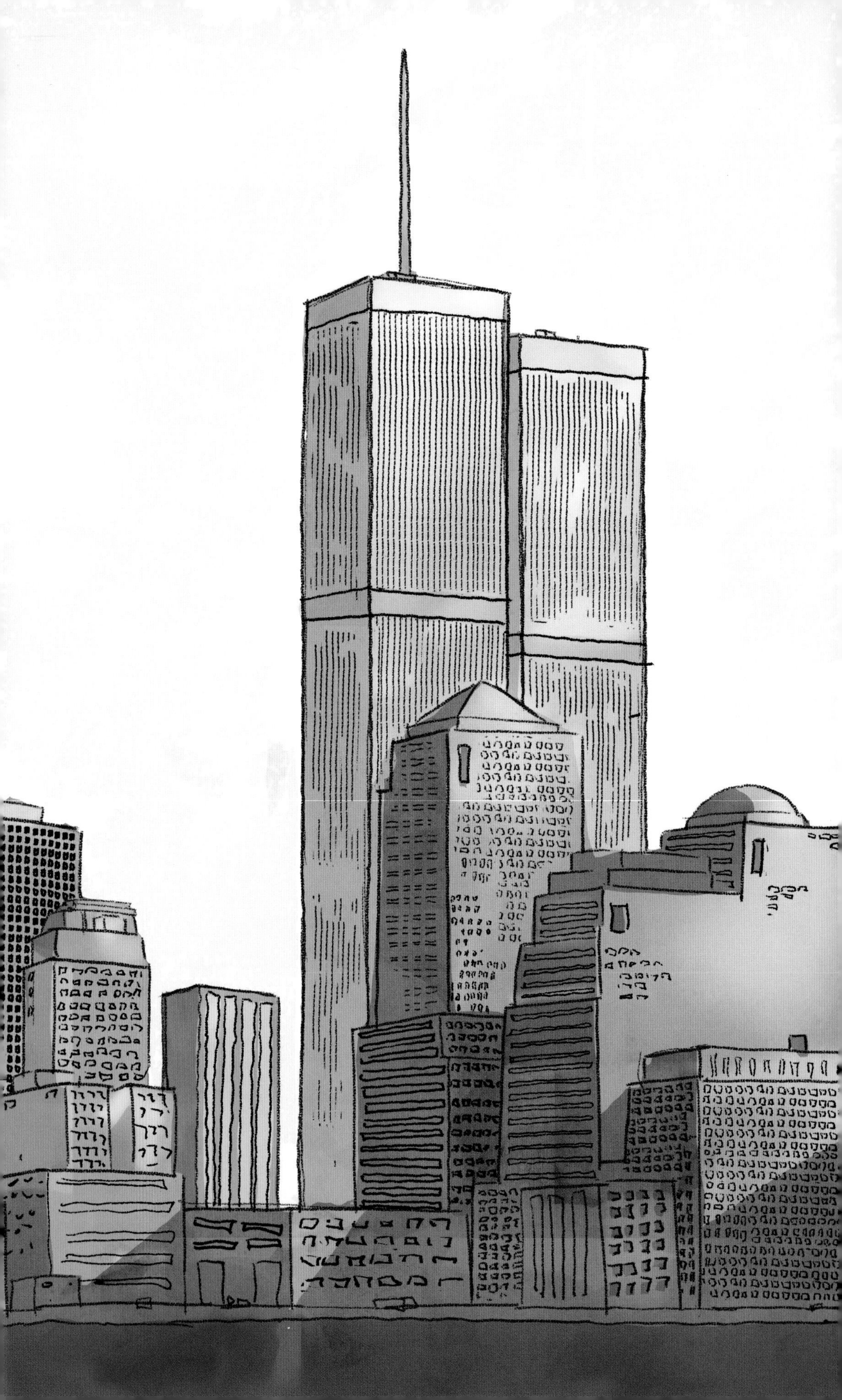

In the
SHADOW
of the
FALLEN
TOWERS

The Seconds, Minutes, Hours, Days, Weeks, Months, and Years after the 9/11 Attacks

Written and illustrated by
DON BROWN

Clarion Books
Imprints of HarperCollins*Publishers*

HARPER
alley

Dedicated to all those who are suffering as

a consequence of their work at the Pile

Clarion Books is an imprint of HarperCollins Publishers.
HarperAlley is an imprint of HarperCollins Publishers.

In the Shadow of the Fallen Towers
Copyright © 2021 by Don Brown
O'Sullivan family photo (p. 65) courtesy of Kate O'Sullivan

Library of Congress Control Number: 2023944598
ISBN 978-0-06-336098-3

The artist used pen and ink with digital paint to create the illustrations for this book.
Typography by Whitney Leader-Picone and Catherine Kung
24 25 26 27 28   COS   10 9 8 7 6 5 4 3 2 1

First paperback edition, 2024

9-11-01 10:28:00

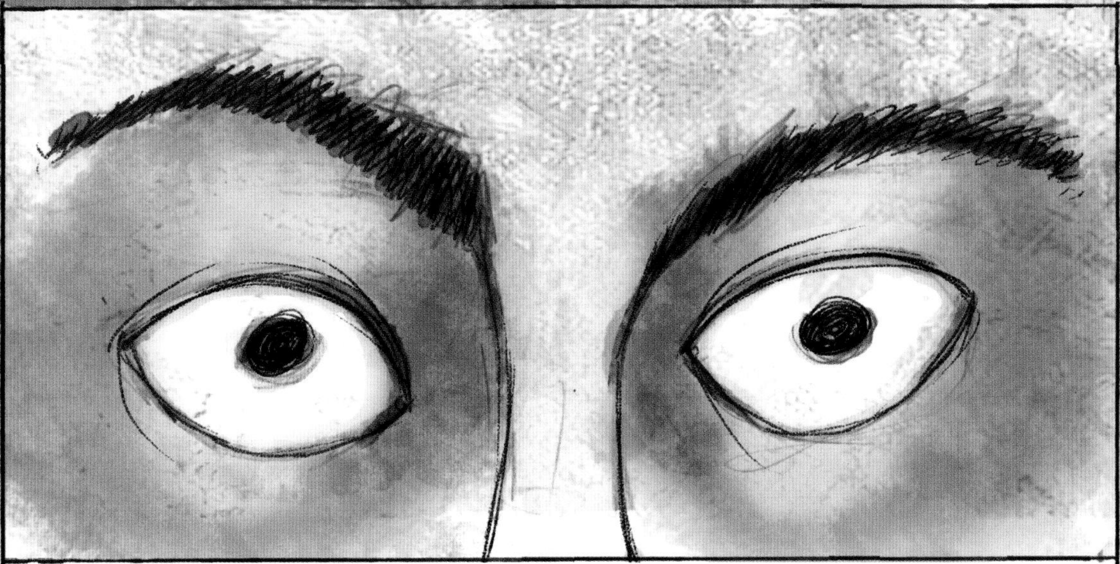

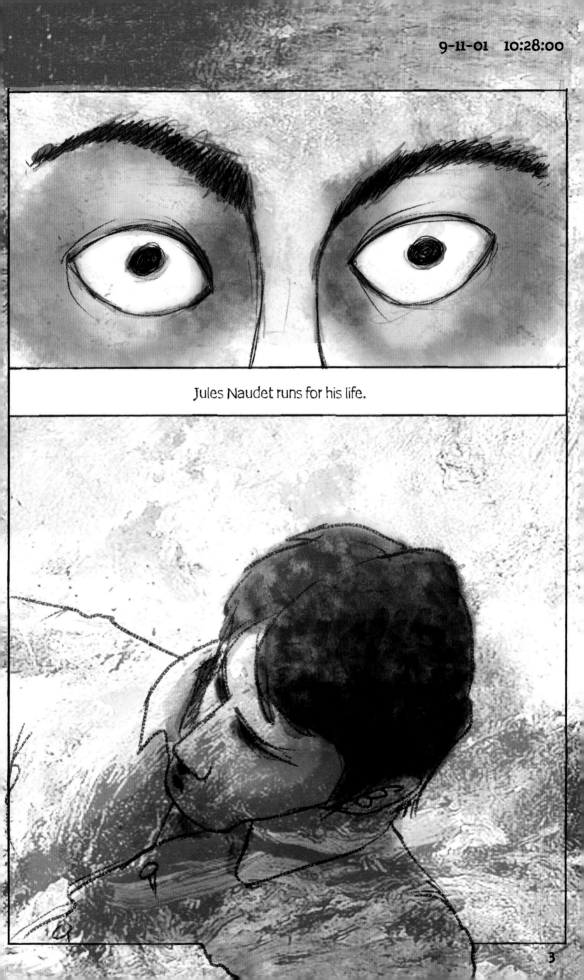

Jules Naudet runs for his life.

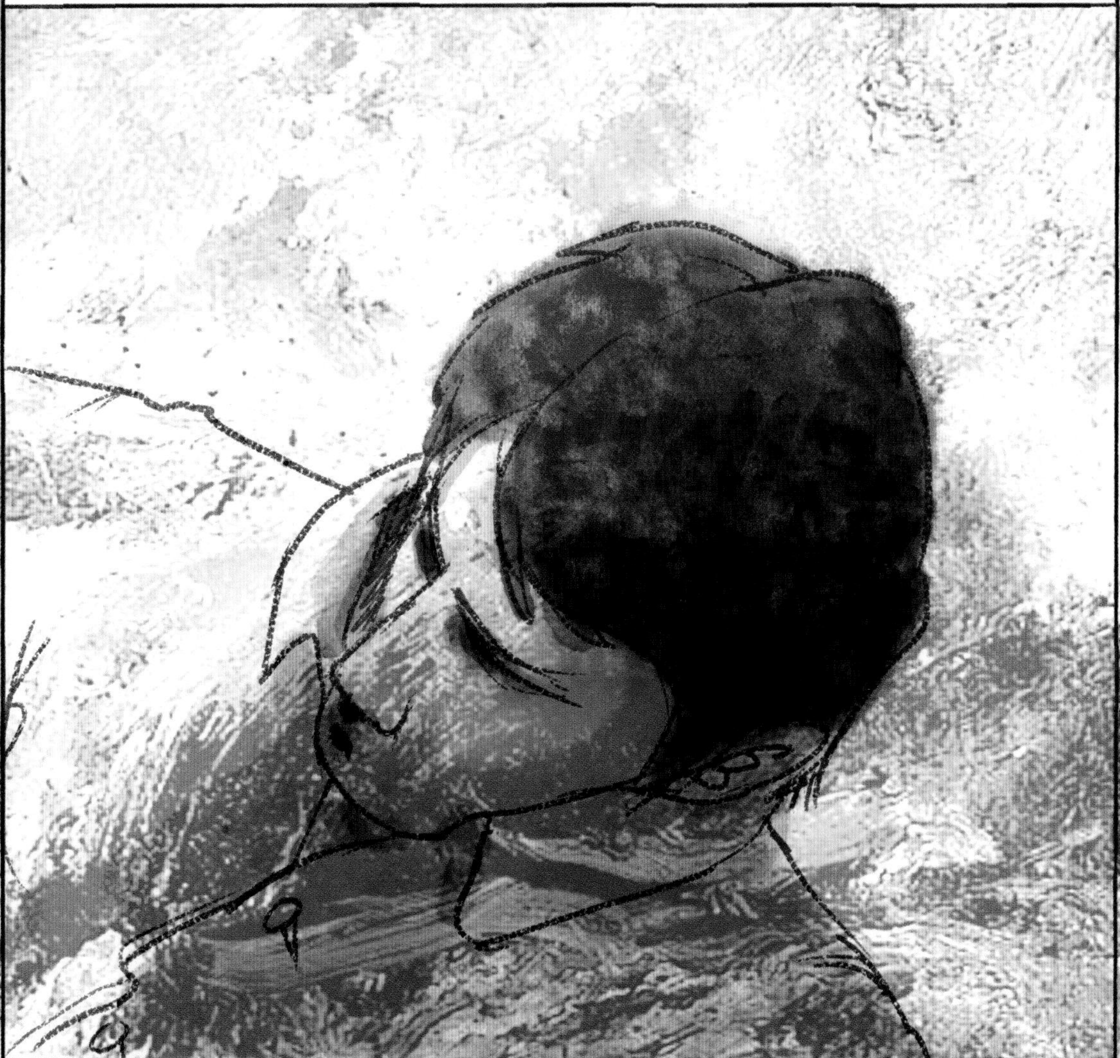

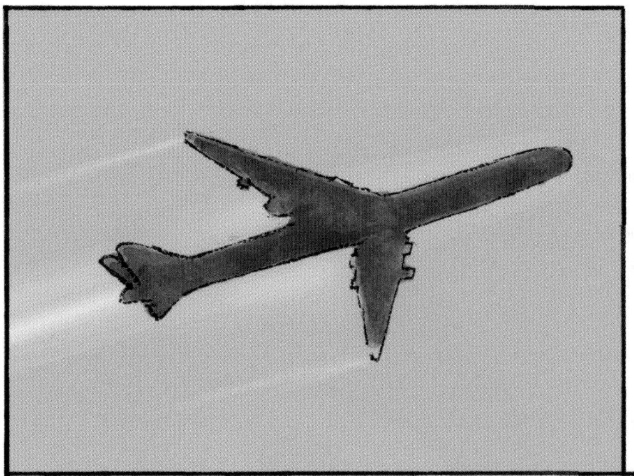

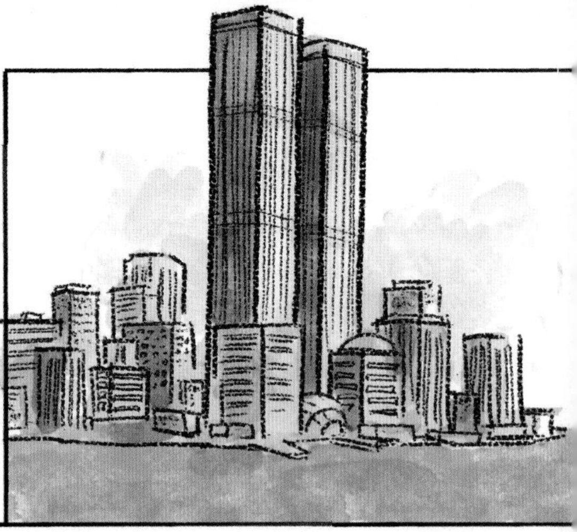

That morning, Jules had been with New York City Fire Department Chief Joseph Pfeifer and his firefighting crew in Lower Manhattan filming a documentary about the Fire Department. When the sound of a low-flying jet caught everyone's attention, Naudet swung his camera skyward and filmed a jetliner slamming into the North Tower of the World Trade Center.

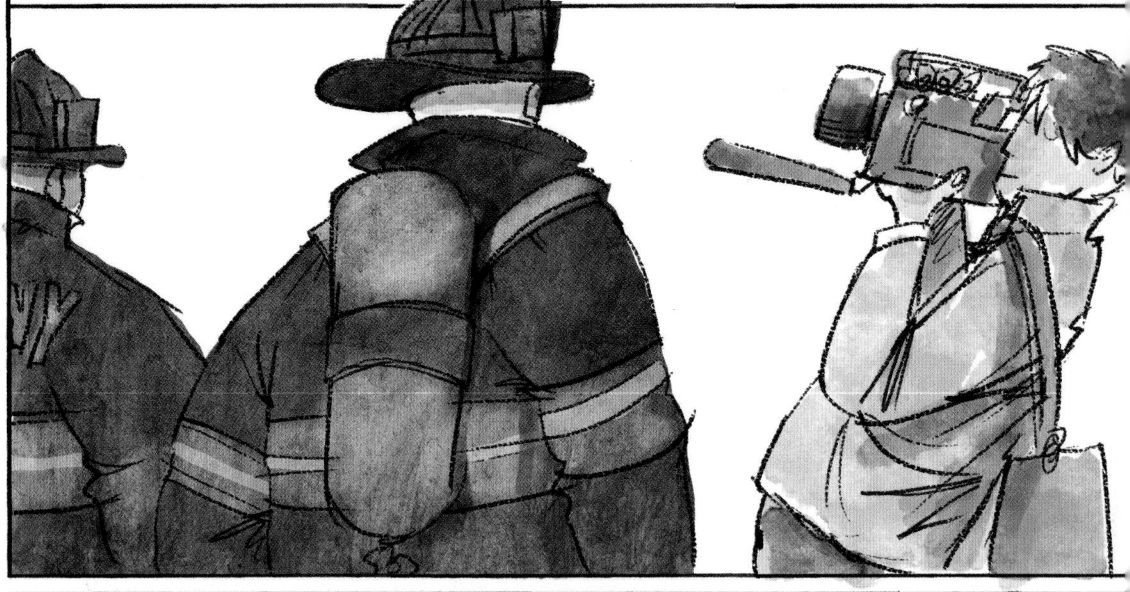

He followed the firefighters into the stricken building and was there when the South Tower of the World Trade Center collapsed after it, too, was struck by an airliner.

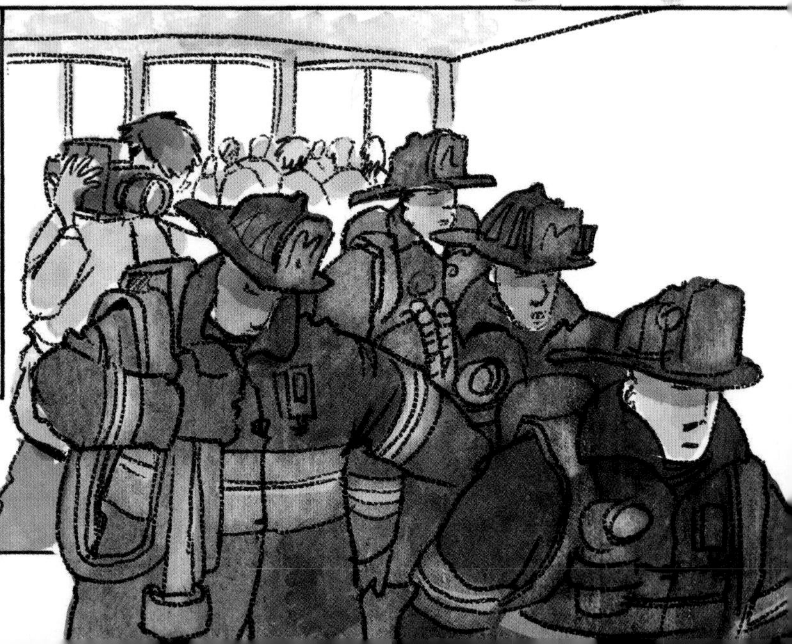

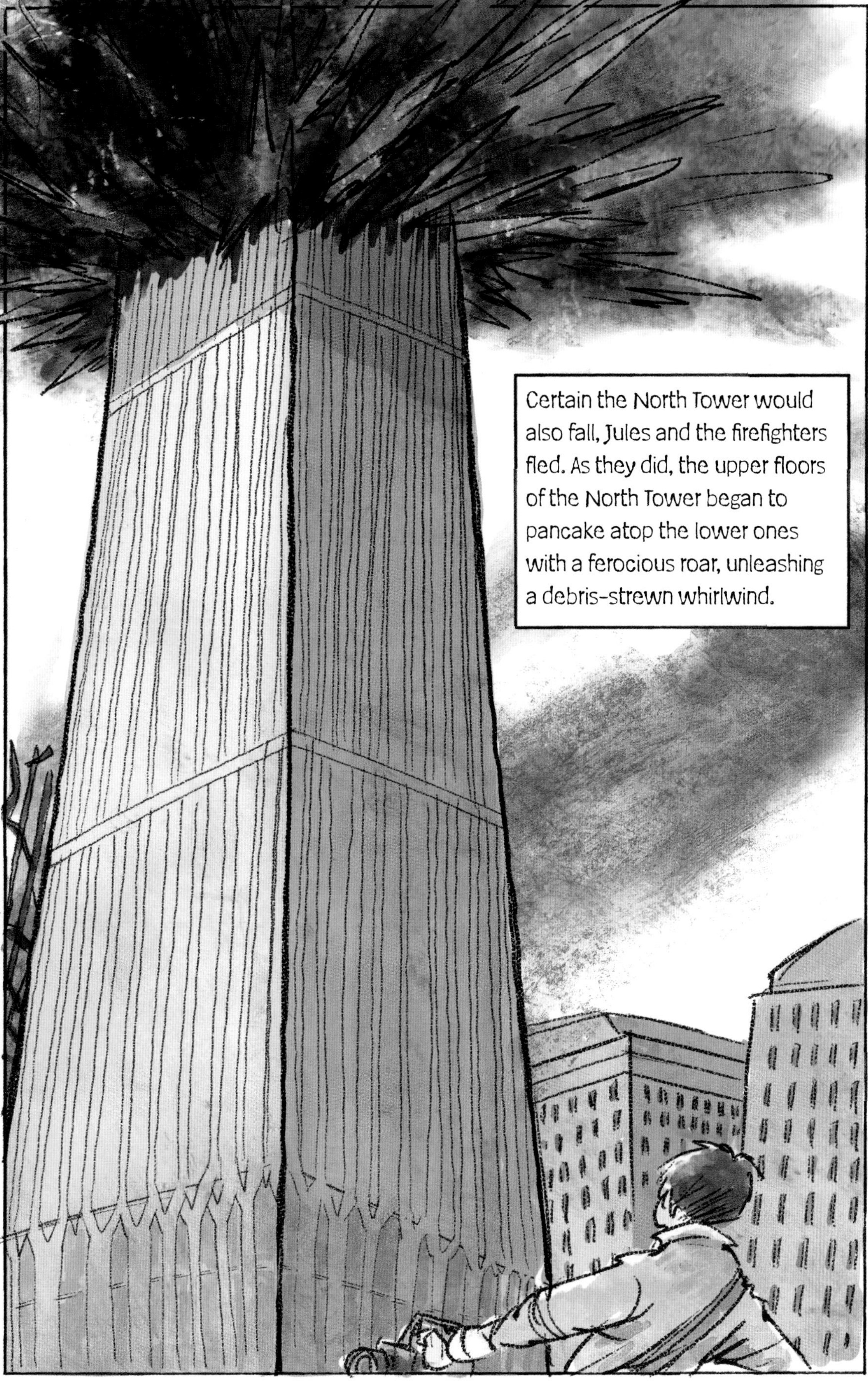
Certain the North Tower would also fall, Jules and the firefighters fled. As they did, the upper floors of the North Tower began to pancake atop the lower ones with a ferocious roar, unleashing a debris-strewn whirlwind.

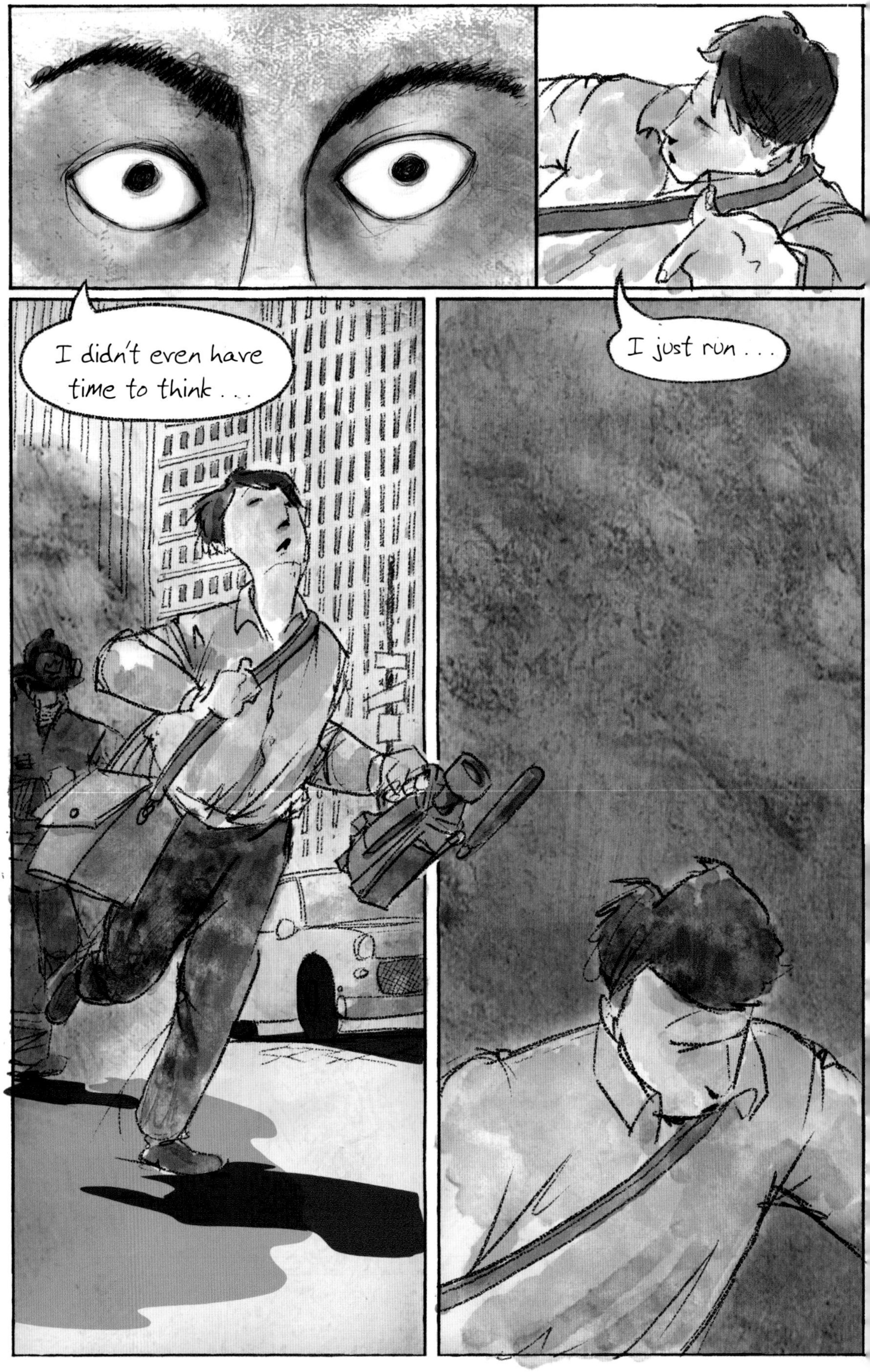
I didn't even have time to think . . .
I just run . . .

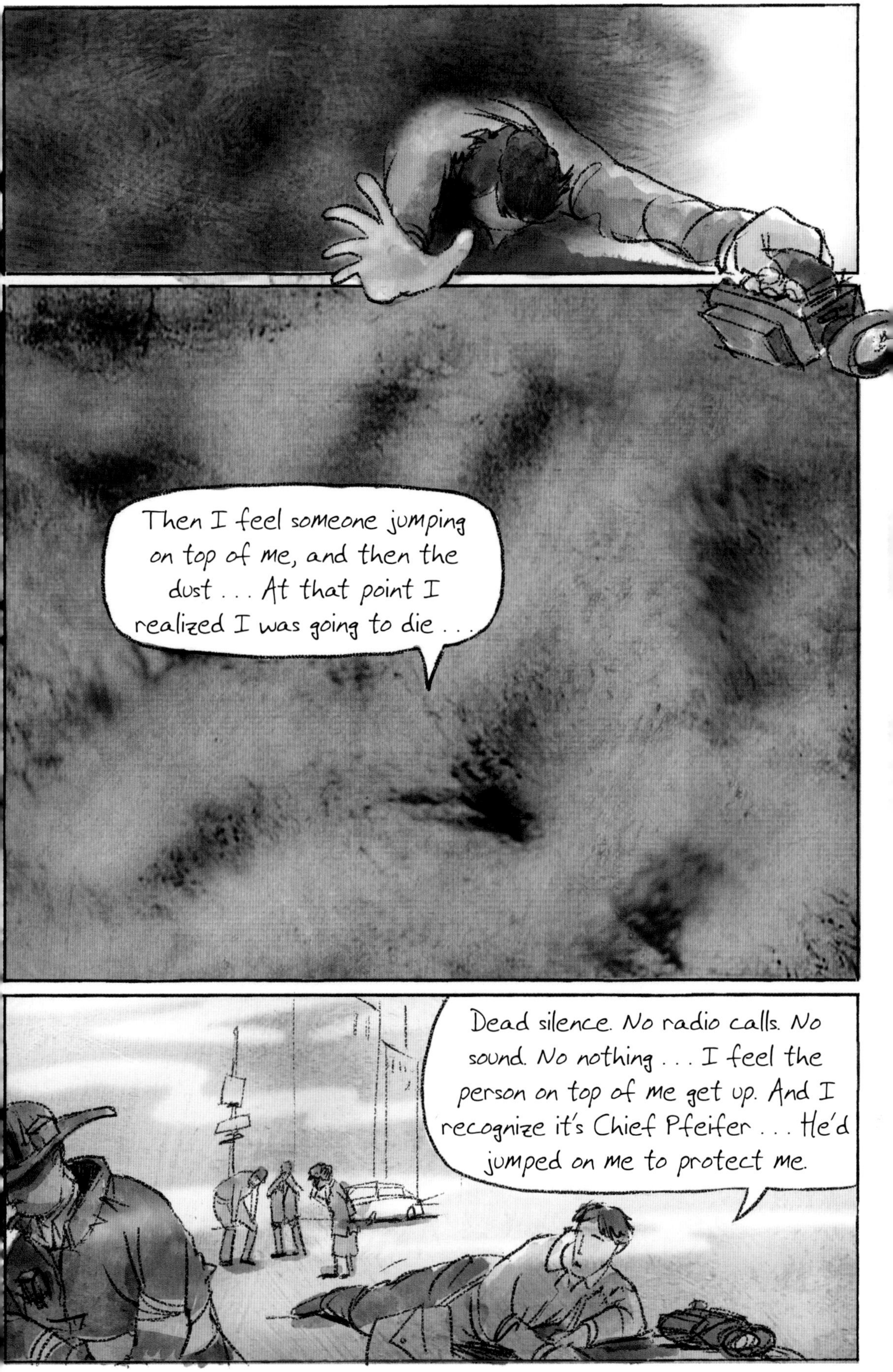

Then I feel someone jumping on top of me, and then the dust . . . At that point I realized I was going to die . . .
Dead silence. No radio calls. No sound. No nothing . . . I feel the person on top of me get up. And I recognize it's Chief Pfeifer . . . He'd jumped on me to protect me.

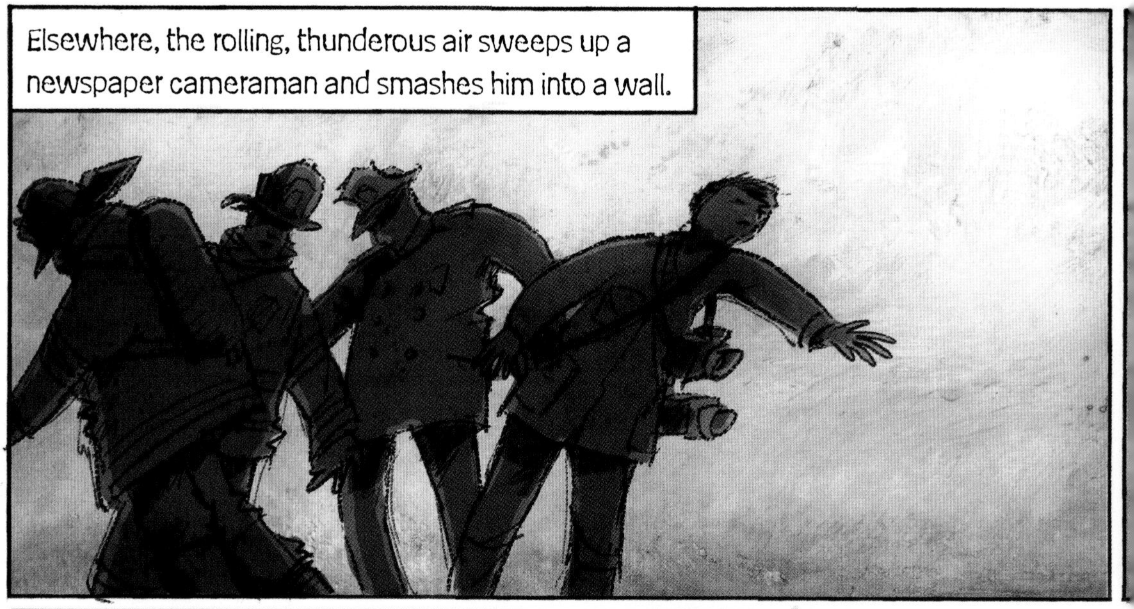
Elsewhere, the rolling, thunderous air sweeps up a newspaper cameraman and smashes him into a wall.

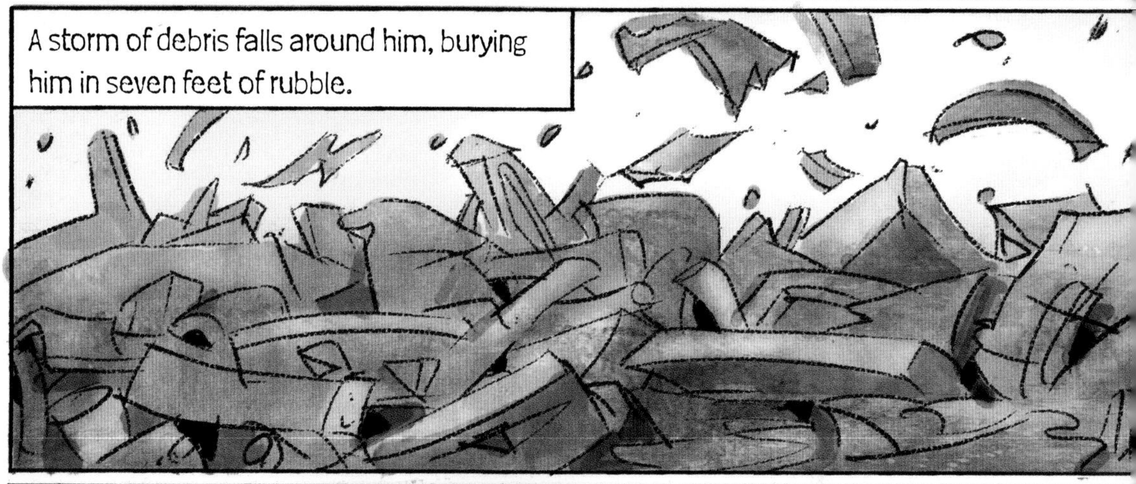
A storm of debris falls around him, burying him in seven feet of rubble.

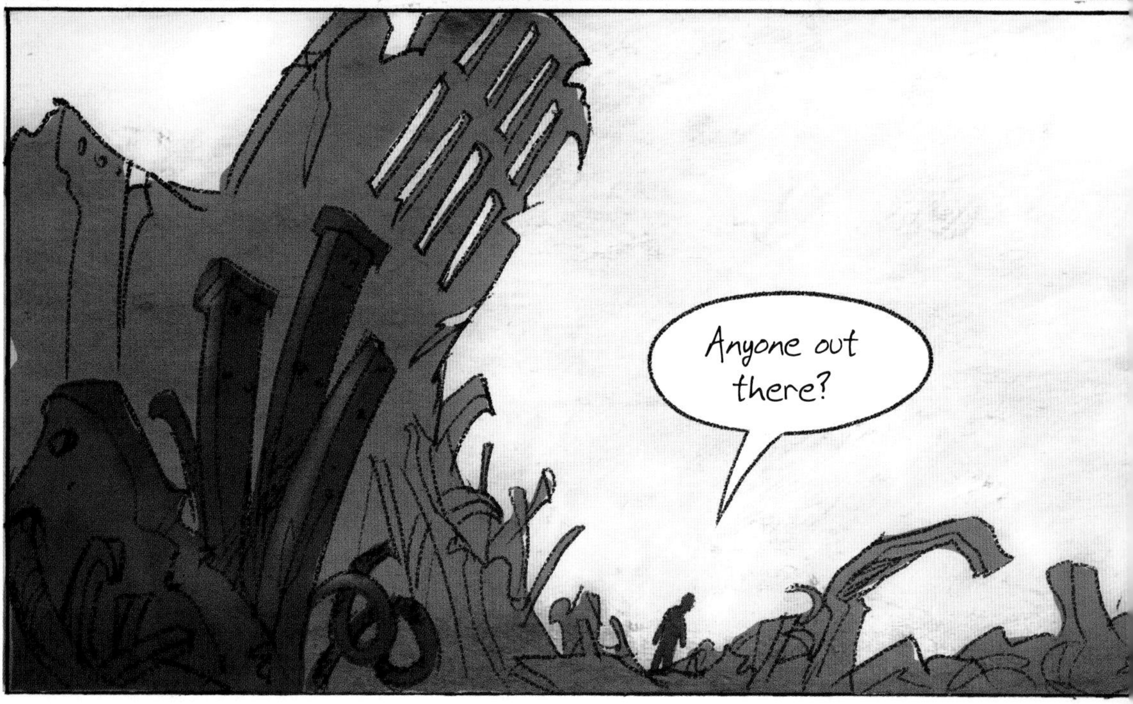
Anyone out there?

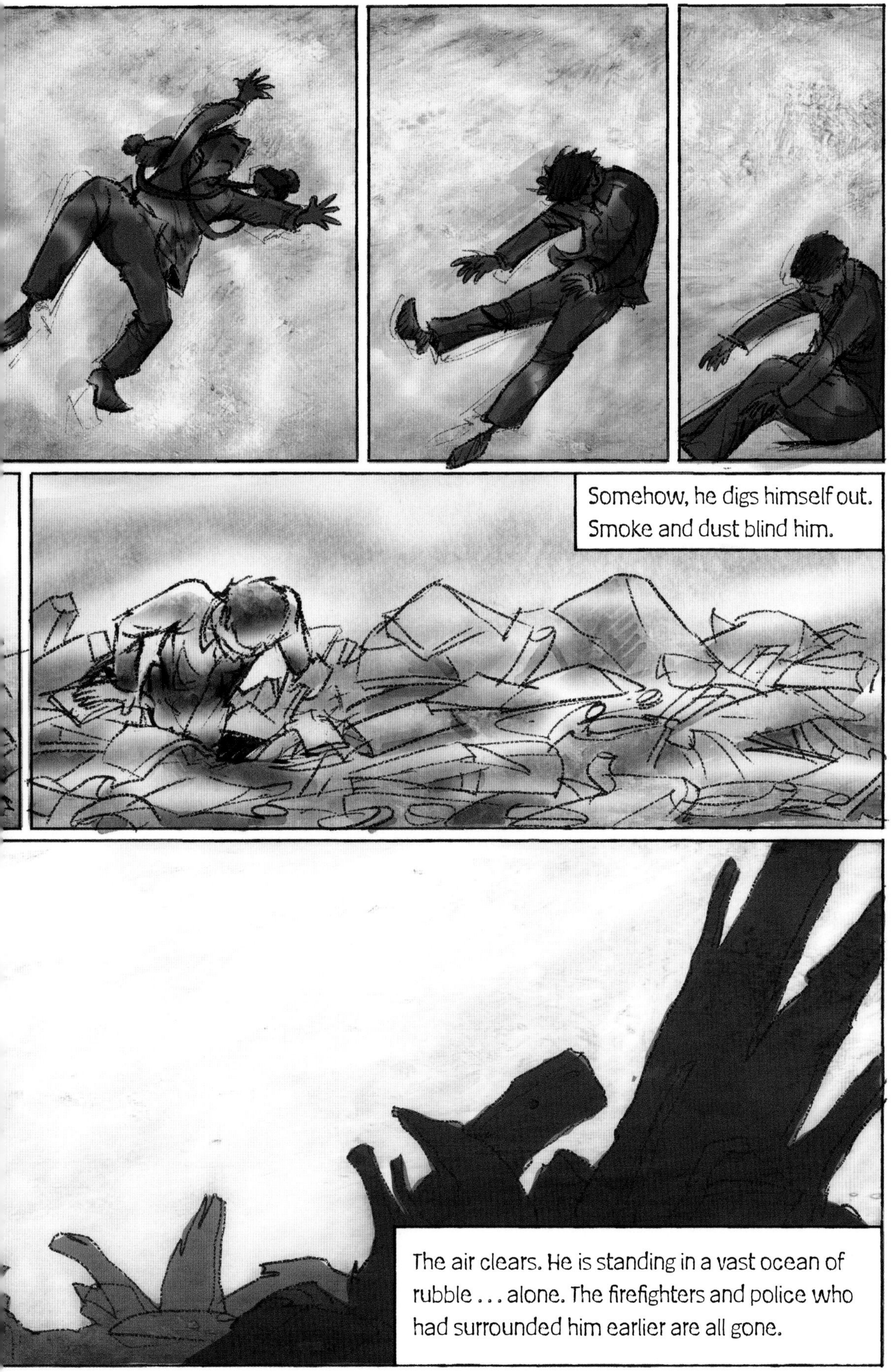
Somehow, he digs himself out. Smoke and dust blind him.
The air clears. He is standing in a vast ocean of rubble . . . alone. The firefighters and police who had surrounded him earlier are all gone.

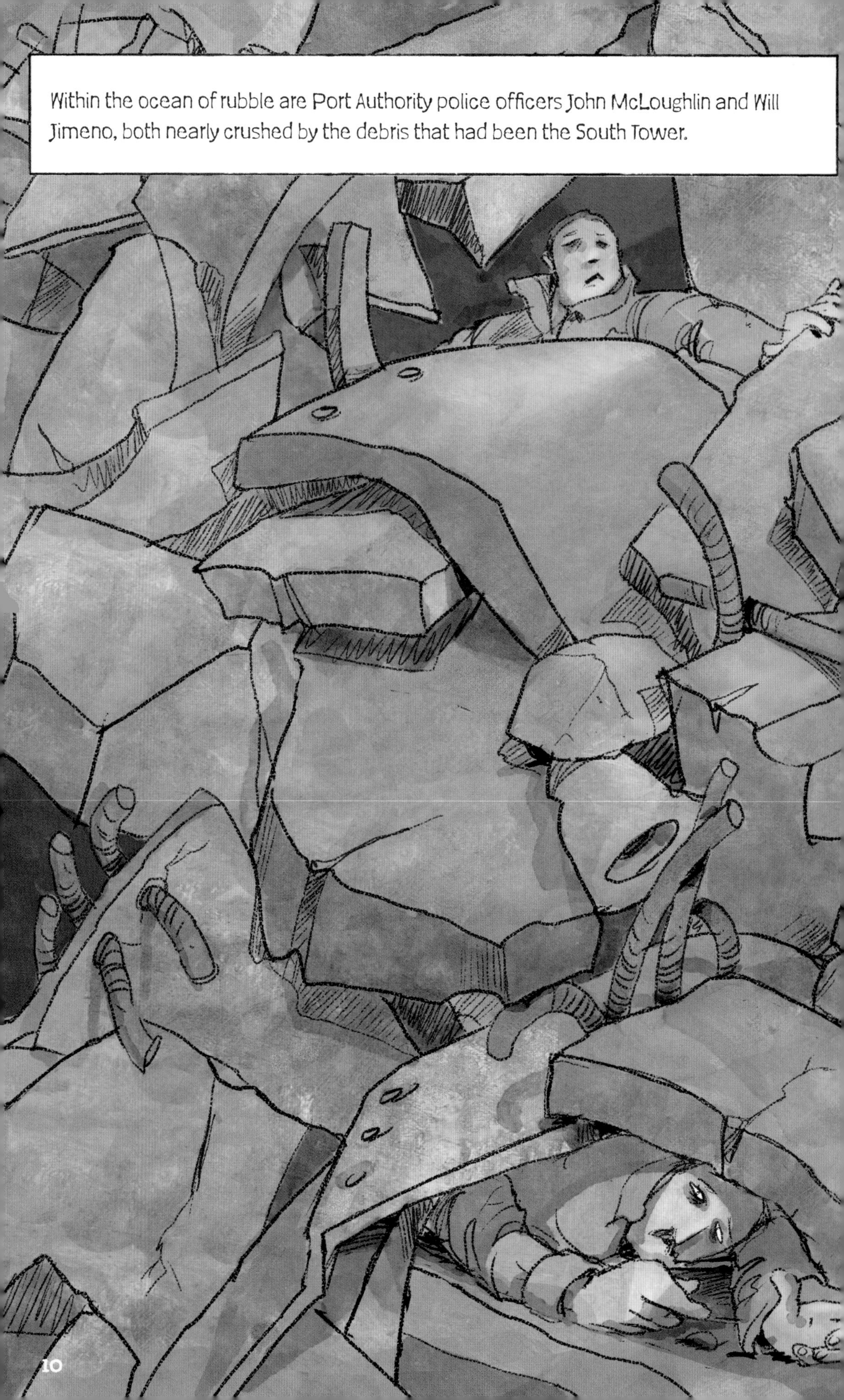
Within the ocean of rubble are Port Authority police officers John McLoughlin and Will Jimeno, both nearly crushed by the debris that had been the South Tower.

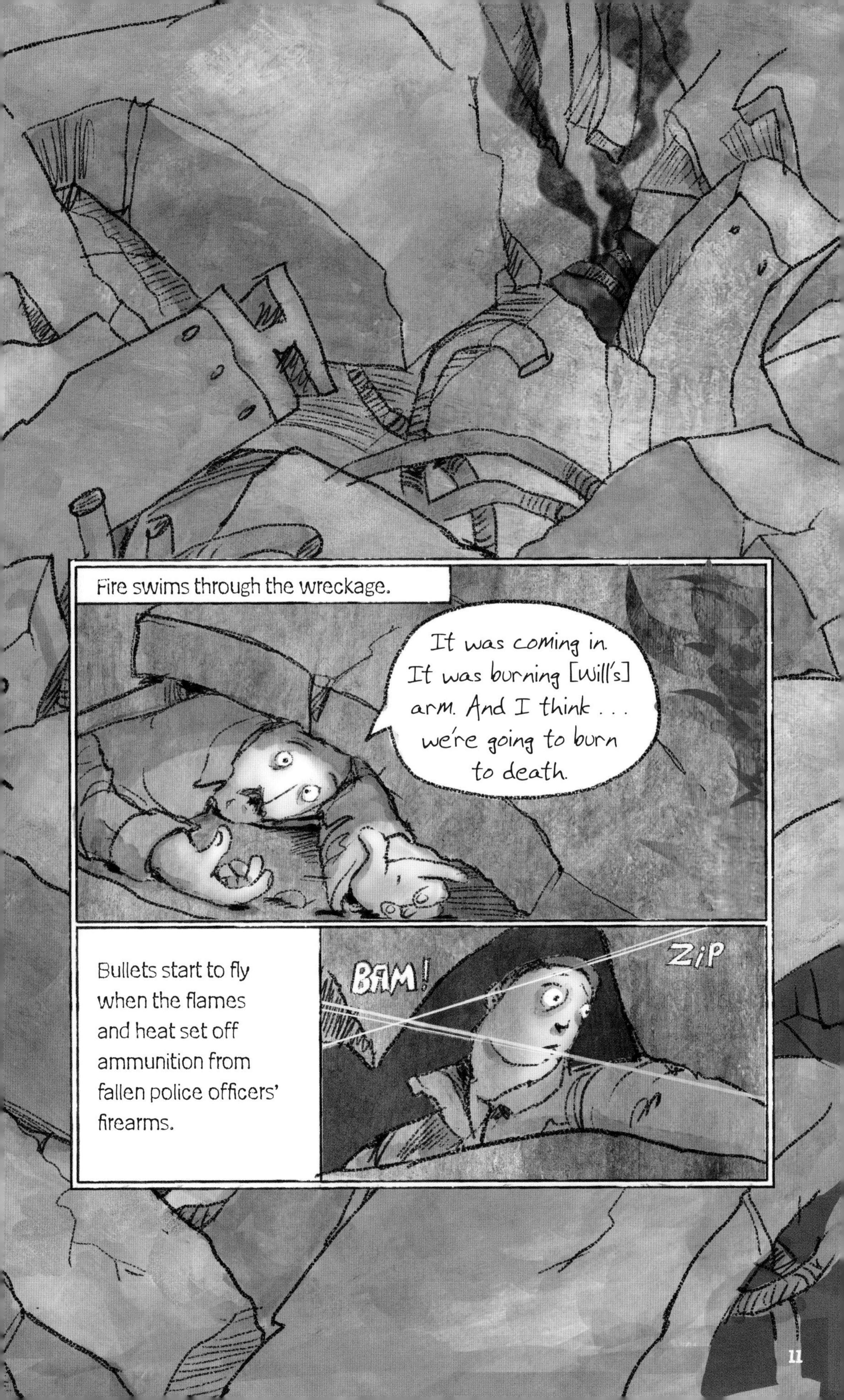
Fire swims through the wreckage.
It was coming in. It was burning [Will's] arm. And I think . . . we're going to burn to death.
Bullets start to fly when the flames and heat set off ammunition from fallen police officers' firearms.
BAM!
ZIP

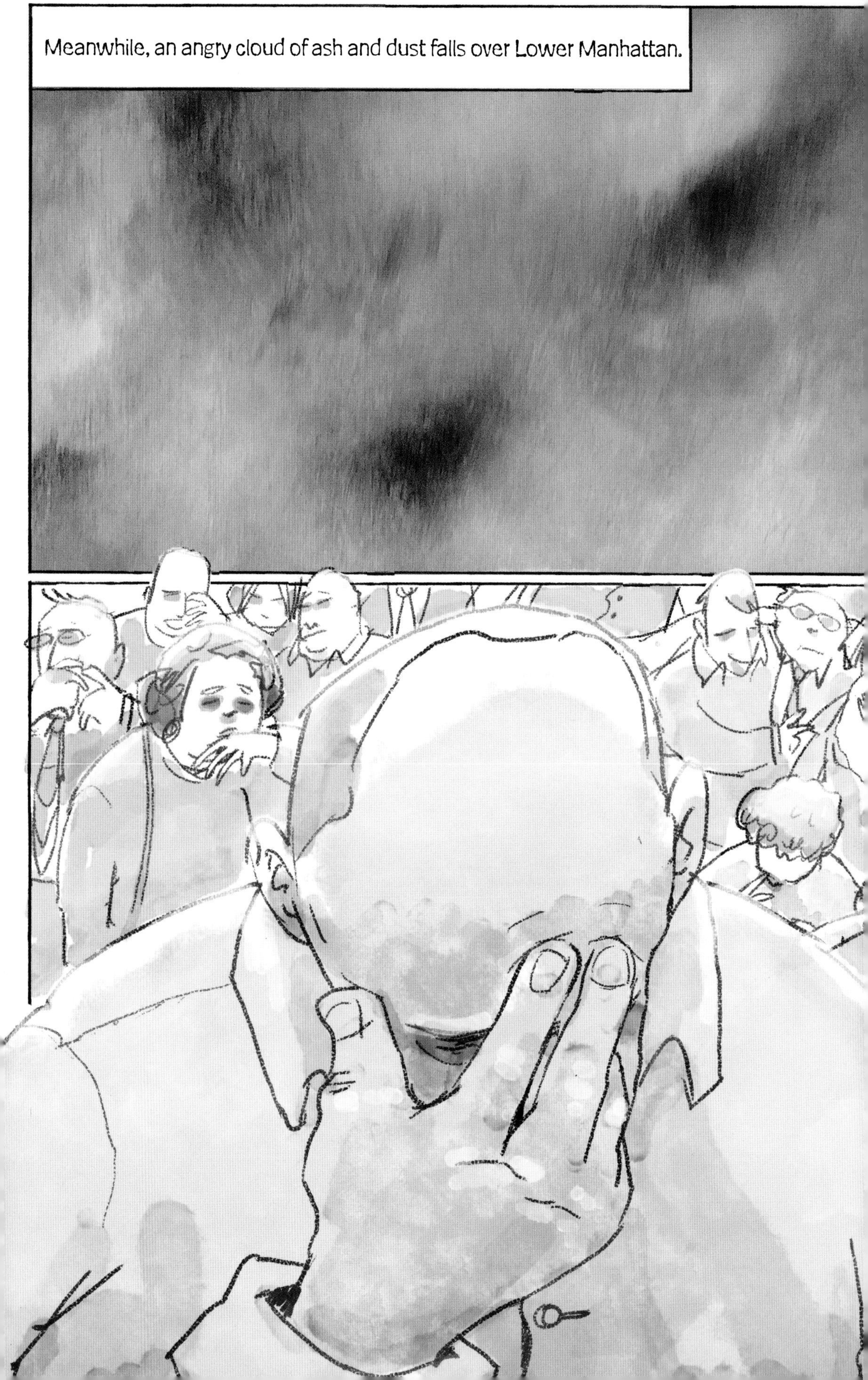
Meanwhile, an angry cloud of ash and dust falls over Lower Manhattan.

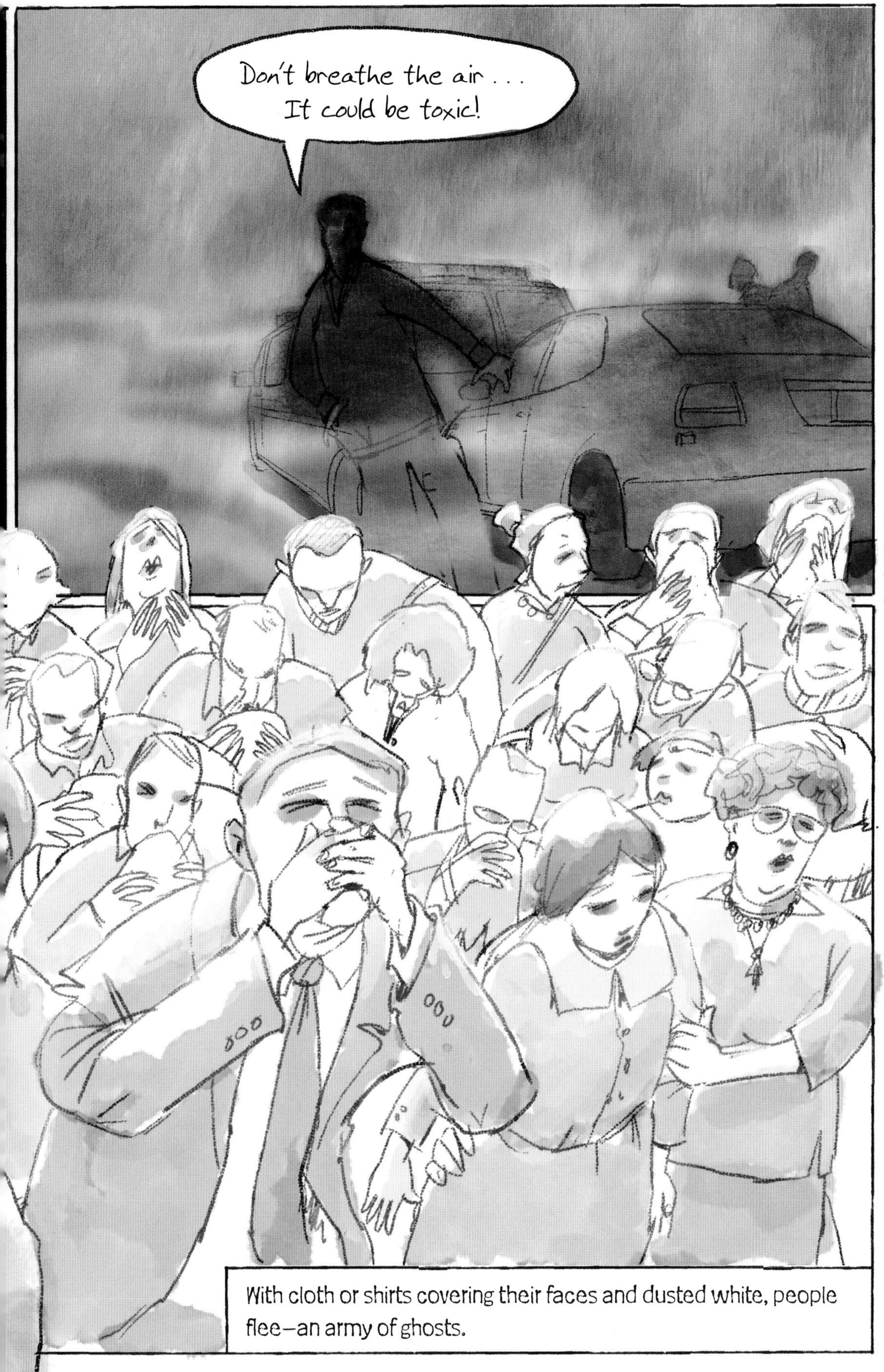
Don't breathe the air . . .
It could be toxic!
With cloth or shirts covering their faces and dusted white, people flee—an army of ghosts.

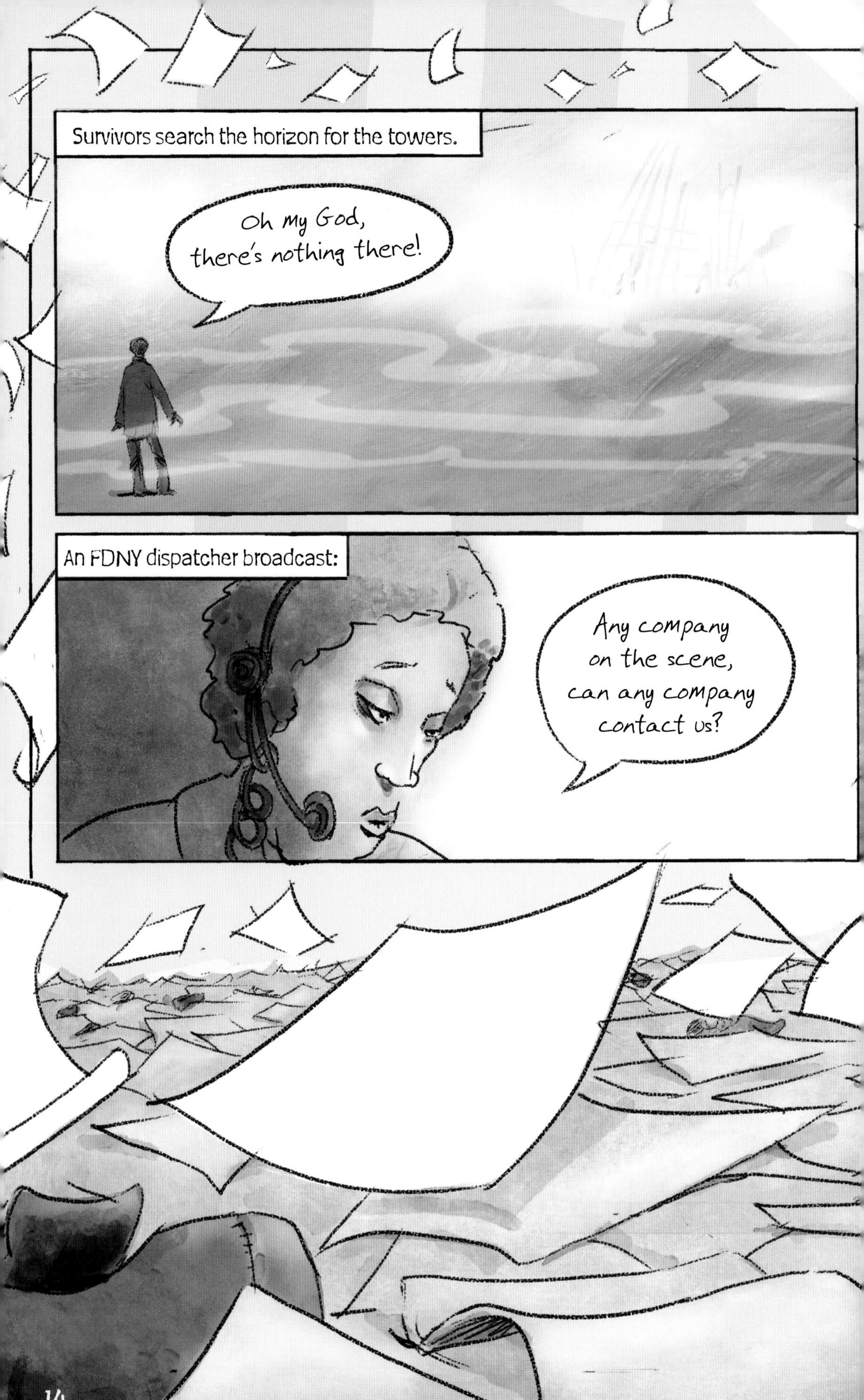
Survivors search the horizon for the towers.
Oh my God, there's nothing there!
An FDNY dispatcher broadcast:
Any company on the scene, can any company contact us?

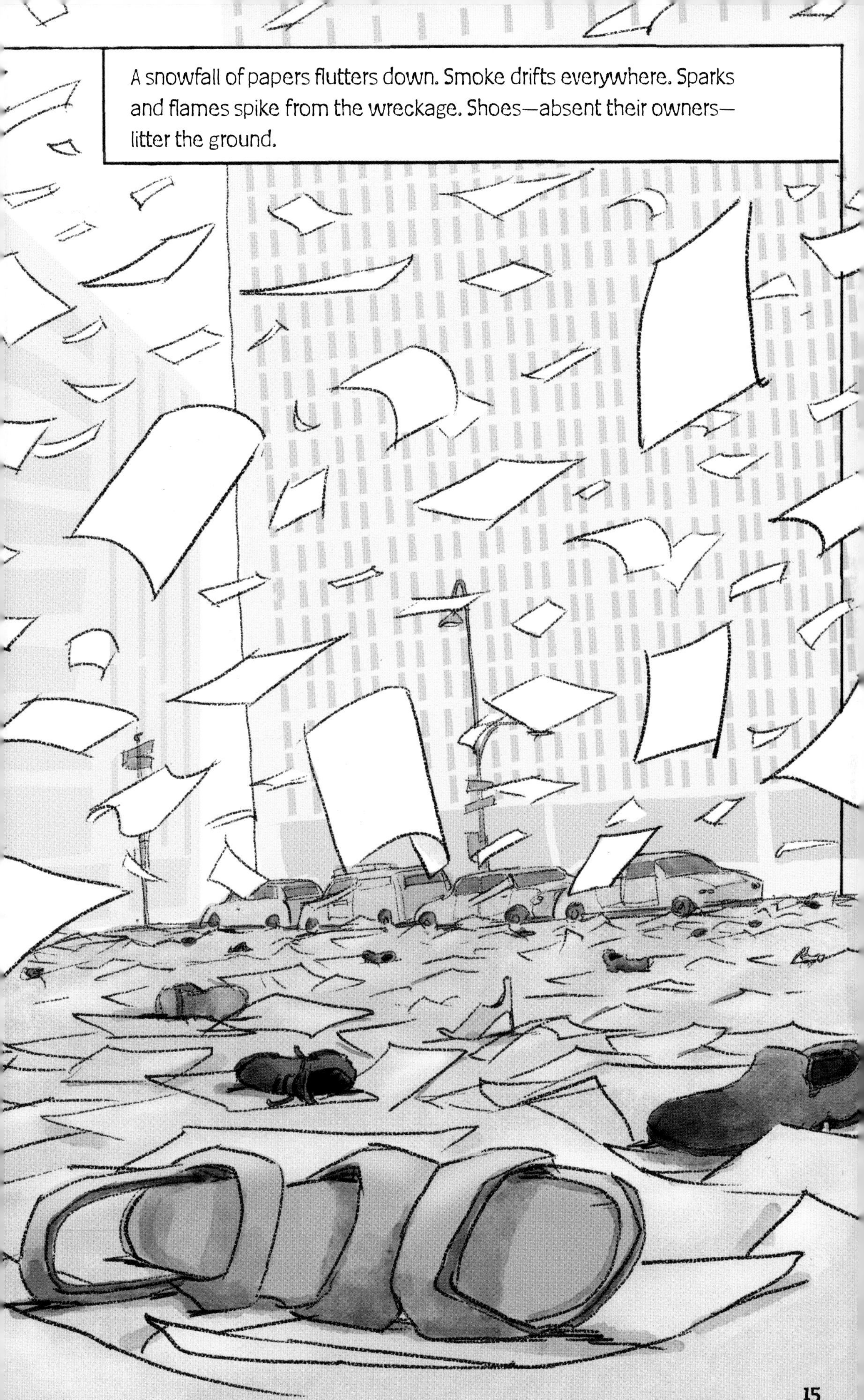
A snowfall of papers flutters down. Smoke drifts everywhere. Sparks and flames spike from the wreckage. Shoes—absent their owners—litter the ground.

Sixteen people are trapped in the remnants of the North Tower's Stairwell B. Captain Jay Jonas, five other firefighters, a Port Authority police officer, and office worker Josephine Harris are spread out over three floors. The group had been slowed by Harris's injured leg and were gradually making their way down when the building collapsed, sending everyone tumbling. Nearby are other firefighters, including Fire Chief Richard Picciotto.

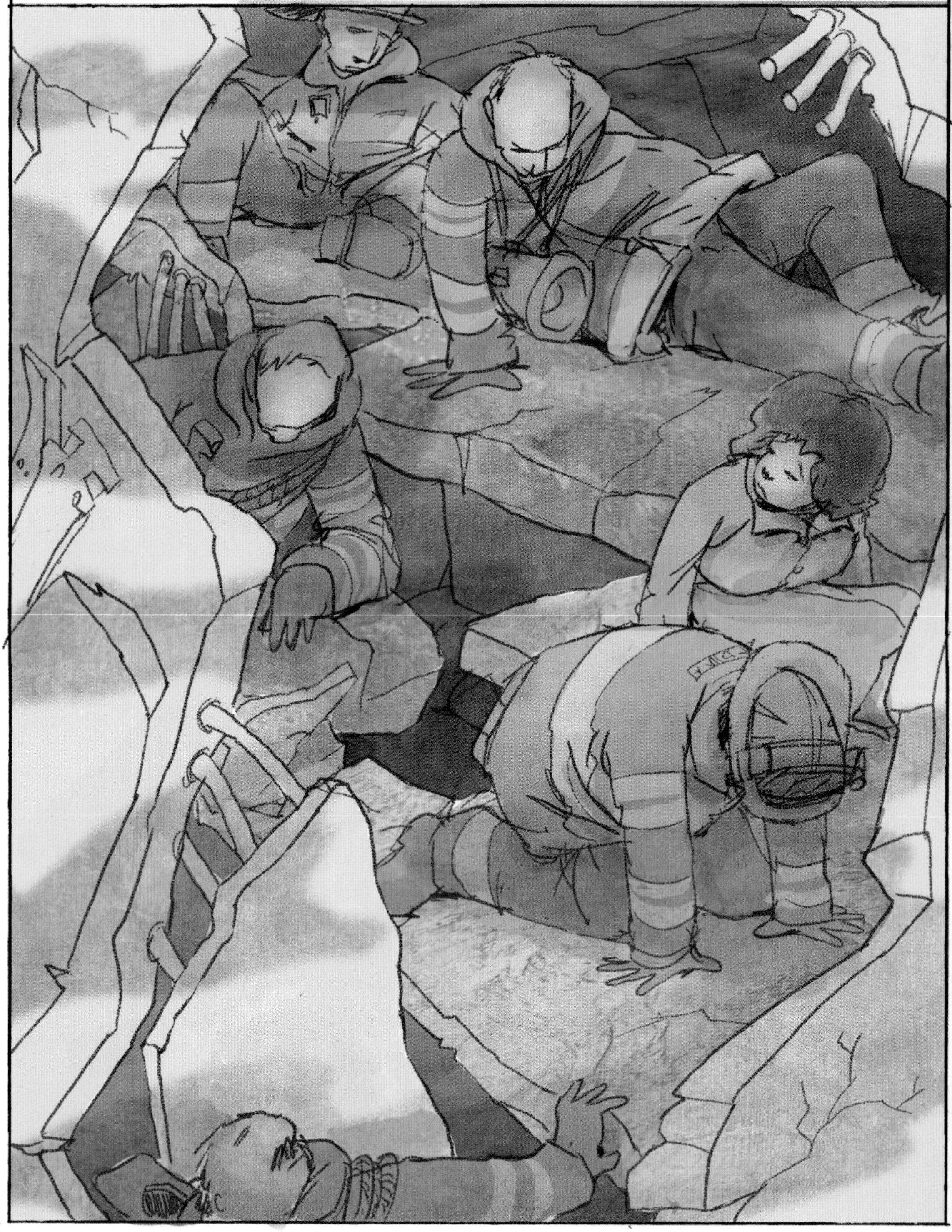

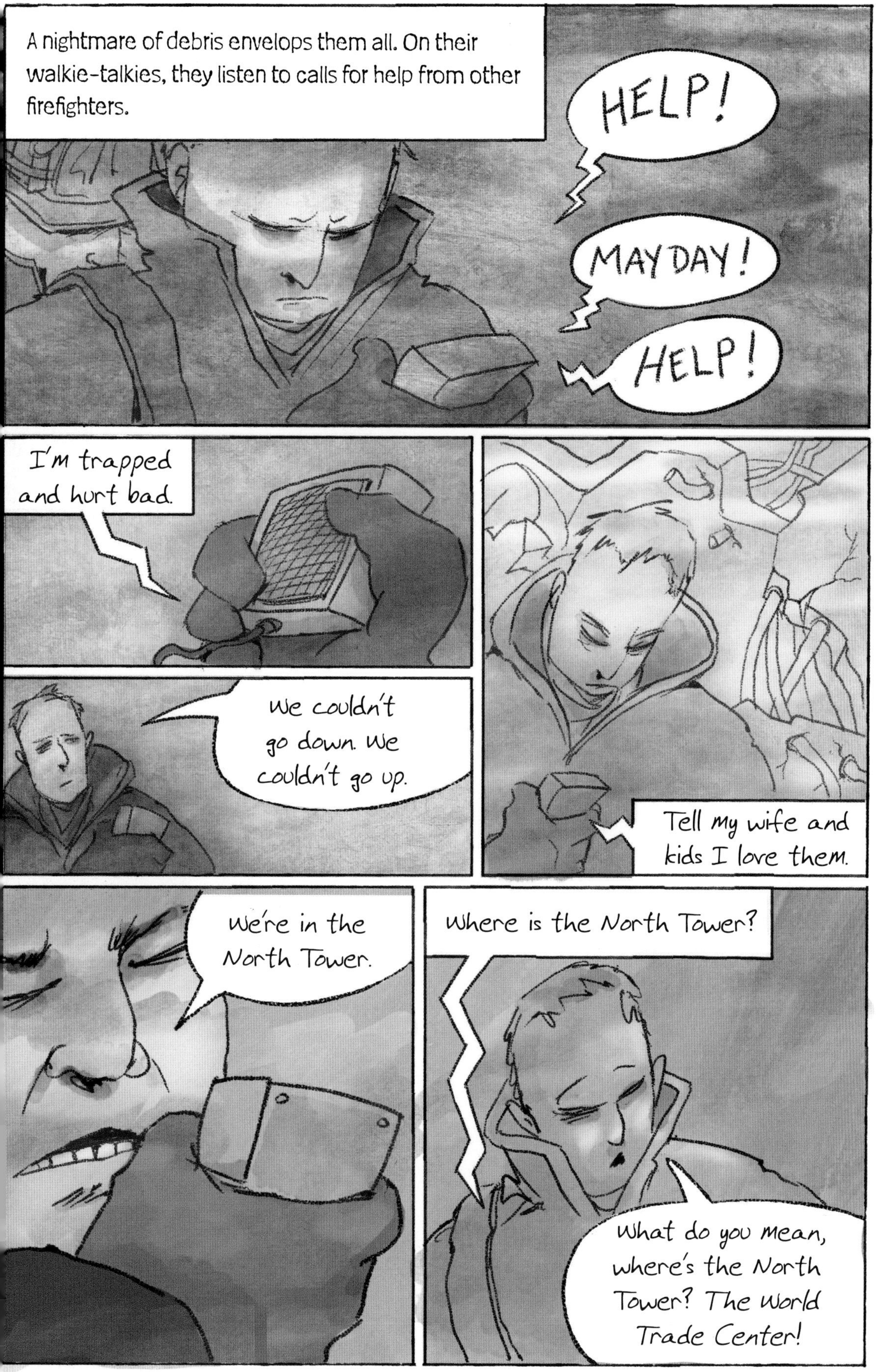
A nightmare of debris envelops them all. On their walkie-talkies, they listen to calls for help from other firefighters.
HELP!
MAYDAY!
HELP!
I'm trapped and hurt bad.
We couldn't go down. We couldn't go up.
Tell my wife and kids I love them.
We're in the North Tower.
Where is the North Tower?
What do you mean, where's the North Tower? The World Trade Center!

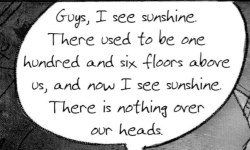

Guys, I see sunshine. There used to be one hundred and six floors above us, and now I see sunshine. There is nothing over our heads.

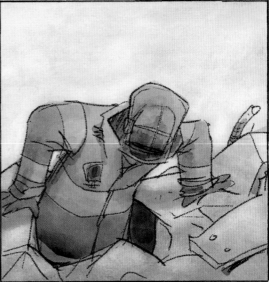

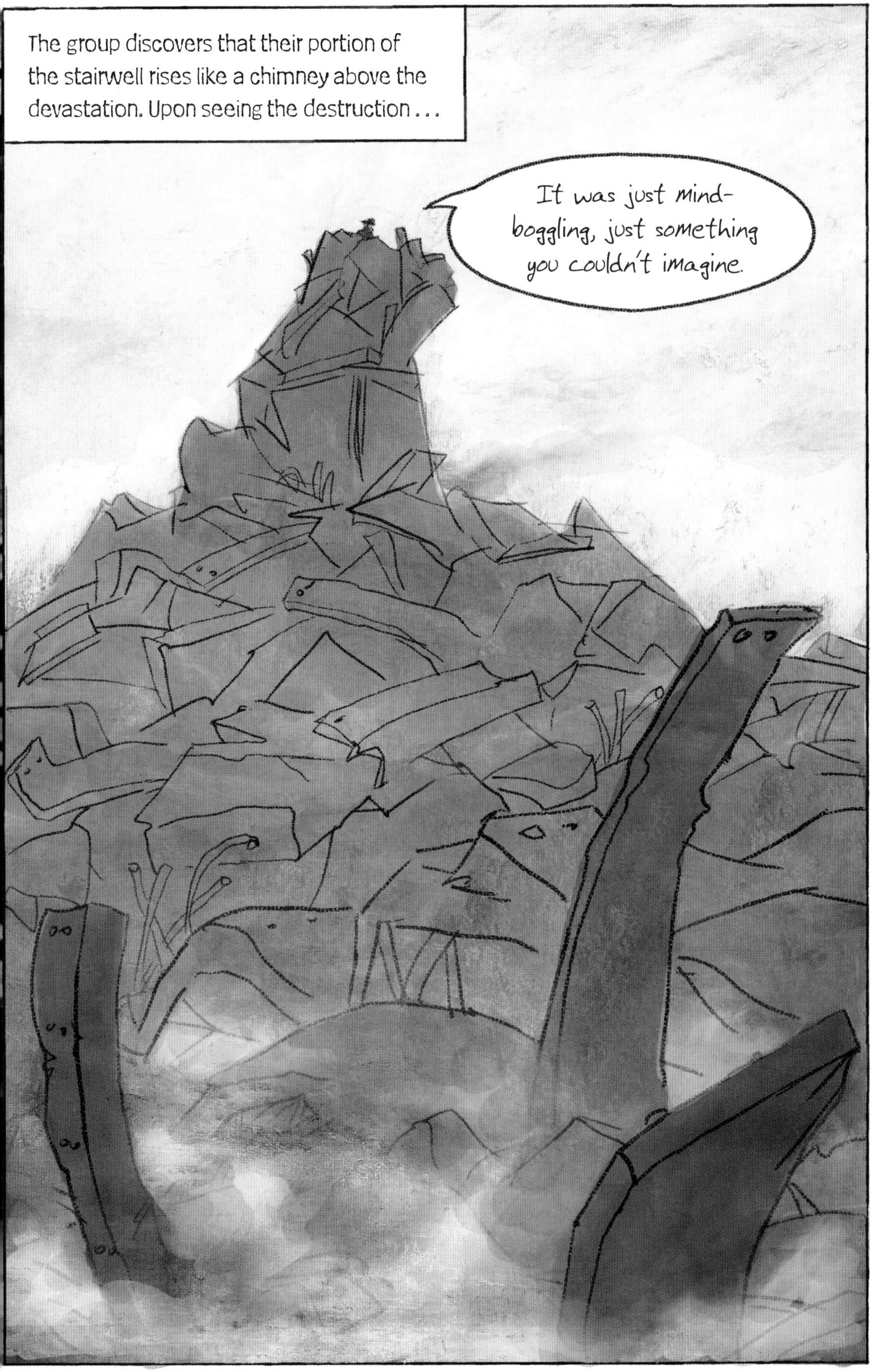
The group discovers that their portion of the stairwell rises like a chimney above the devastation. Upon seeing the destruction . . .
It was just mind-boggling, just something you couldn't imagine.

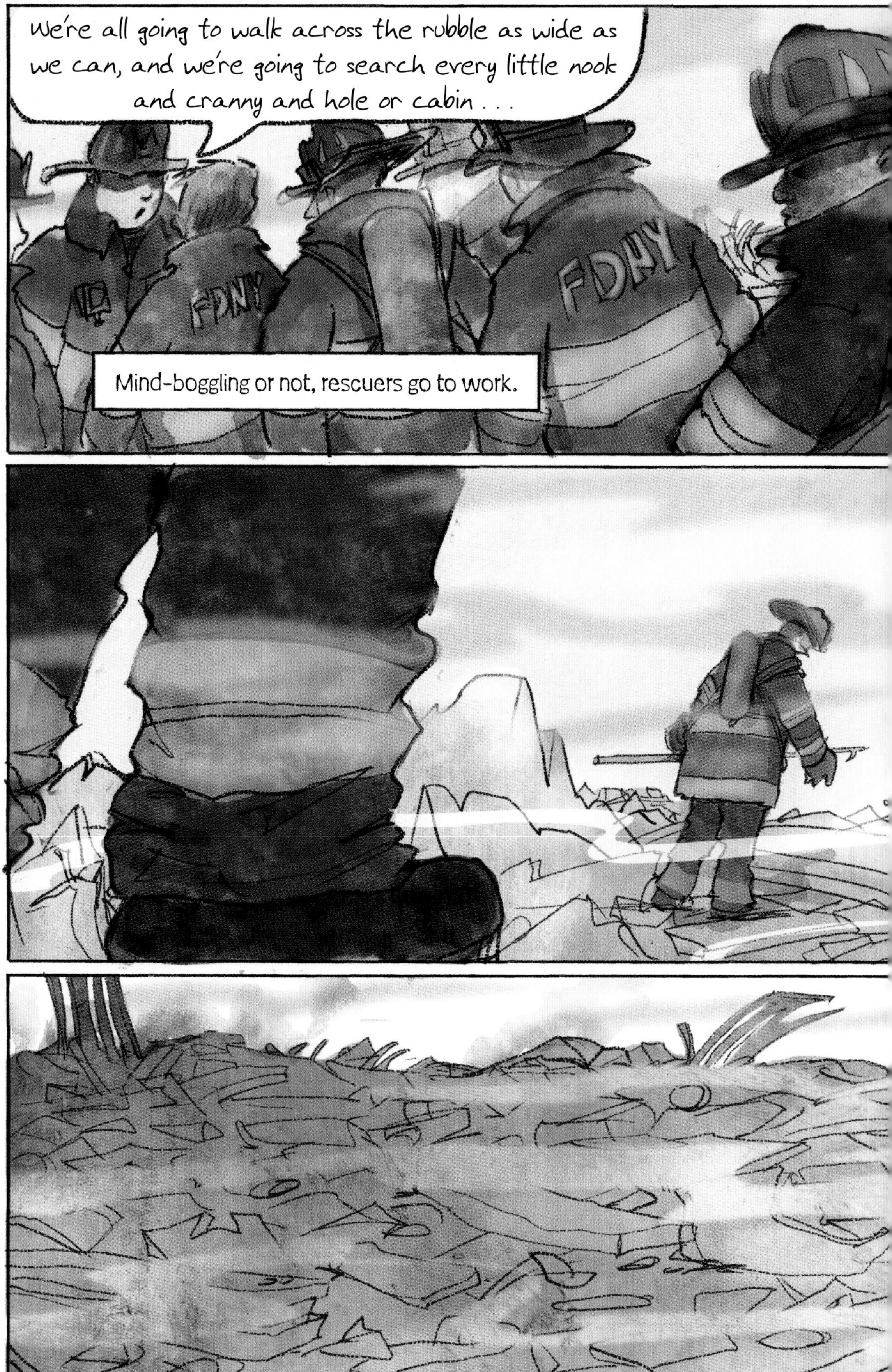
We're all going to walk across the rubble as wide as we can, and we're going to search every little nook and cranny and hole or cabin . . .
FDNY
FDNY
Mind-boggling or not, rescuers go to work.

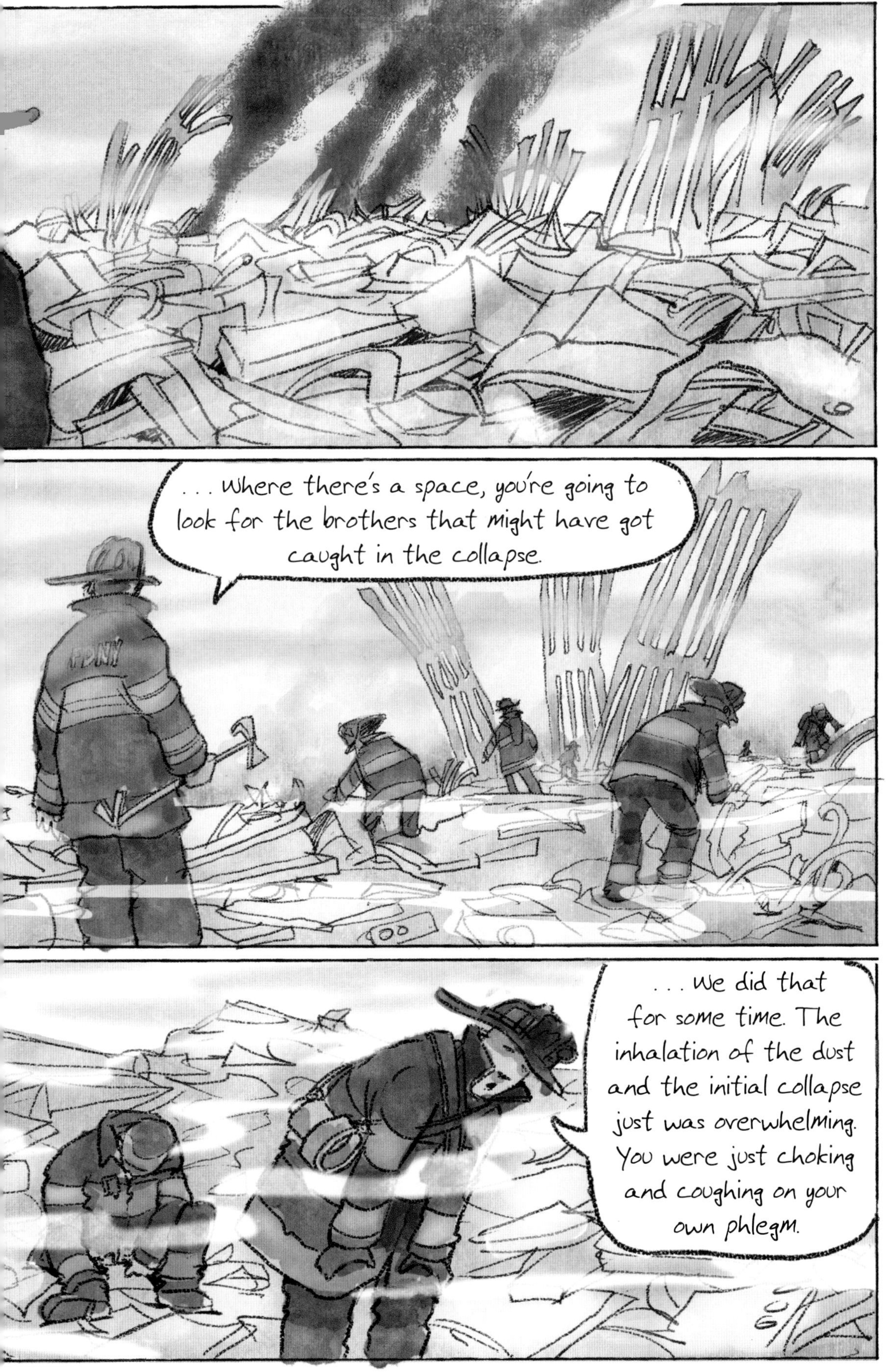
. . . Where there's a space, you're going to look for the brothers that might have got caught in the collapse.
FDNY
. . . We did that for some time. The inhalation of the dust and the initial collapse just was overwhelming. You were just choking and coughing on your own phlegm.

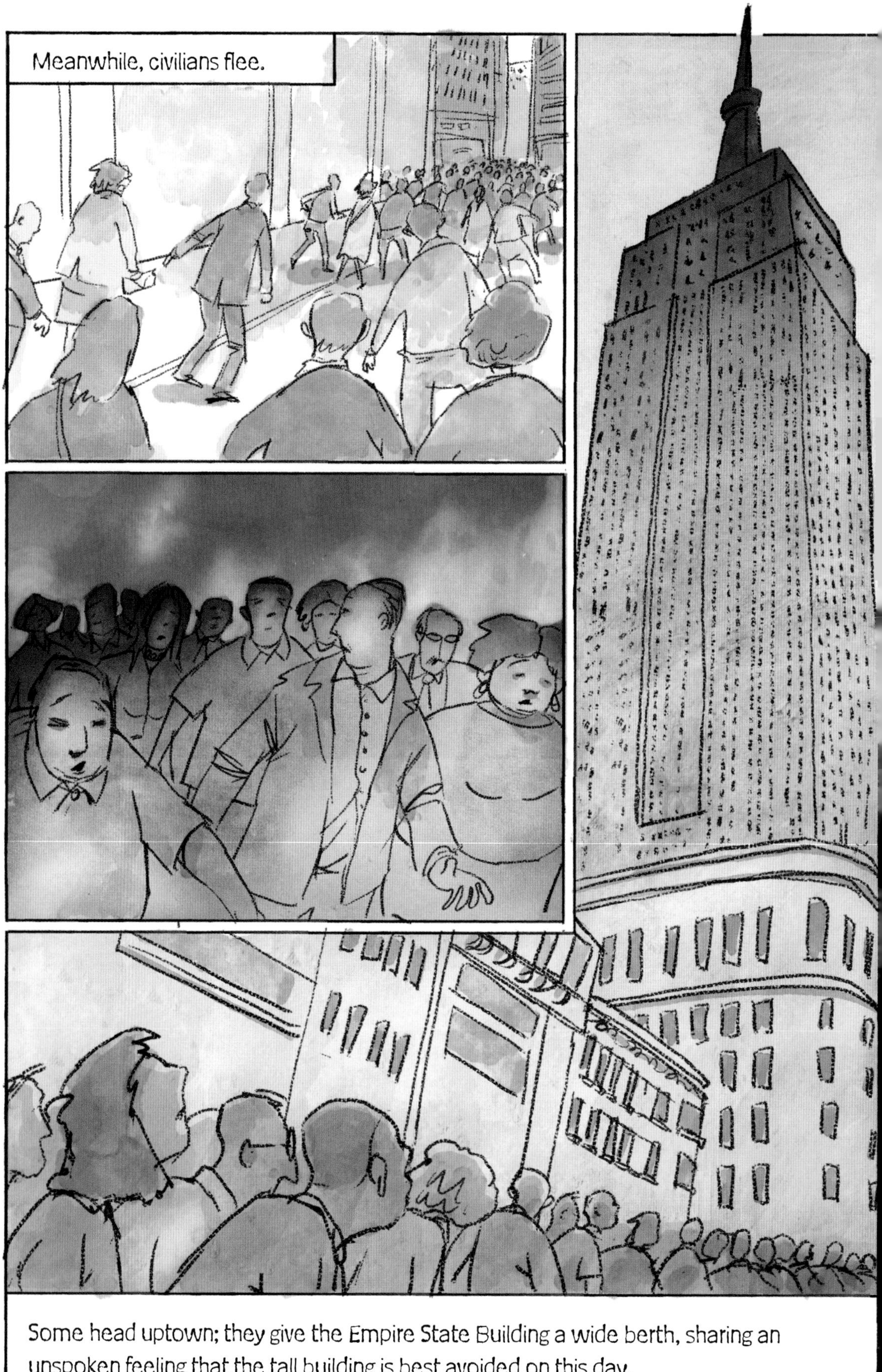
Meanwhile, civilians flee.
Some head uptown; they give the Empire State Building a wide berth, sharing an unspoken feeling that the tall building is best avoided on this day.

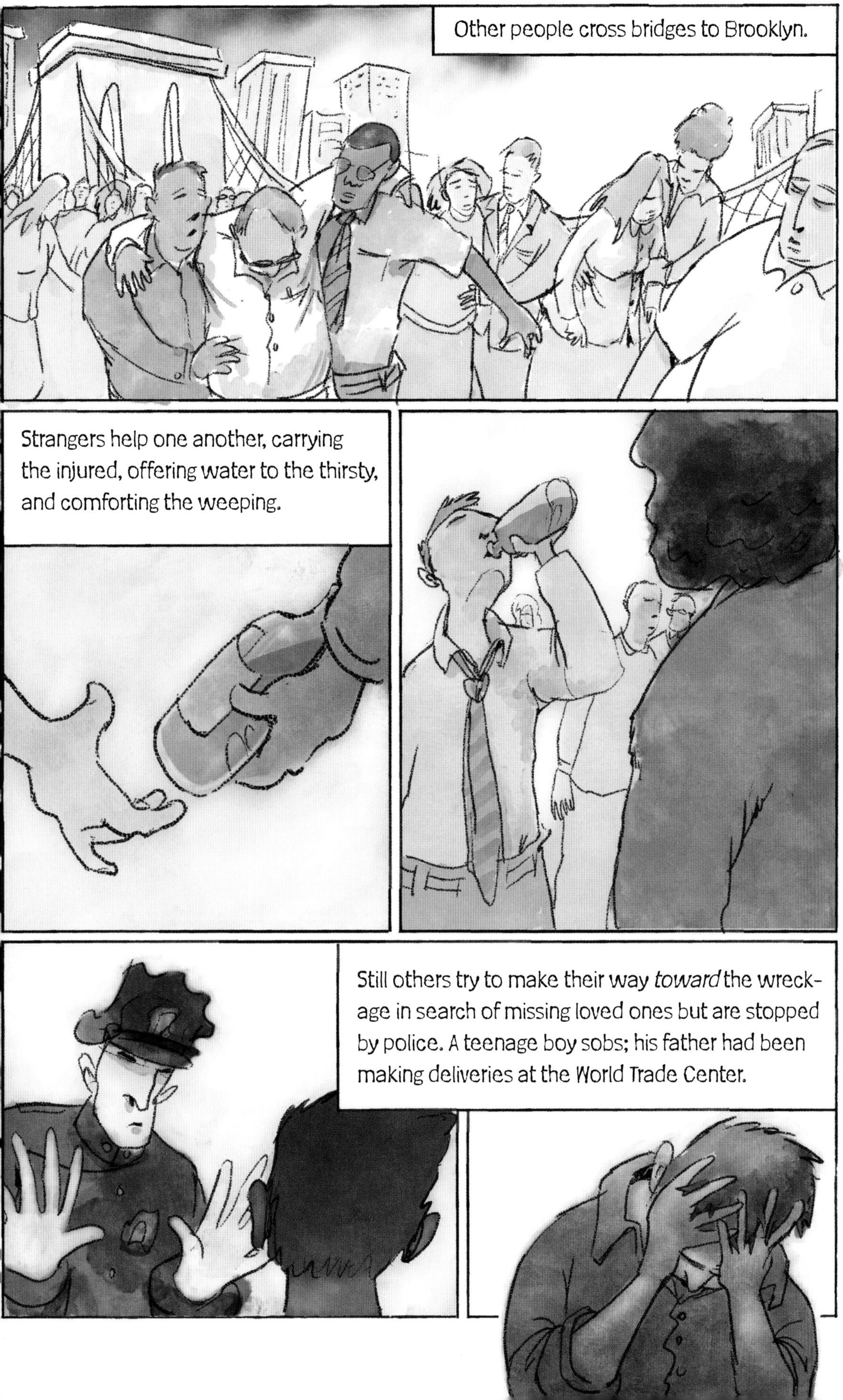
Other people cross bridges to Brooklyn.
Strangers help one another, carrying the injured, offering water to the thirsty, and comforting the weeping.
Still others try to make their way *toward* the wreckage in search of missing loved ones but are stopped by police. A teenage boy sobs; his father had been making deliveries at the World Trade Center.

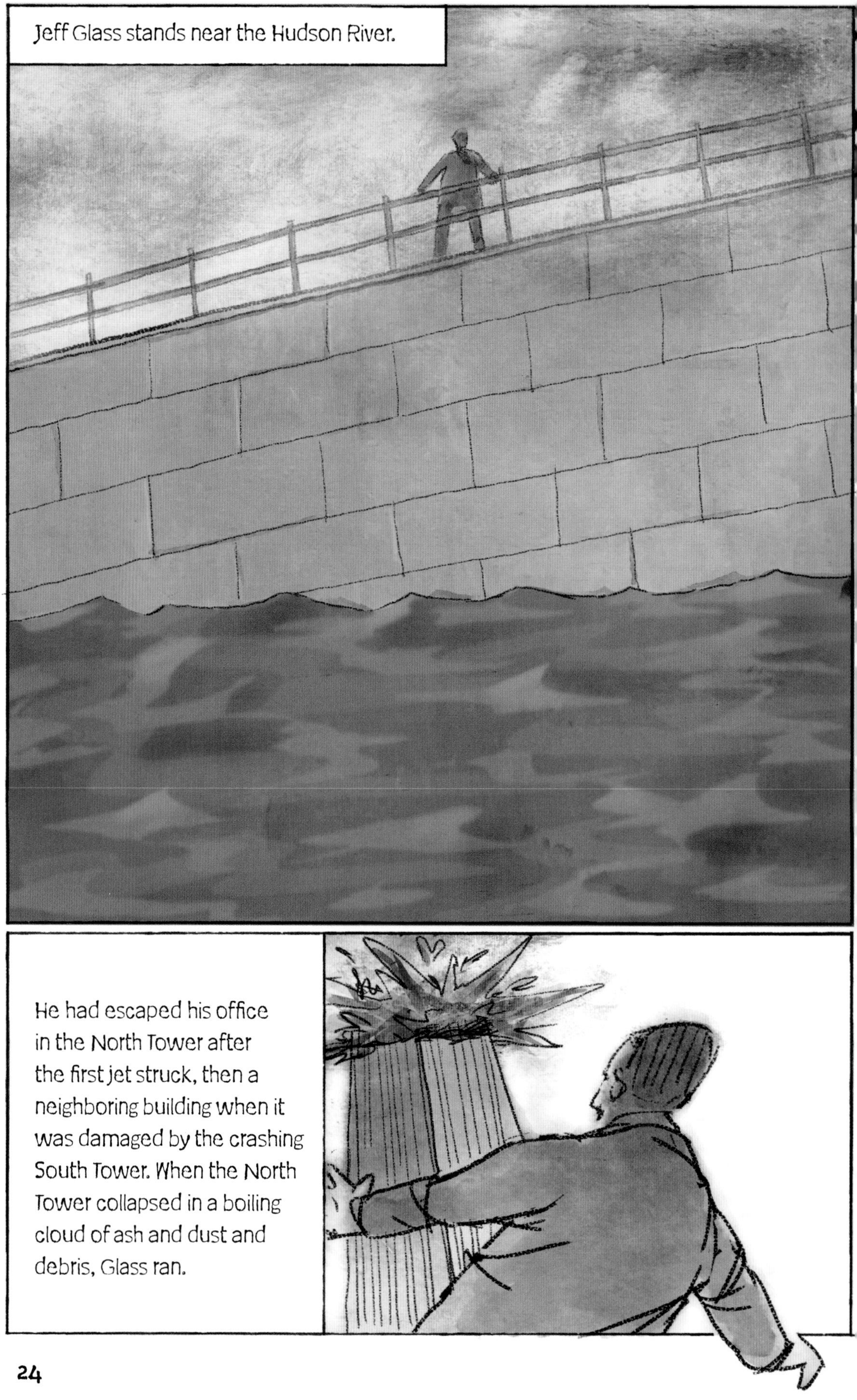
Jeff Glass stands near the Hudson River.
He had escaped his office in the North Tower after the first jet struck, then a neighboring building when it was damaged by the crashing South Tower. When the North Tower collapsed in a boiling cloud of ash and dust and debris, Glass ran.

Covered in ash, he now comes upon a boat at the seawall. He hops the seawall fence and the boat rail and escapes over the water to New Jersey.

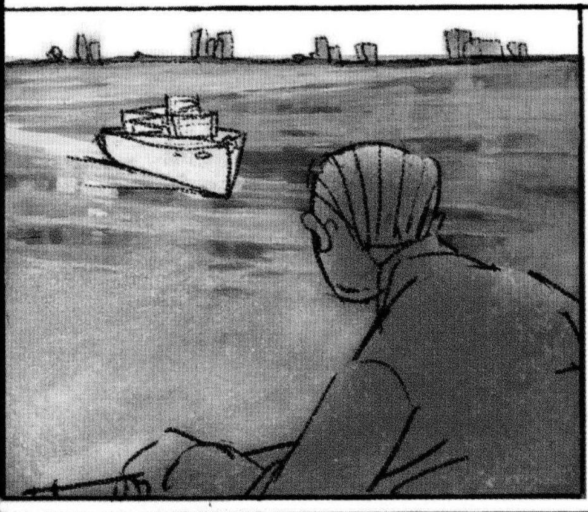

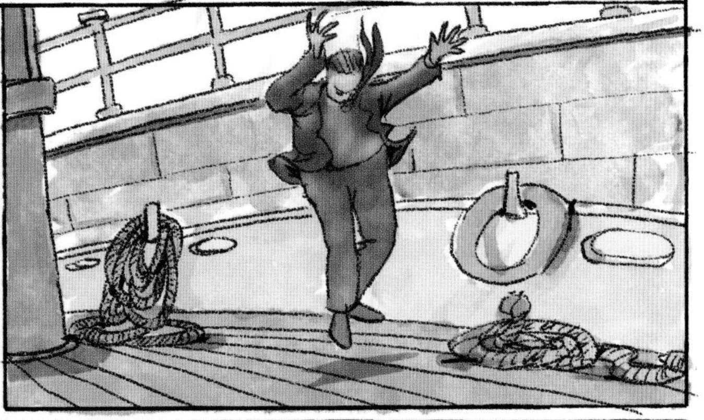

He is not alone. Thousands escape Lower Manhattan on all manner of boats—ferries, fireboats, party boats, tugboats, and private boats.

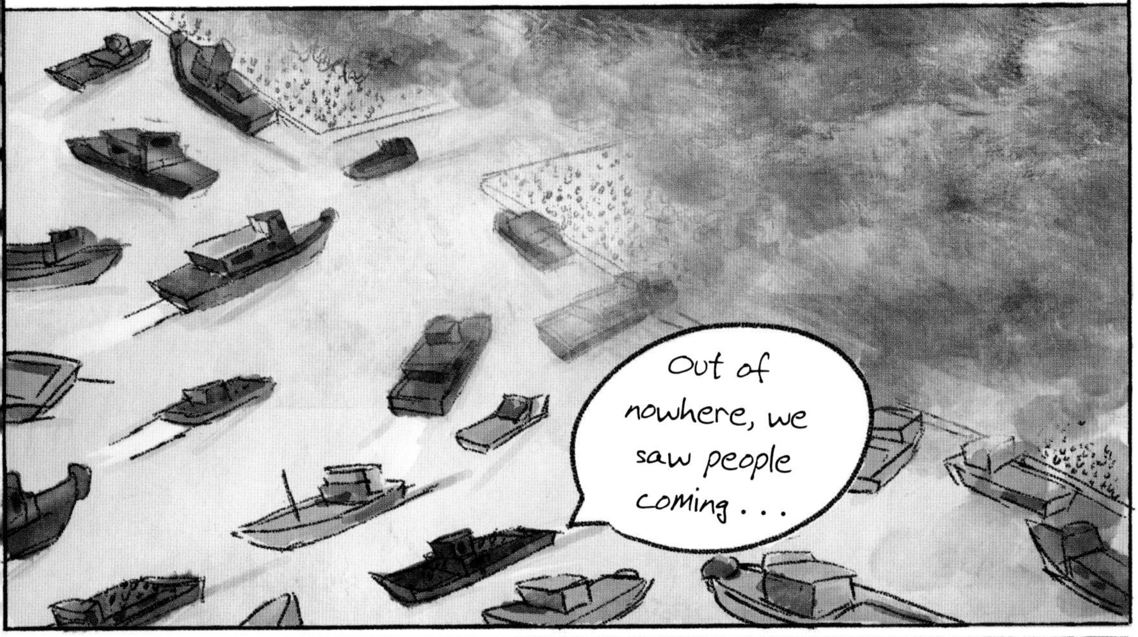
Out of nowhere, we saw people coming . . .

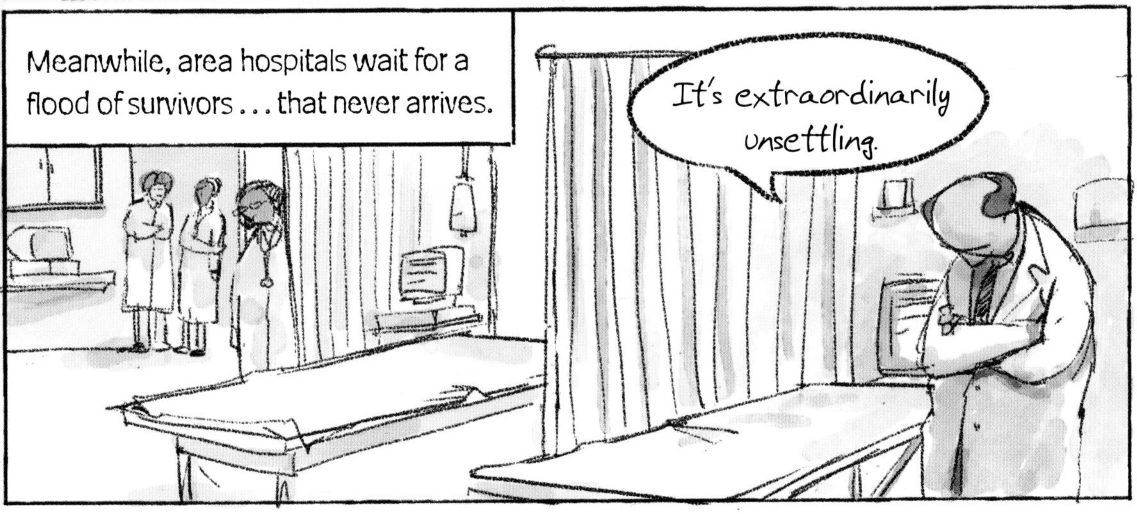
Meanwhile, area hospitals wait for a flood of survivors . . . that never arrives.
It's extraordinarily unsettling.

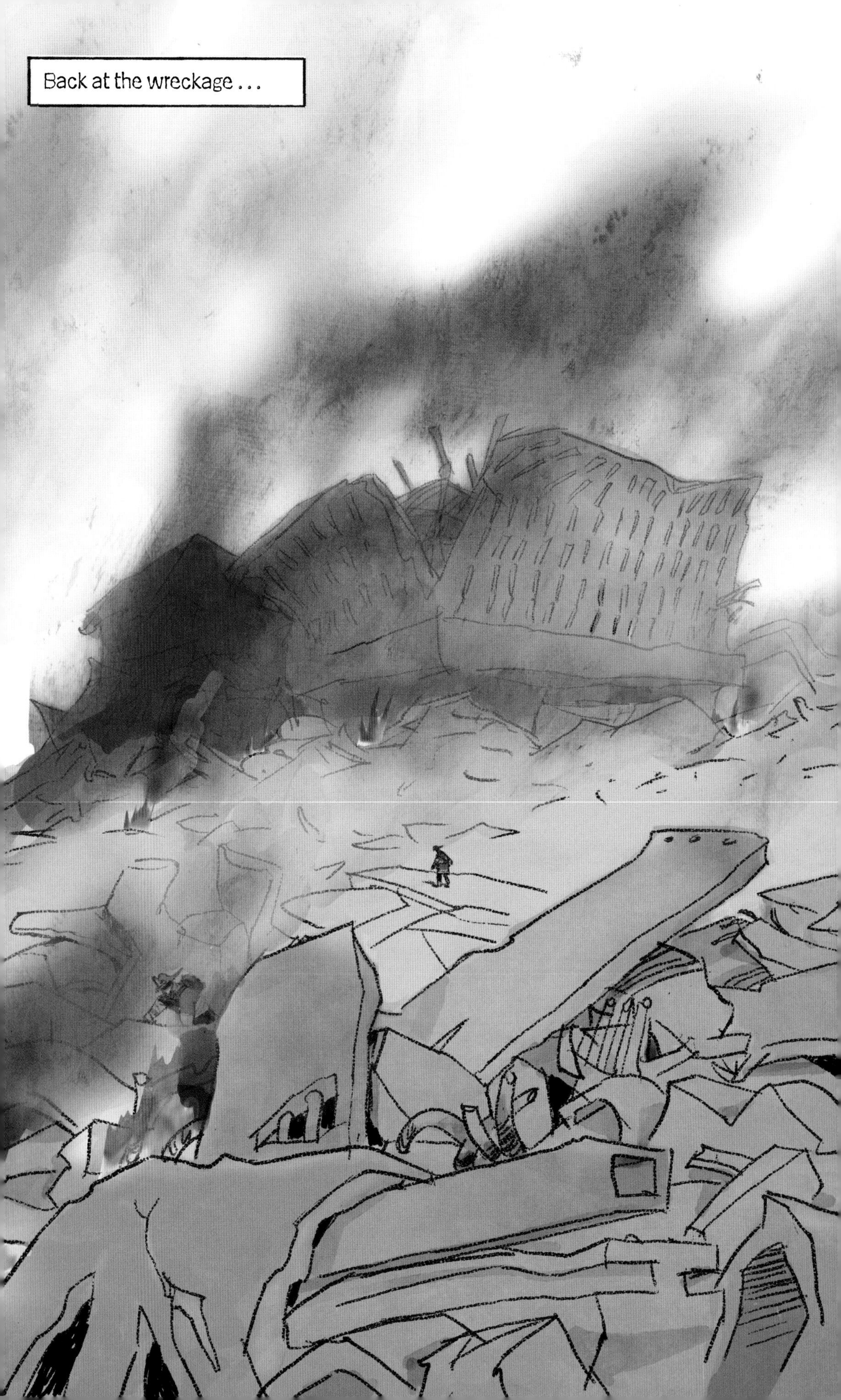
Back at the wreckage . . .

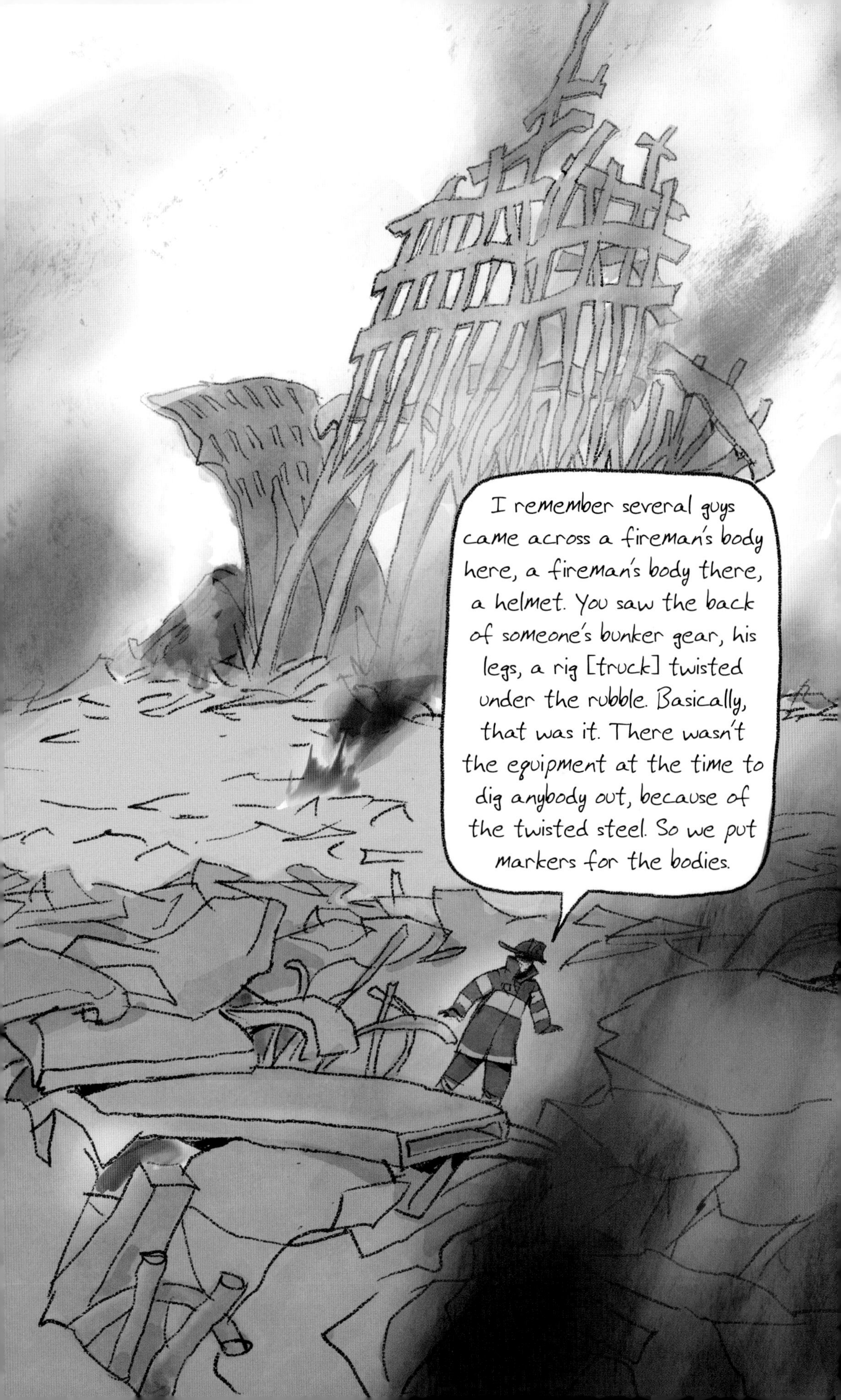
I remember several guys came across a fireman's body here, a fireman's body there, a helmet. You saw the back of someone's bunker gear, his legs, a rig [truck] twisted under the rubble. Basically, that was it. There wasn't the equipment at the time to dig anybody out, because of the twisted steel. So we put markers for the bodies.

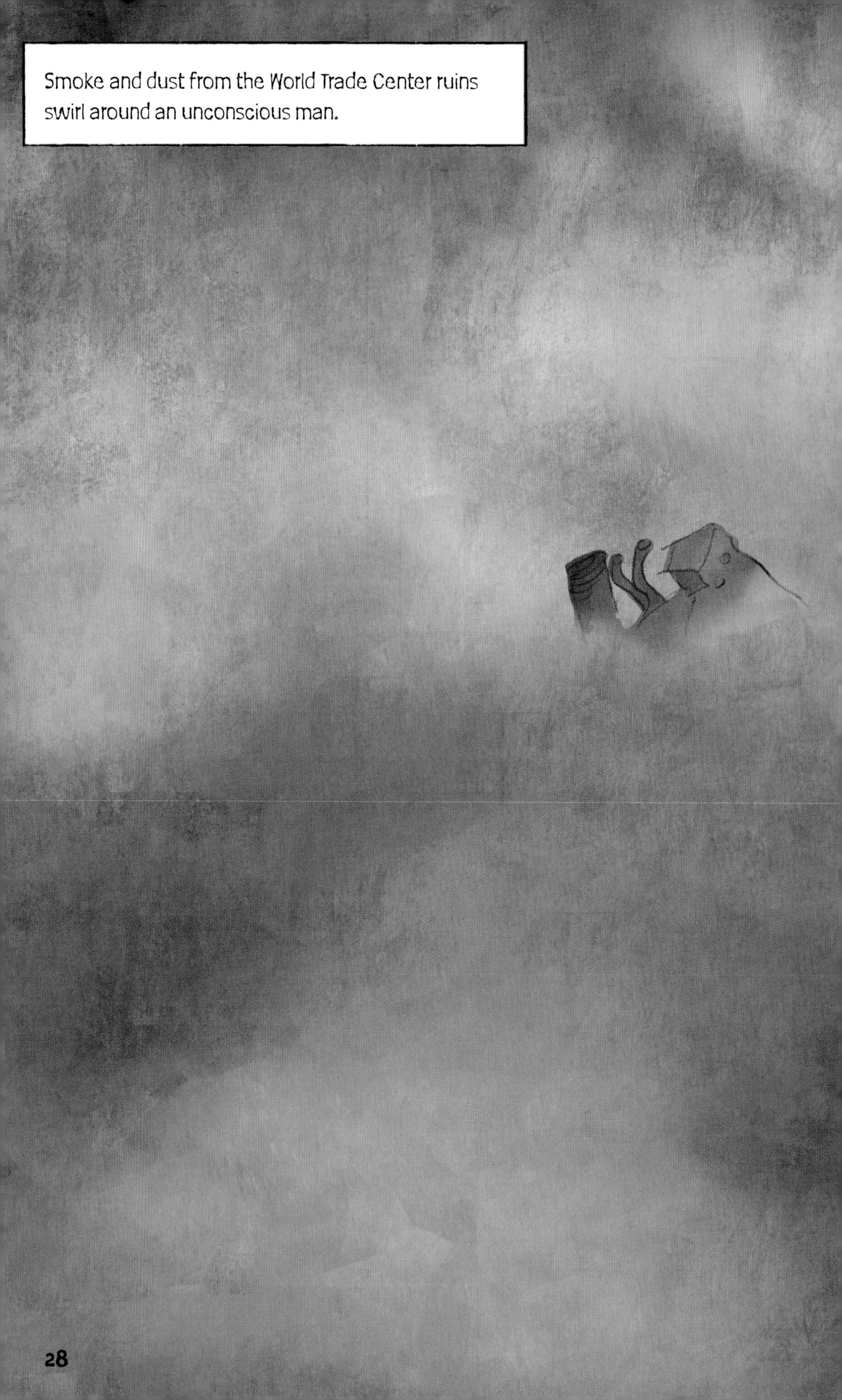
Smoke and dust from the World Trade Center ruins swirl around an unconscious man.

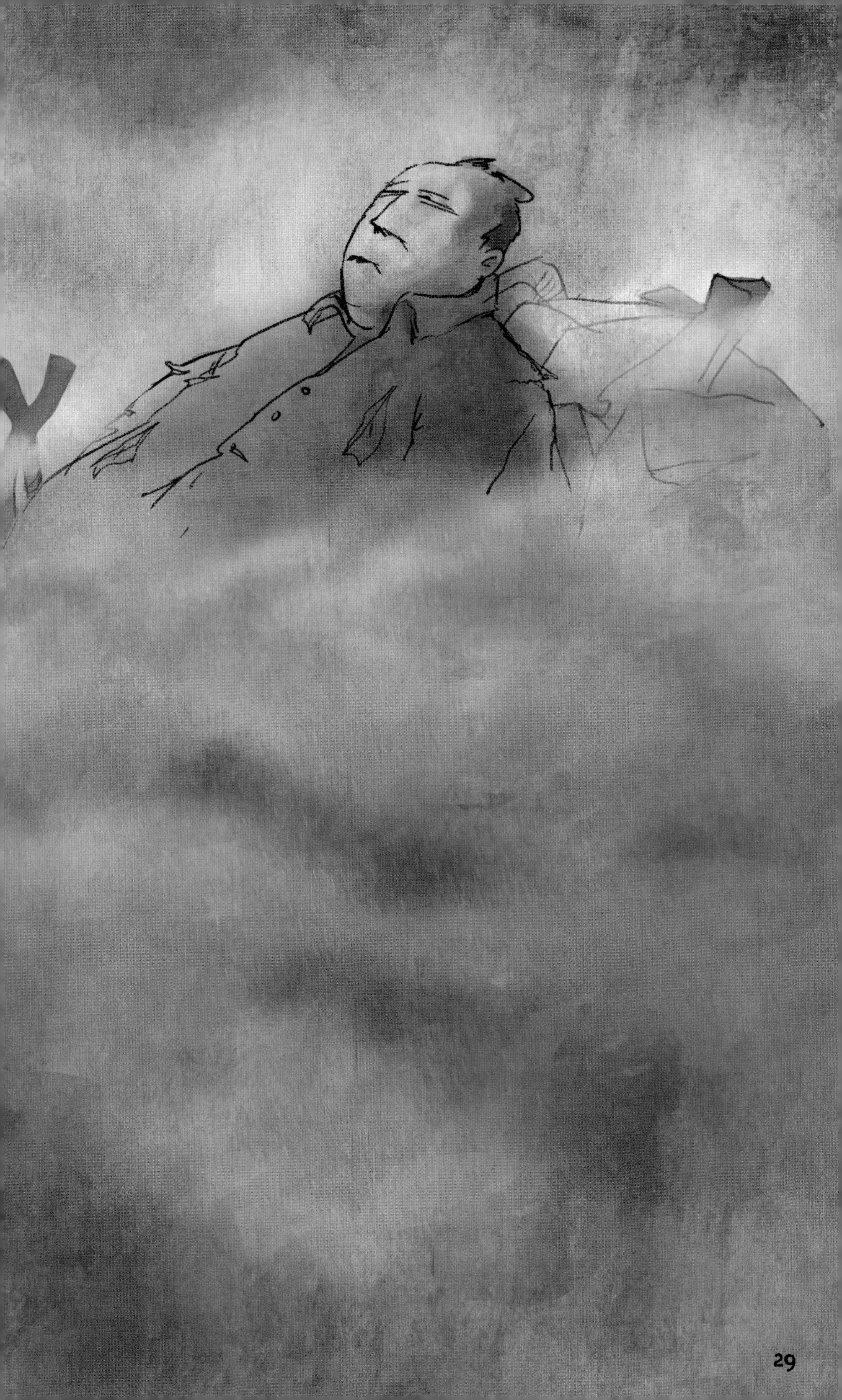

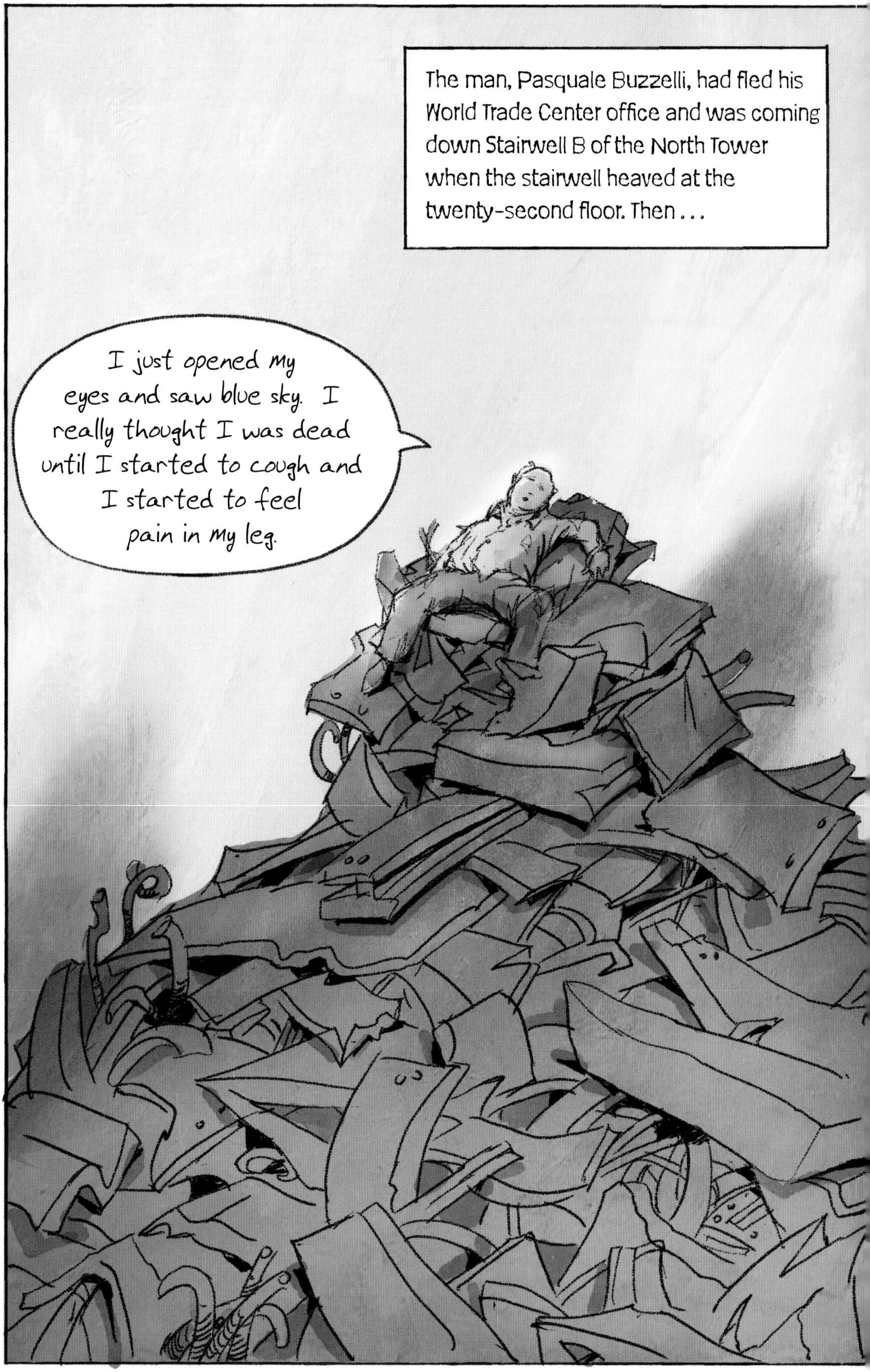
The man, Pasquale Buzzelli, had fled his World Trade Center office and was coming down Stairwell B of the North Tower when the stairwell heaved at the twenty-second floor. Then . . .
I just opened my eyes and saw blue sky. I really thought I was dead until I started to cough and I started to feel pain in my leg.

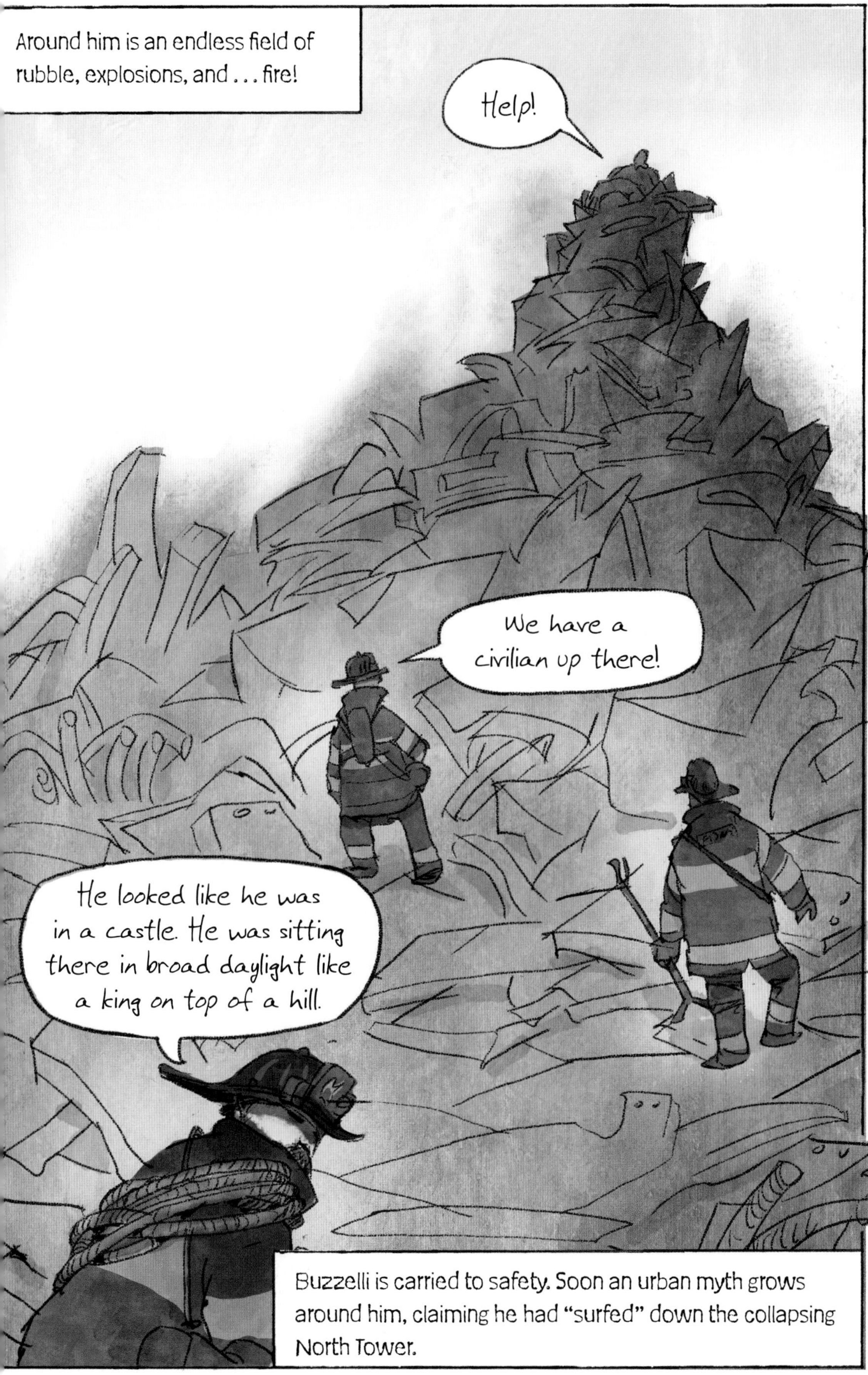

Around him is an endless field of rubble, explosions, and . . . fire!
Help!
We have a civilian up there!
He looked like he was in a castle. He was sitting there in broad daylight like a king on top of a hill.
Buzzelli is carried to safety. Soon an urban myth grows around him, claiming he had "surfed" down the collapsing North Tower.

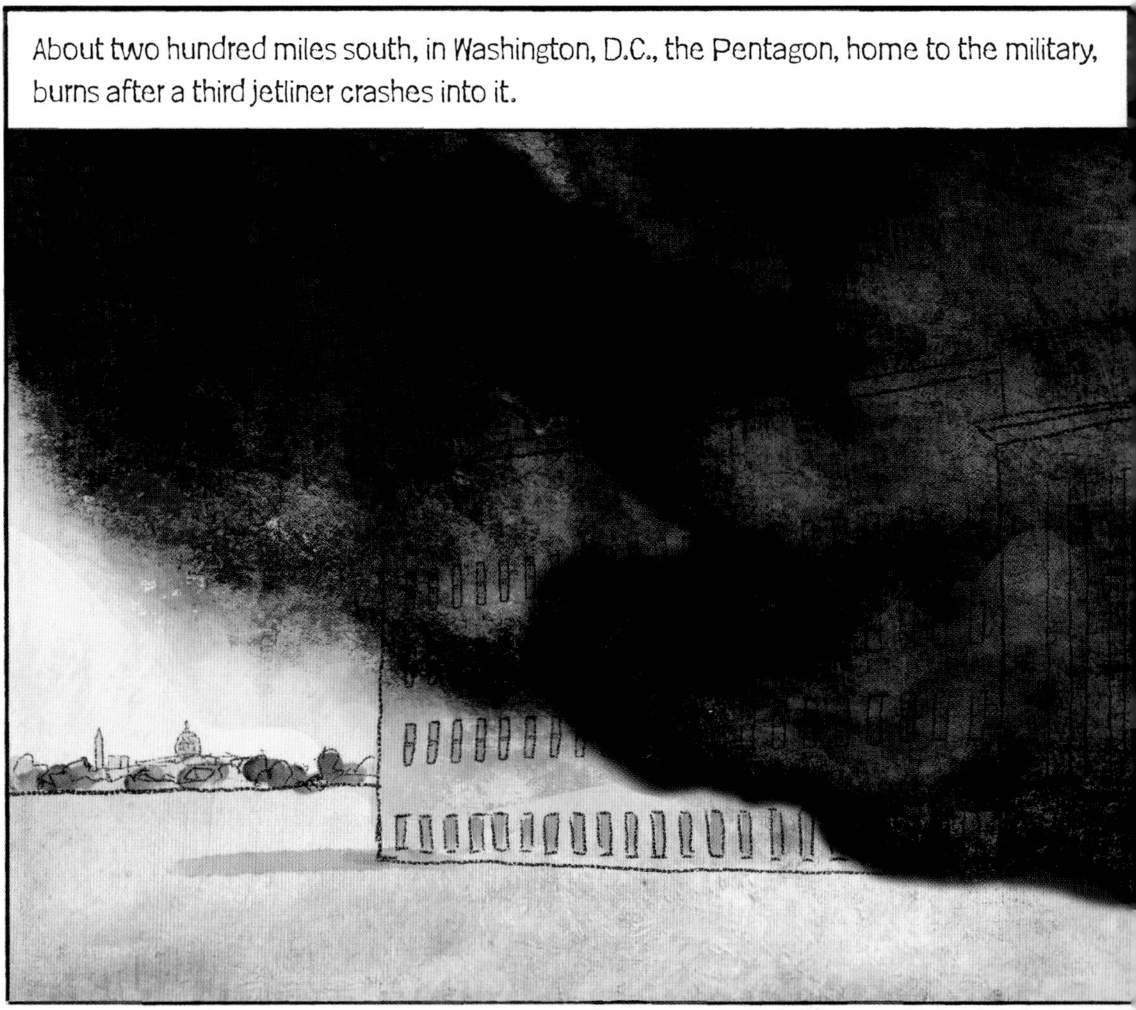
About two hundred miles south, in Washington, D.C., the Pentagon, home to the military, burns after a third jetliner crashes into it.

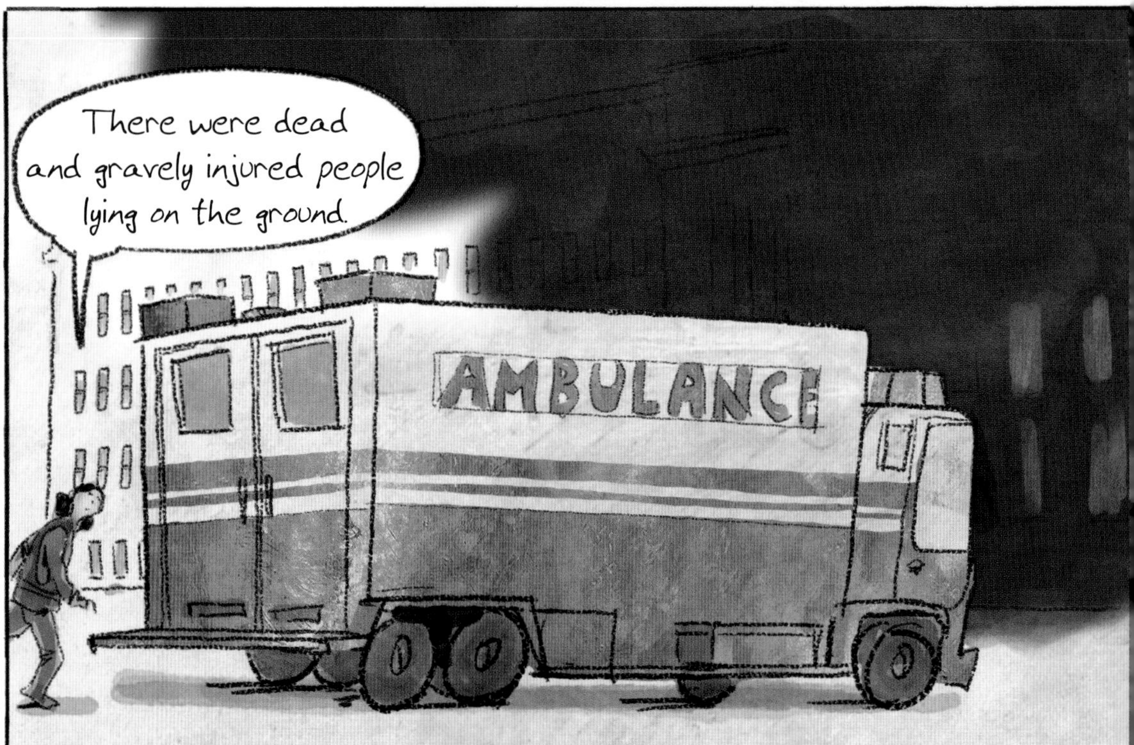
There were dead and gravely injured people lying on the ground.
AMBULANCE

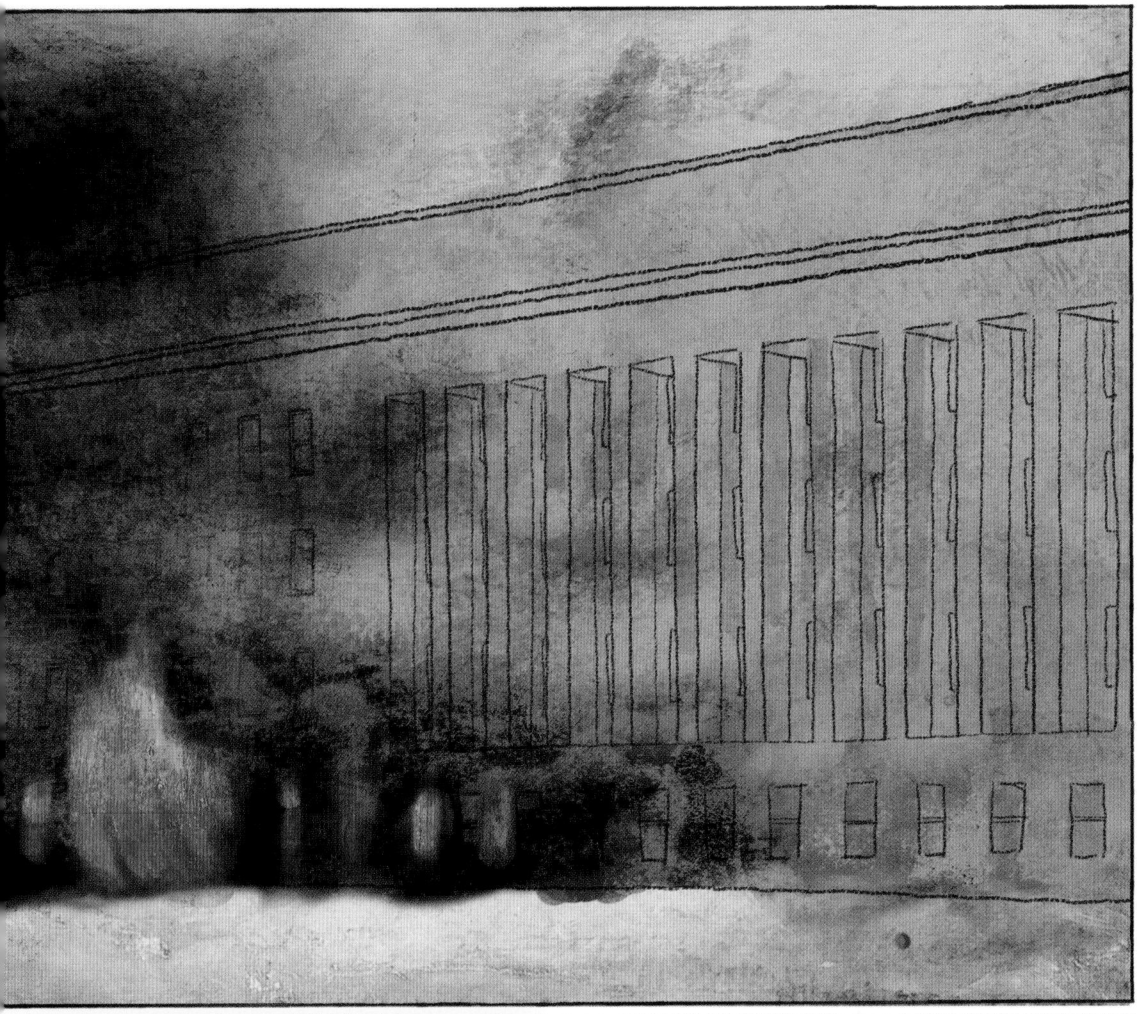

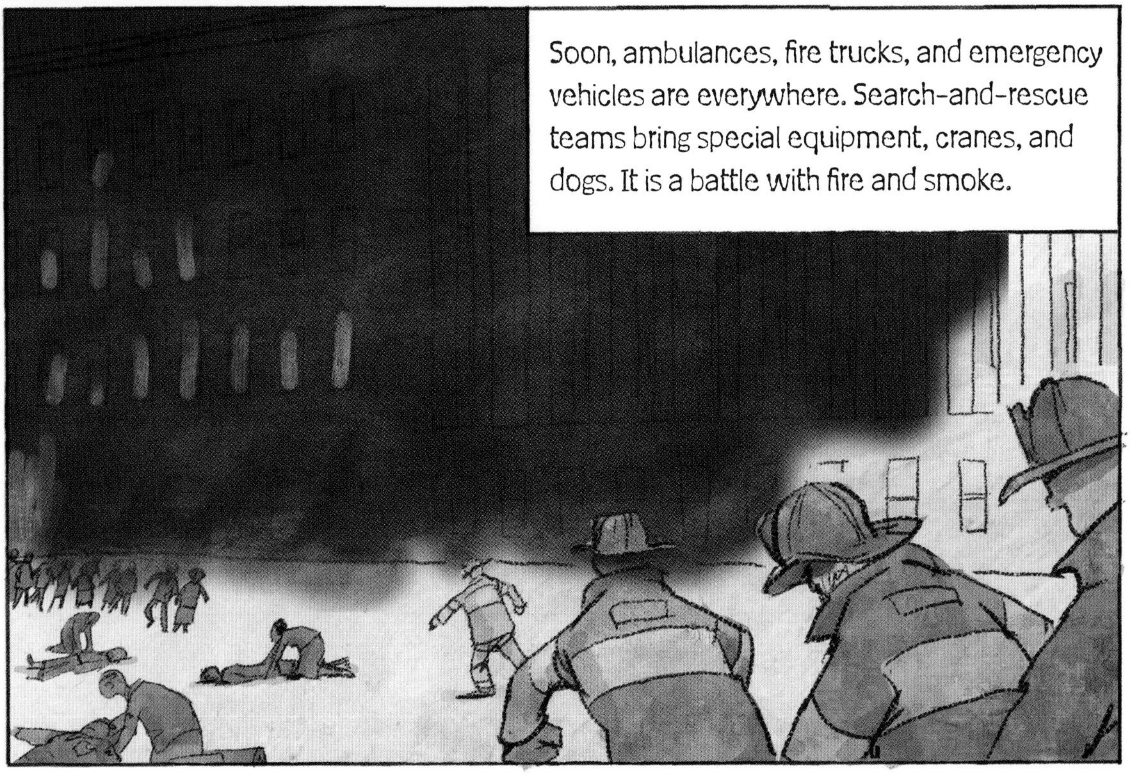
Soon, ambulances, fire trucks, and emergency vehicles are everywhere. Search-and-rescue teams bring special equipment, cranes, and dogs. It is a battle with fire and smoke.

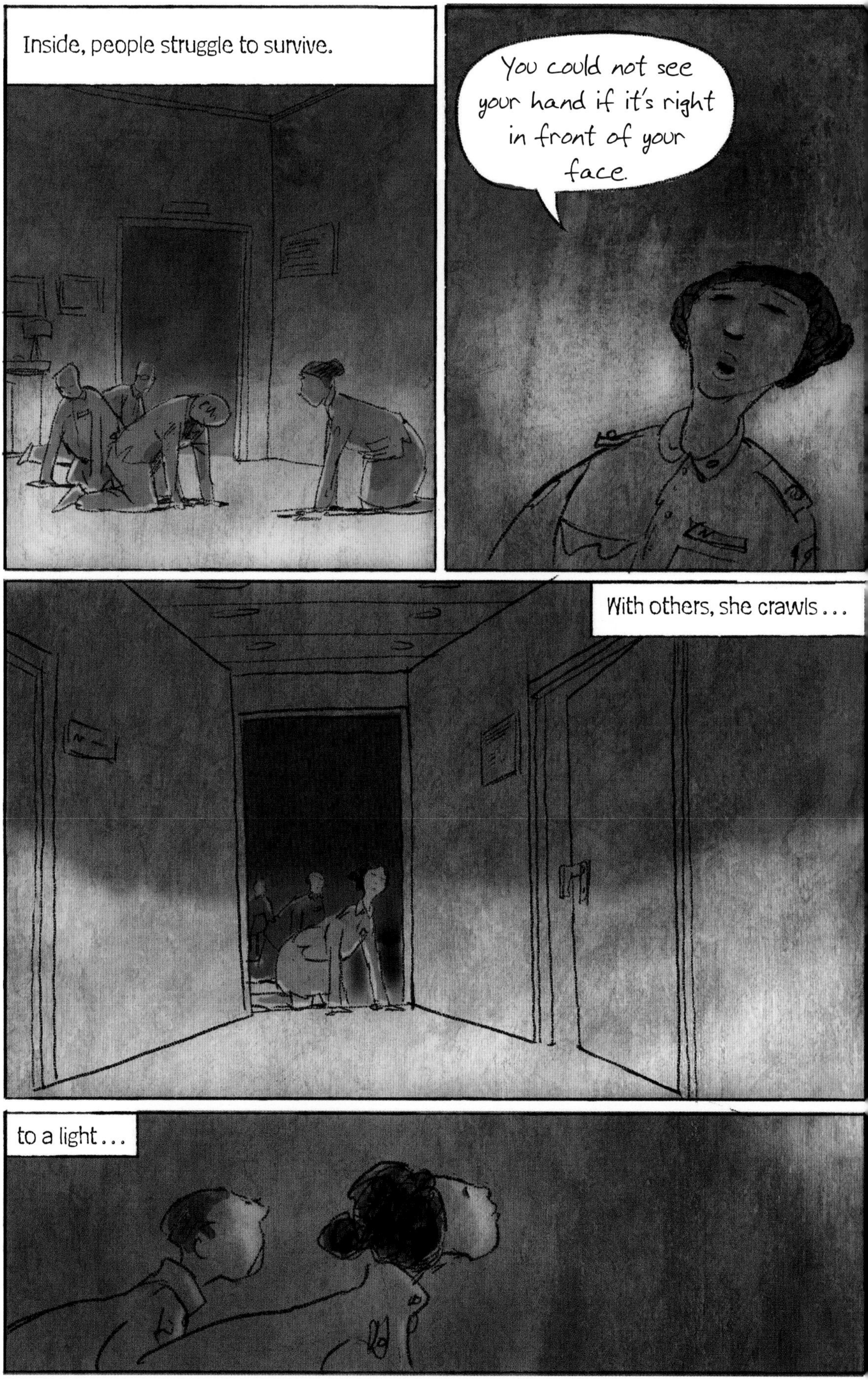
Inside, people struggle to survive.
You could not see your hand if it's right in front of your face.
With others, she crawls . . .
to a light . . .

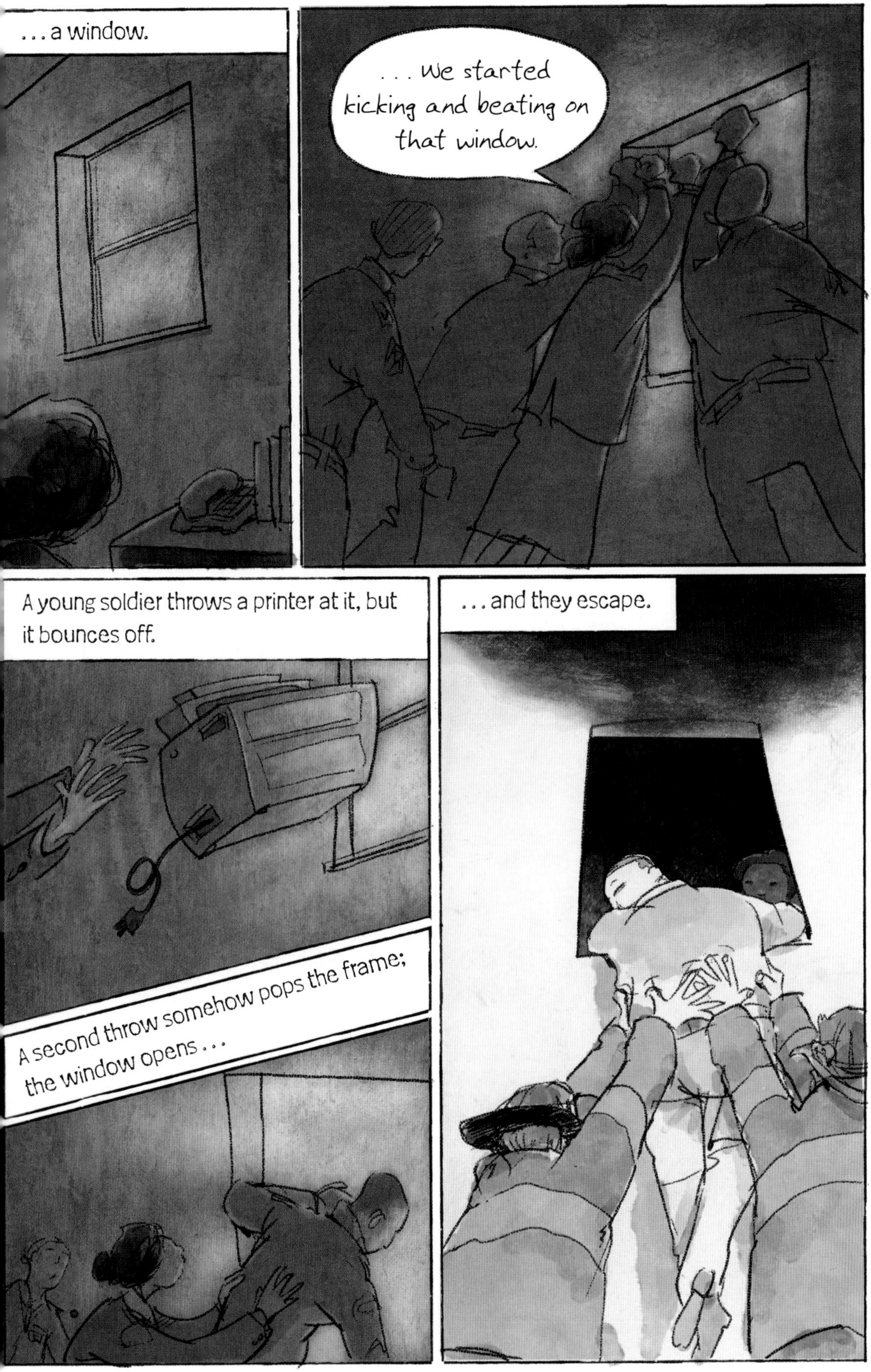

. . . a window.
. . . We started kicking and beating on that window.
A young soldier throws a printer at it, but it bounces off.
A second throw somehow pops the frame; the window opens . . .
. . . and they escape.

Pentagon workers plunge into the smoke-filled building to restore water pressure made feeble by pipes broken in the attack. Without water, there is no firefighting.

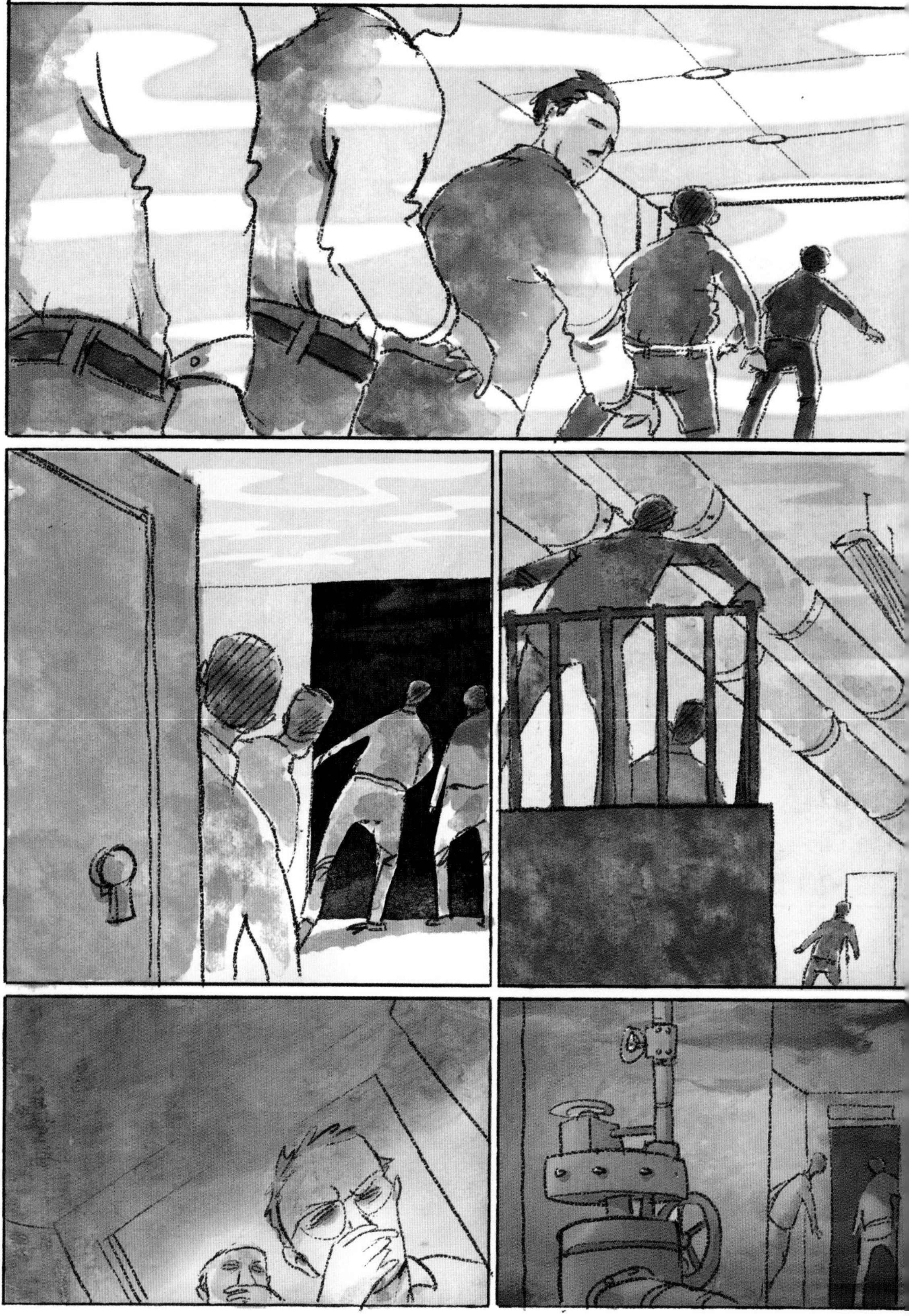

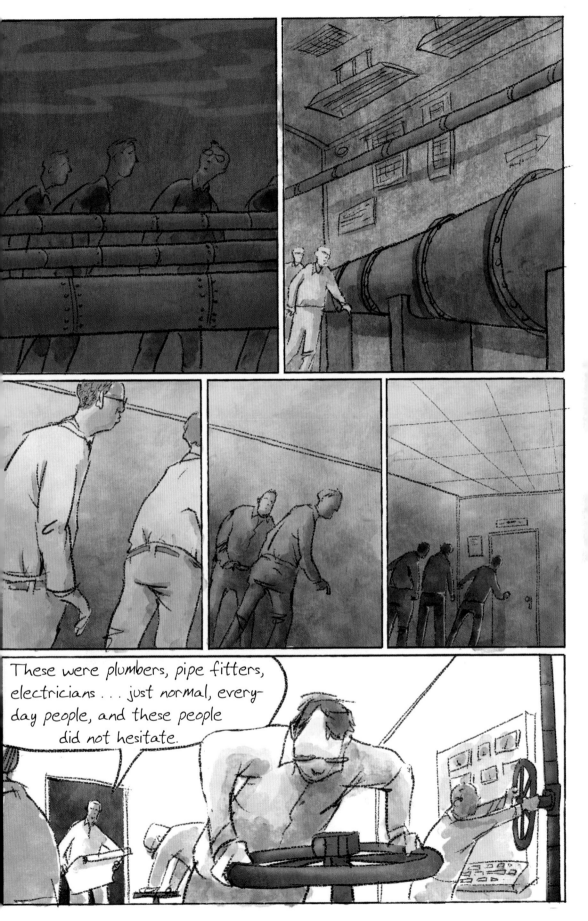

These were plumbers, pipe fitters, electricians . . . just normal, every-day people, and these people did not hesitate.

37

Washington, D.C.—area air-traffic controllers plot more airliners heading toward D.C. They are believed to be hijacked airliners meant for more attacks.

Evacuate five hundred yards away from the building. All Units! Evacuate five hundred yards from the building.

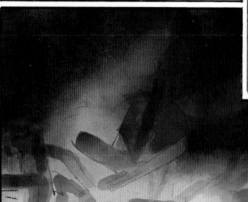

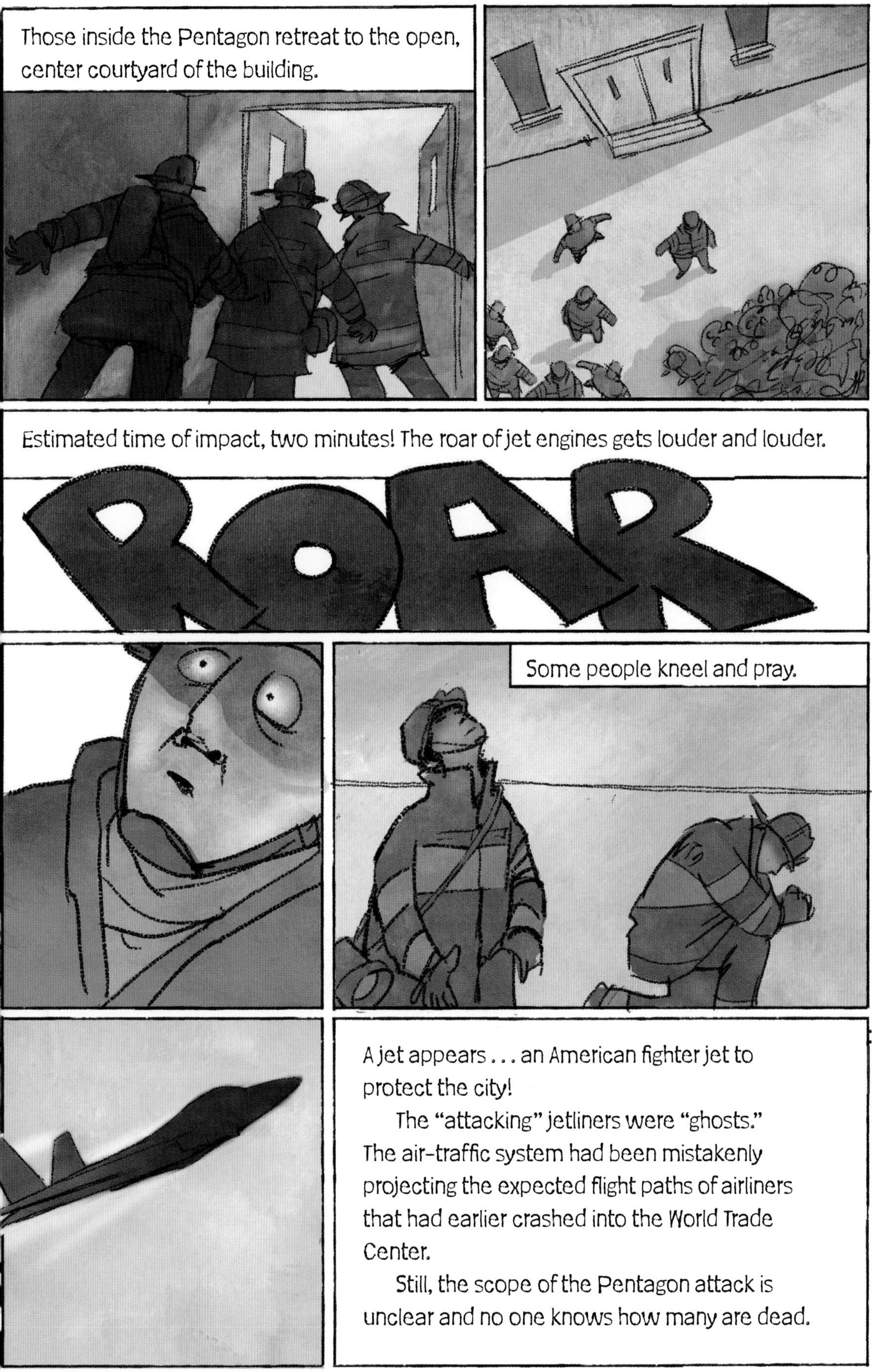
Those inside the Pentagon retreat to the open, center courtyard of the building.
Estimated time of impact, two minutes! The roar of jet engines gets louder and louder.
ROAR
Some people kneel and pray.
A jet appears . . . an American fighter jet to protect the city!
The "attacking" jetliners were "ghosts." The air-traffic system had been mistakenly projecting the expected flight paths of airliners that had earlier crashed into the World Trade Center.
Still, the scope of the Pentagon attack is unclear and no one knows how many are dead.

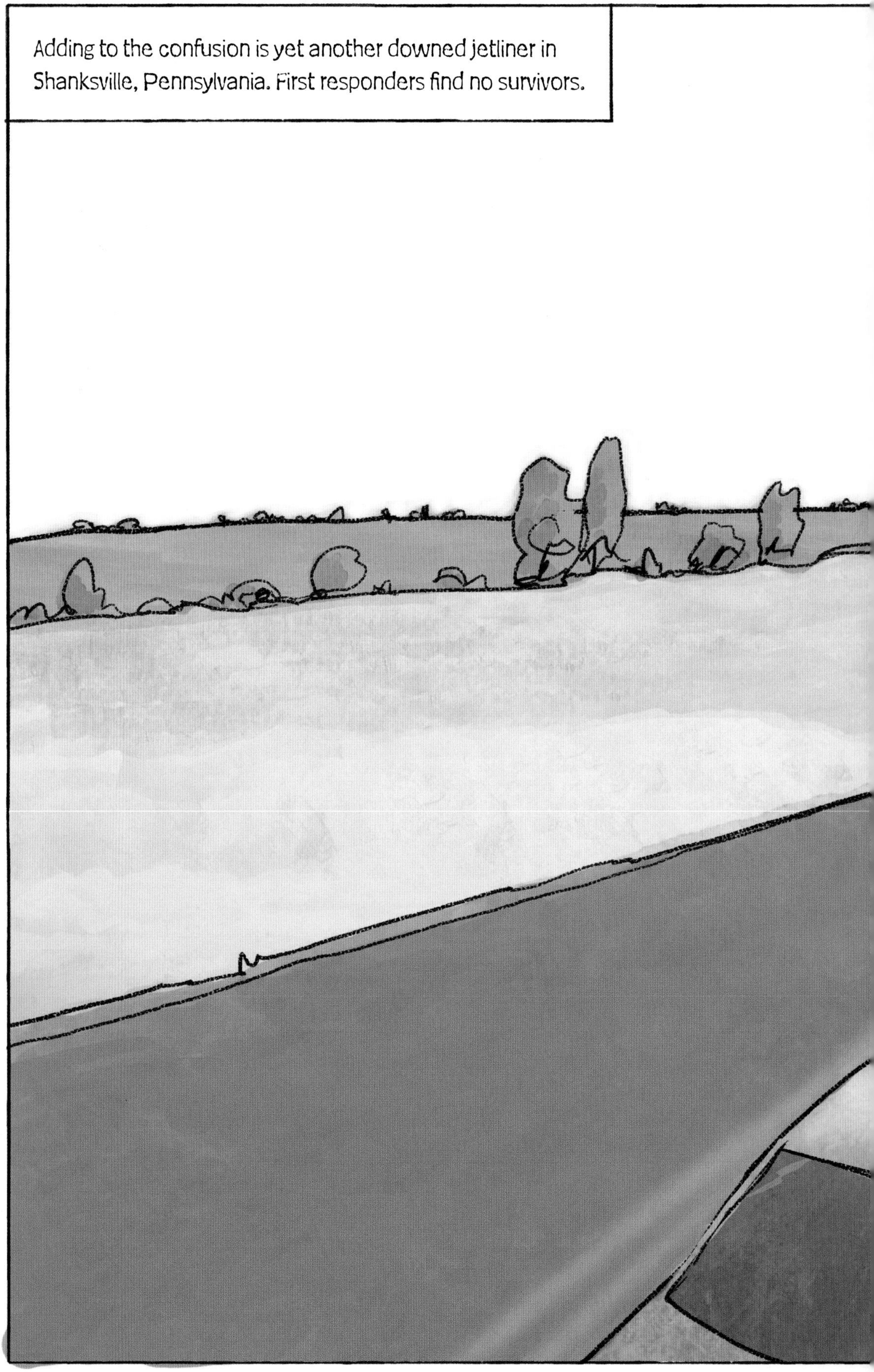
Adding to the confusion is yet another downed jetliner in Shanksville, Pennsylvania. First responders find no survivors.

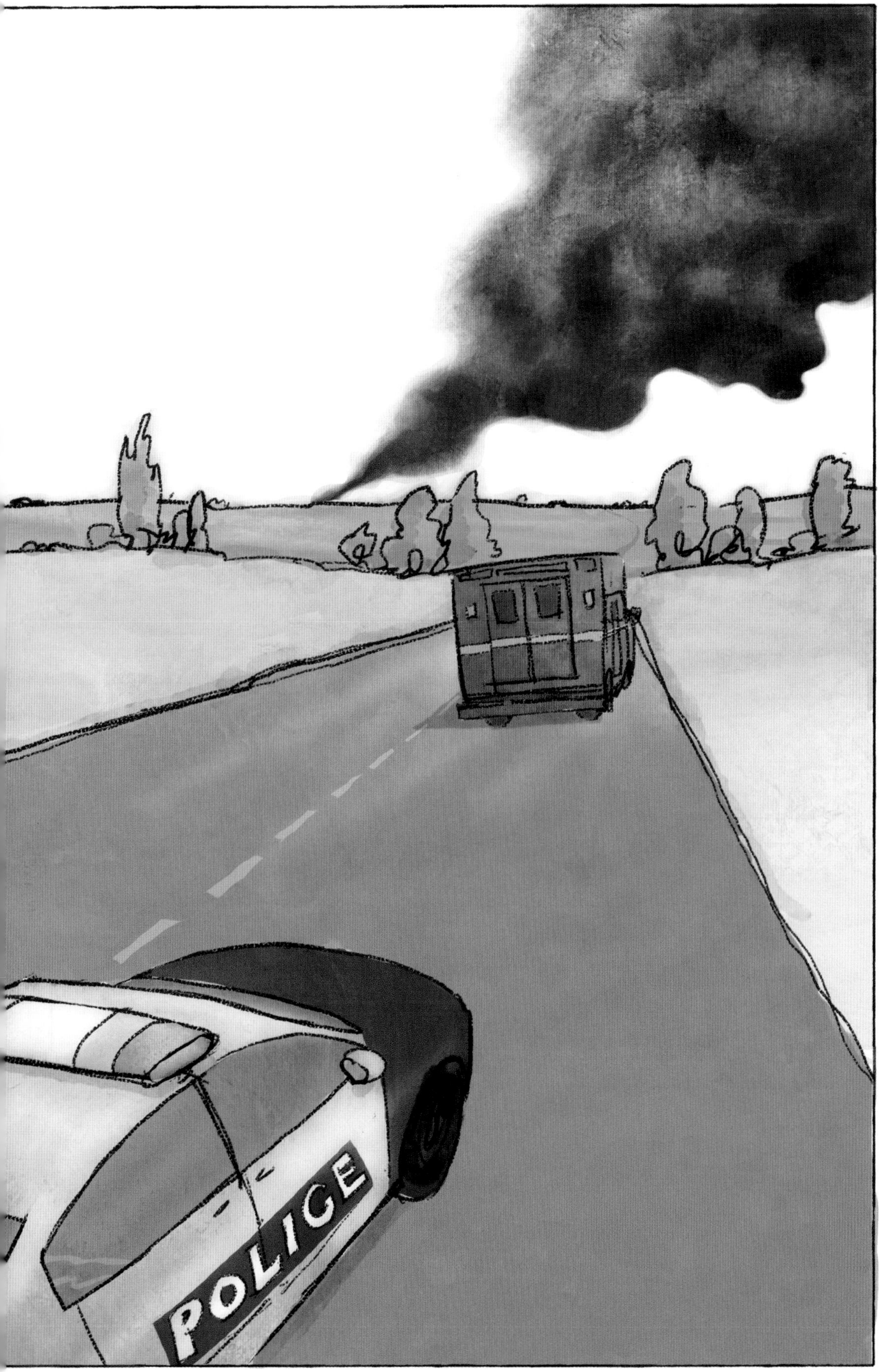
POLICE

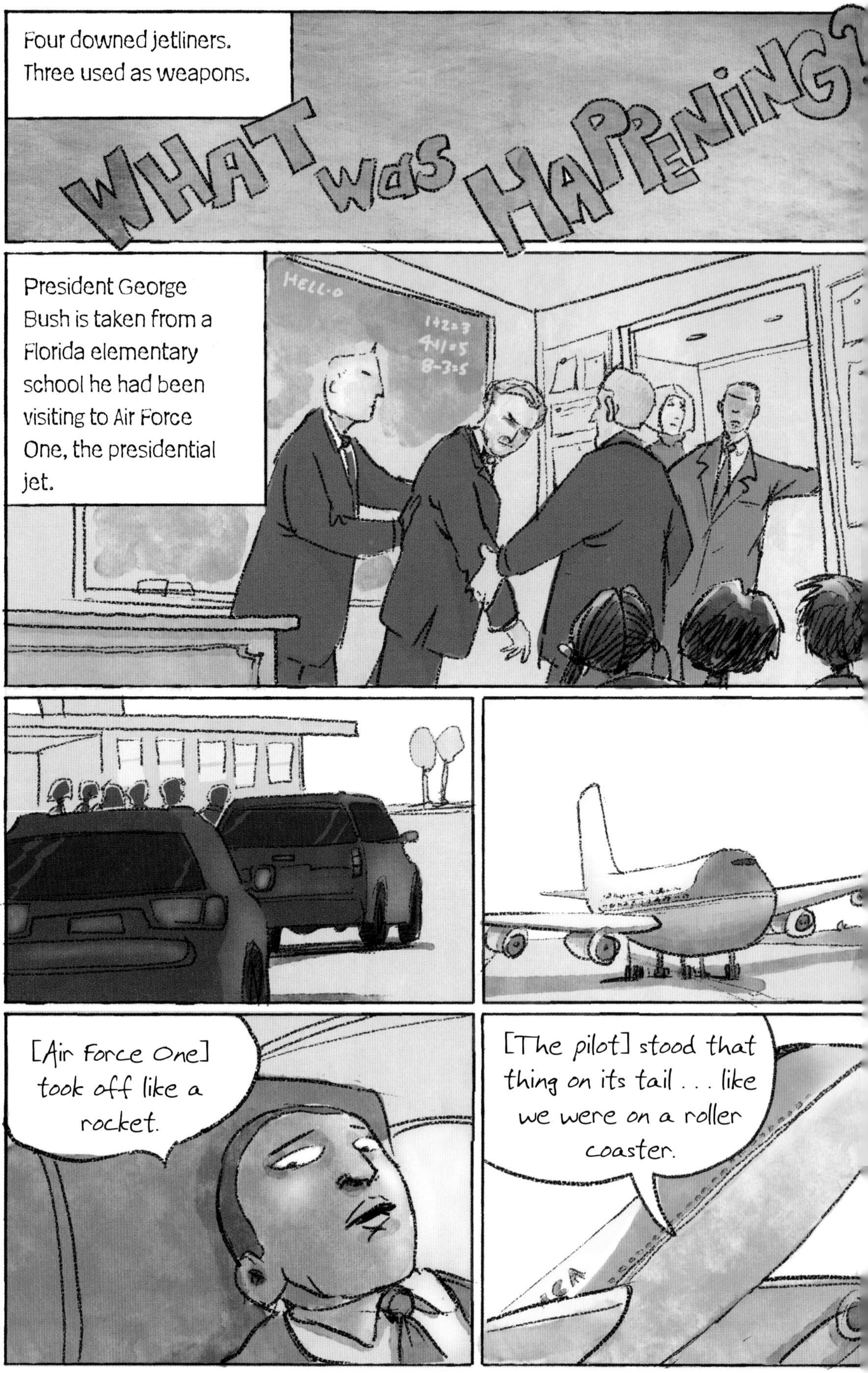
Four downed jetliners.
Three used as weapons.
WHAT was HAPPENING?
President George Bush is taken from a Florida elementary school he had been visiting to Air Force One, the presidential jet.
[Air Force One] took off like a rocket.
[The pilot] stood that thing on its tail . . . like we were on a roller coaster.

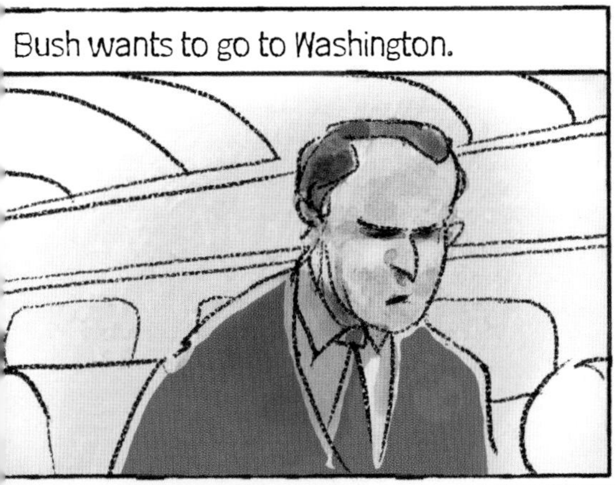
Bush wants to go to Washington.

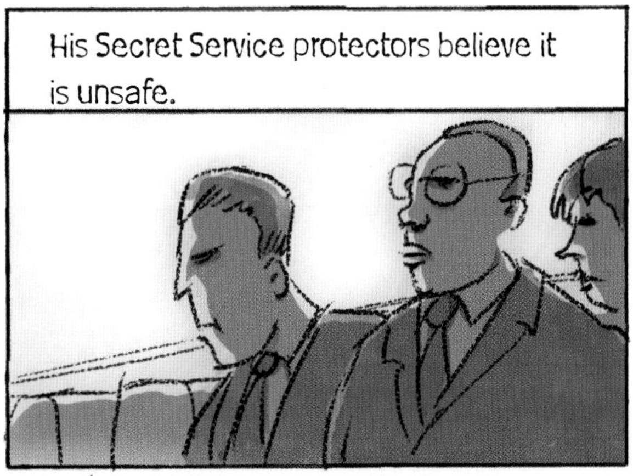
His Secret Service protectors believe it is unsafe.

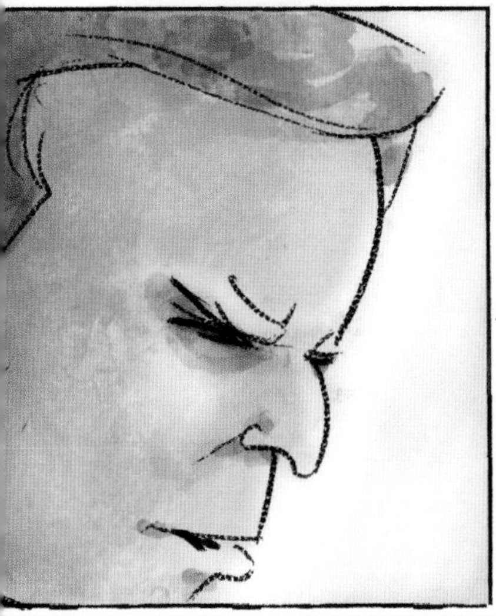

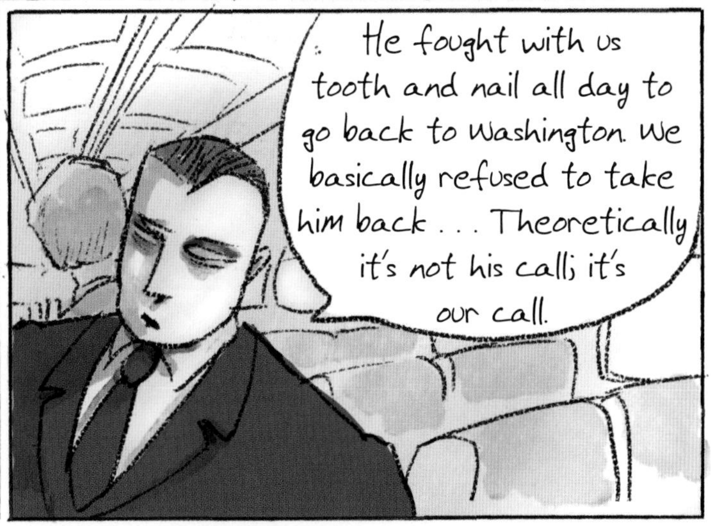
He fought with us tooth and nail all day to go back to Washington. We basically refused to take him back . . . Theoretically it's not his call; it's our call.

On their way to an air force base in Nebraska, Bush asks of the attack, "Who did this?"

Evidence points to Osama bin Laden and his organization, al-Qaeda.

Bin Laden and al-Qaeda are jihadists, believers in violence to promote radical notions of Islam, a religion that shares elements of Judaism and Christianity. Jihadists see America as a religious enemy. Bin Laden and his followers had found refuge in Afghanistan, whose leaders, the Taliban, held similar strict Islamic beliefs and were hostile to foreigners.

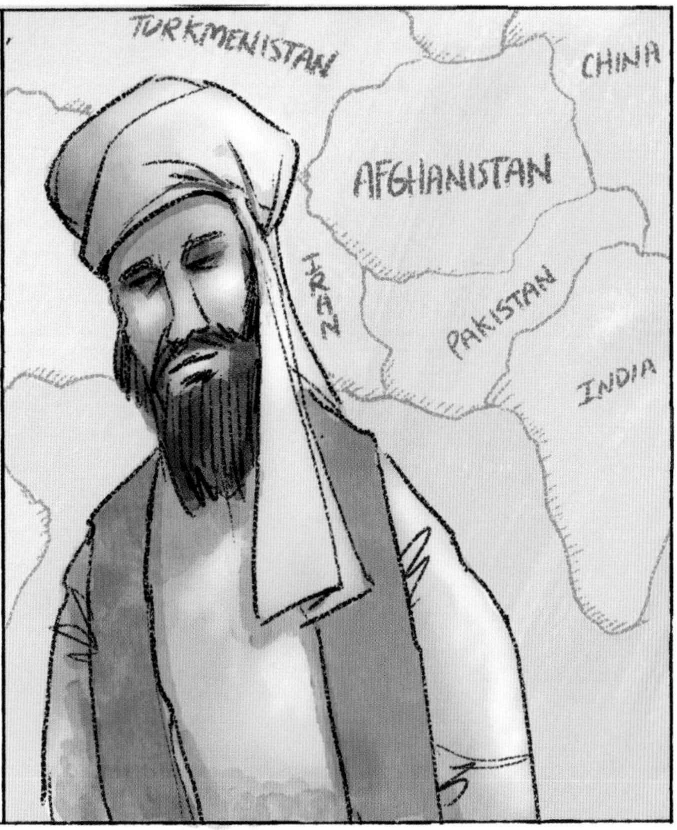
TURKMENISTAN
CHINA
AFGHANISTAN
IRAN
PAKISTAN
INDIA

Soon, Air Force One is the only plane in the sky. All flights in the United States are ordered to land at the nearest airport in fear of additional hijackings. Thirty-eight flights from Europe are rerouted to Newfoundland, a Canadian island in the Atlantic Ocean.

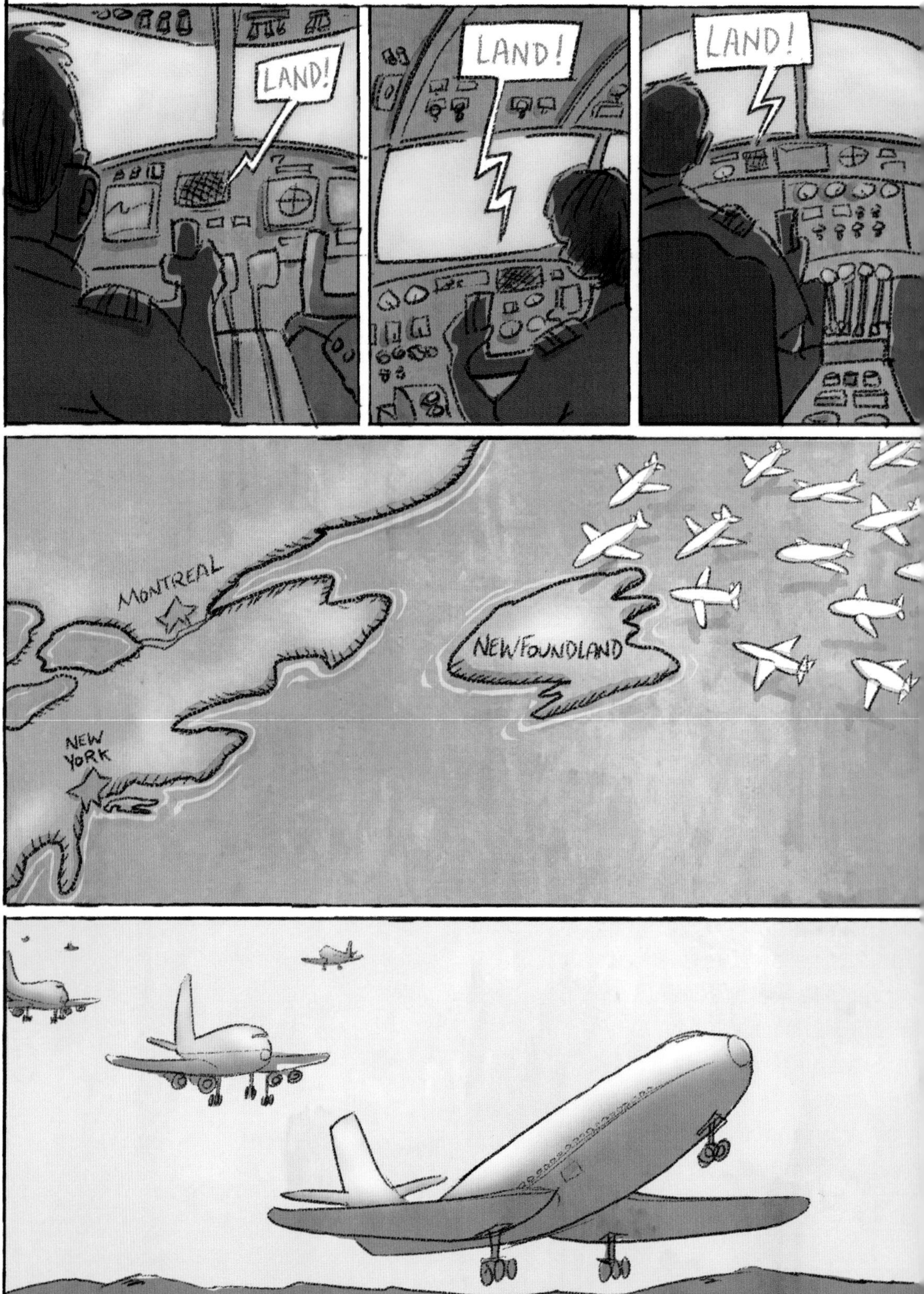

LAND!
LAND!
LAND!
MONTREAL
NEWFOUNDLAND
NEW YORK

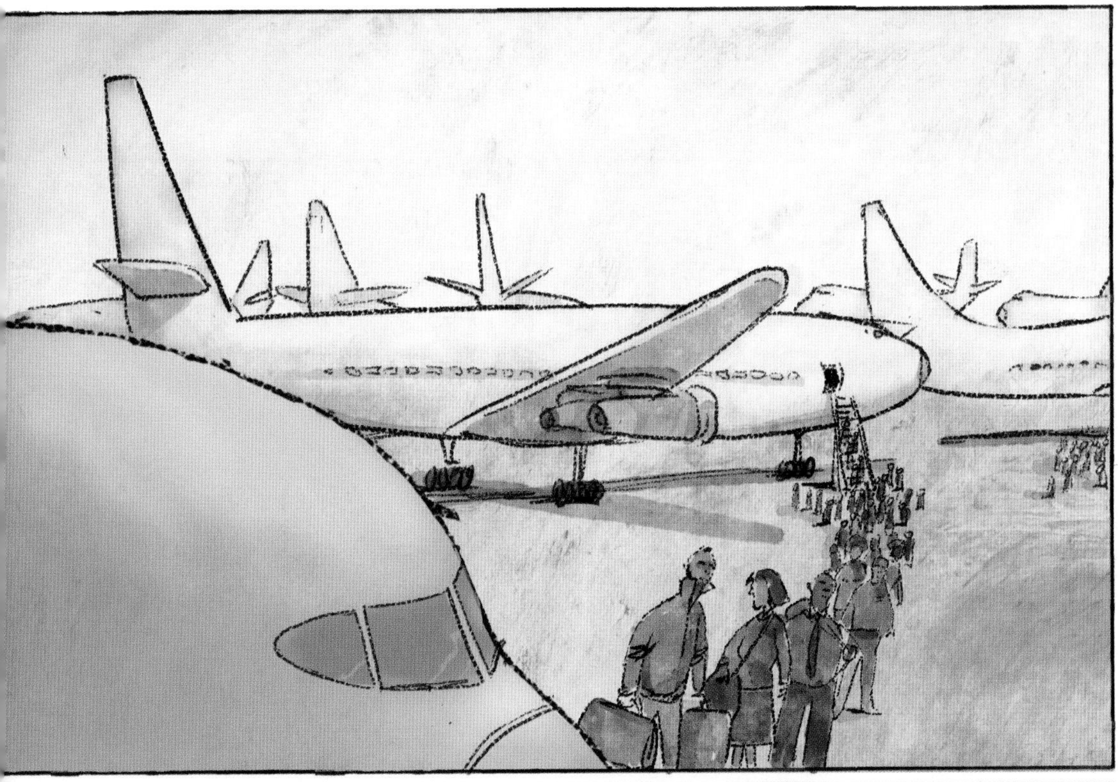

Seven thousand passengers find themselves stranded in the town of Gander with only five hundred hotel rooms, all of which are reserved for the flight crews.

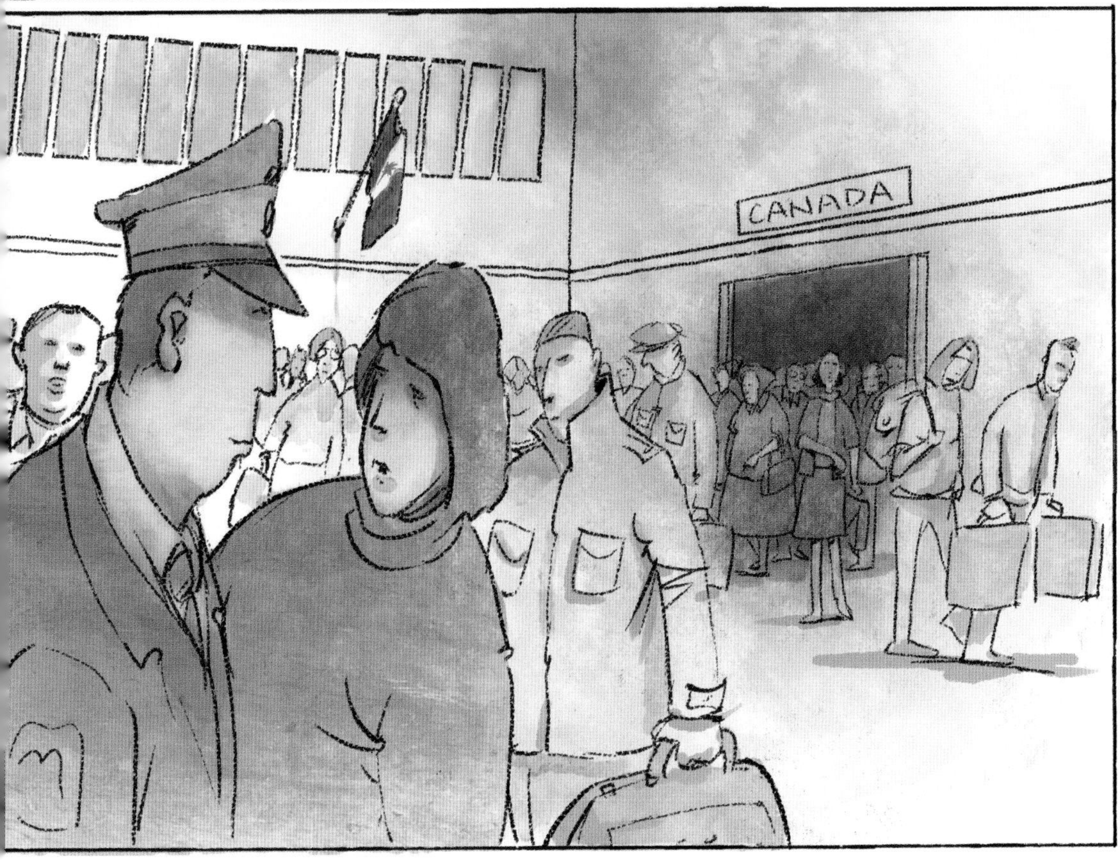
CANADA

Newfoundland schools, gyms, community centers, and churches become makeshift shelters. All manner of personal items such as toiletries, blankets, towels, and toothbrushes are donated. Visitors are fed and clothed.

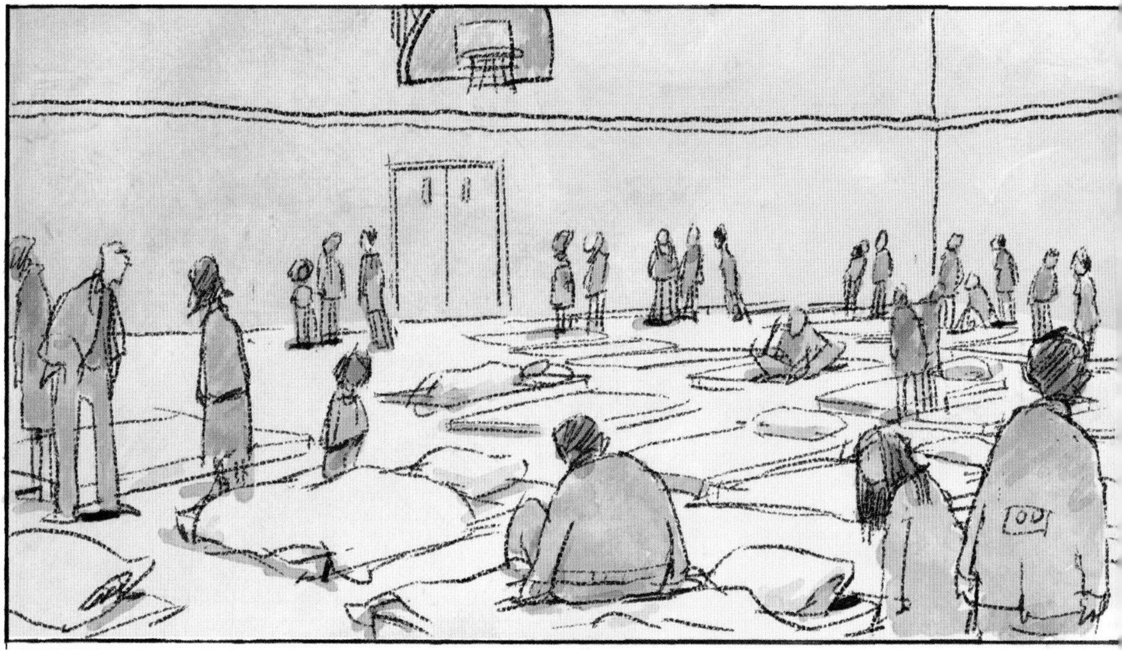

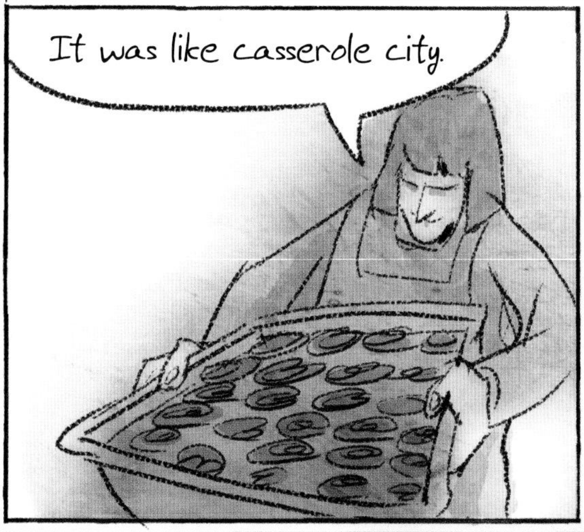
It was like casserole city.

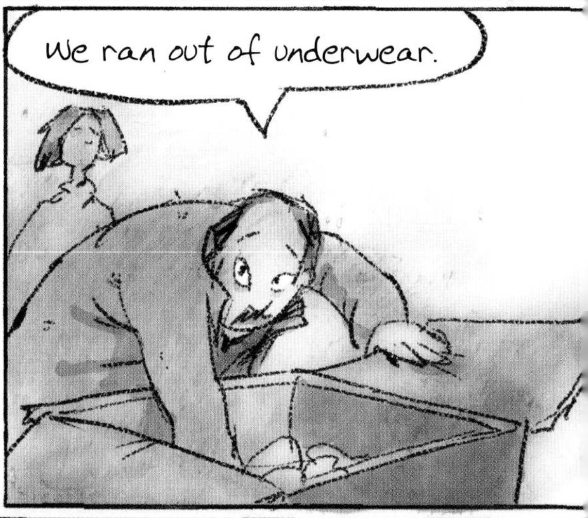
We ran out of underwear.

Animals—including two zoo-bound chimpanzees—in the planes' cargo holds are cared for by a local veterinarian. Regular air traffic resumes a couple of days later.

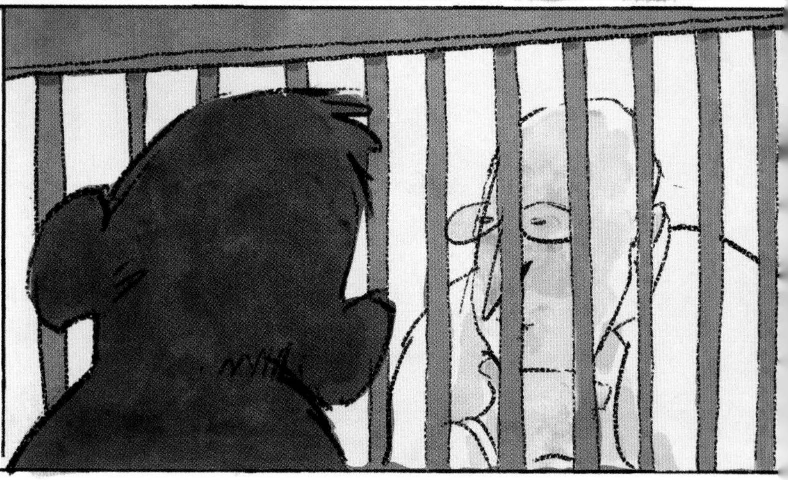

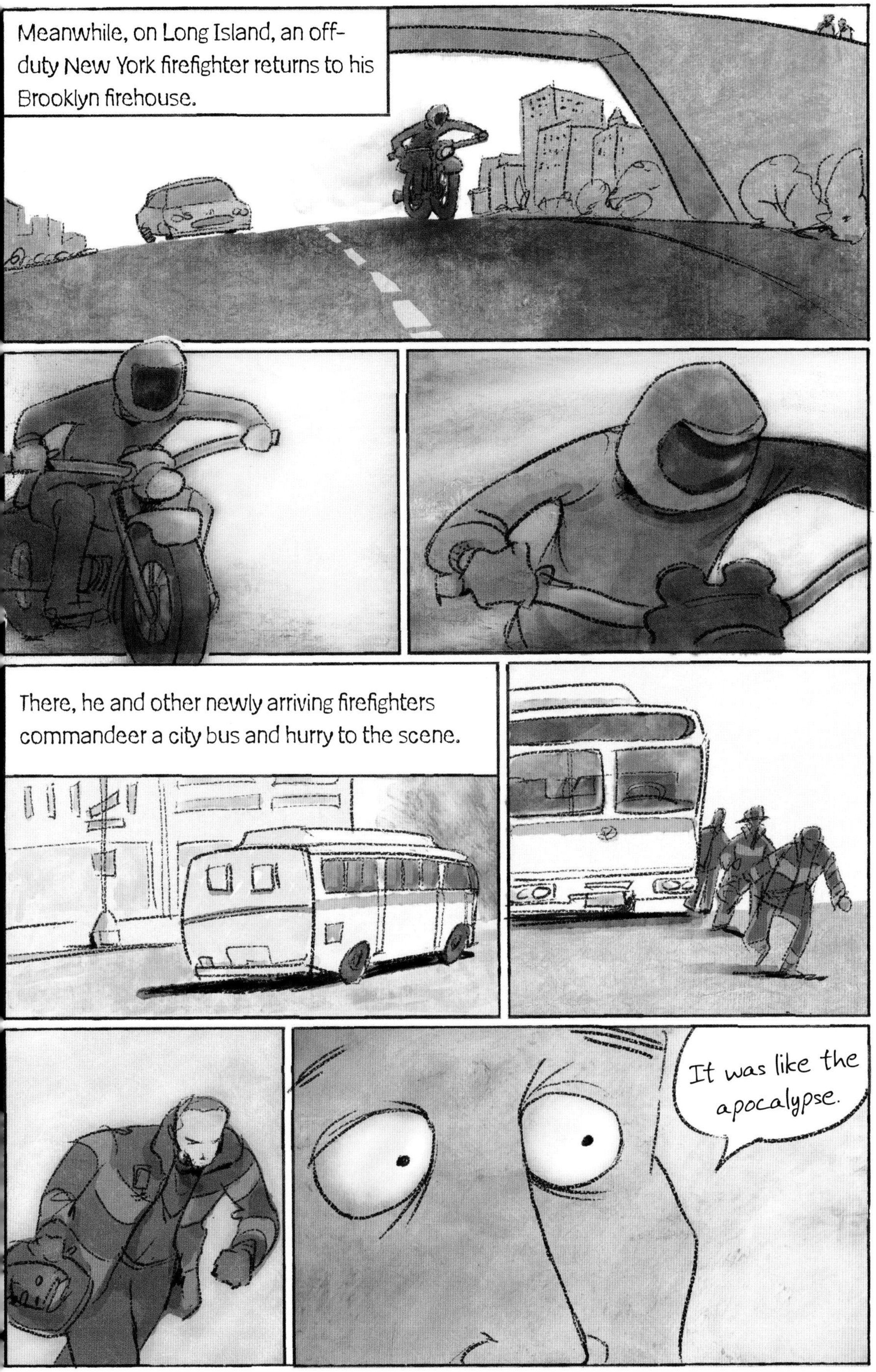
Meanwhile, on Long Island, an off-duty New York firefighter returns to his Brooklyn firehouse.
There, he and other newly arriving firefighters commandeer a city bus and hurry to the scene.
It was like the apocalypse.

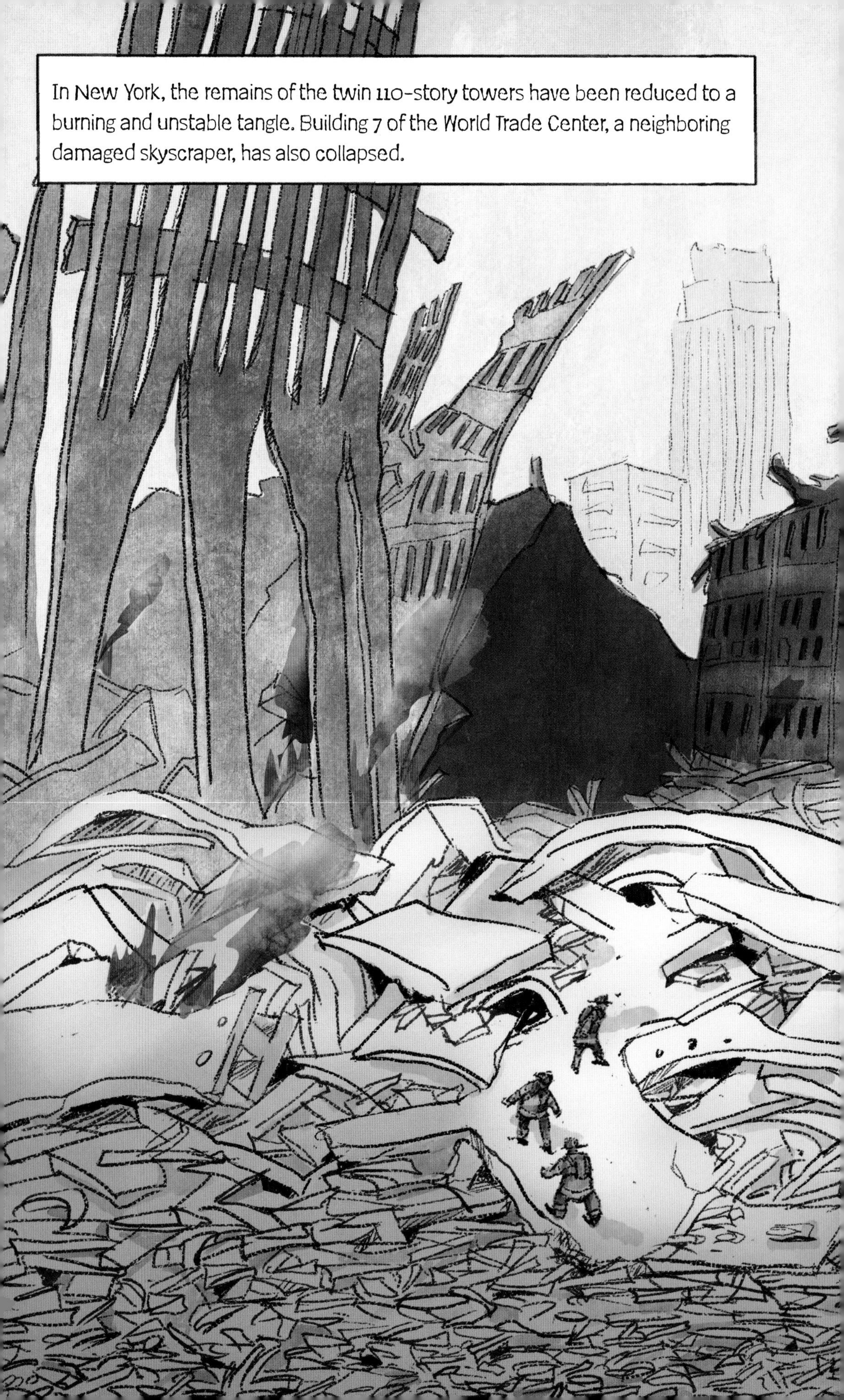
In New York, the remains of the twin 110-story towers have been reduced to a burning and unstable tangle. Building 7 of the World Trade Center, a neighboring damaged skyscraper, has also collapsed.

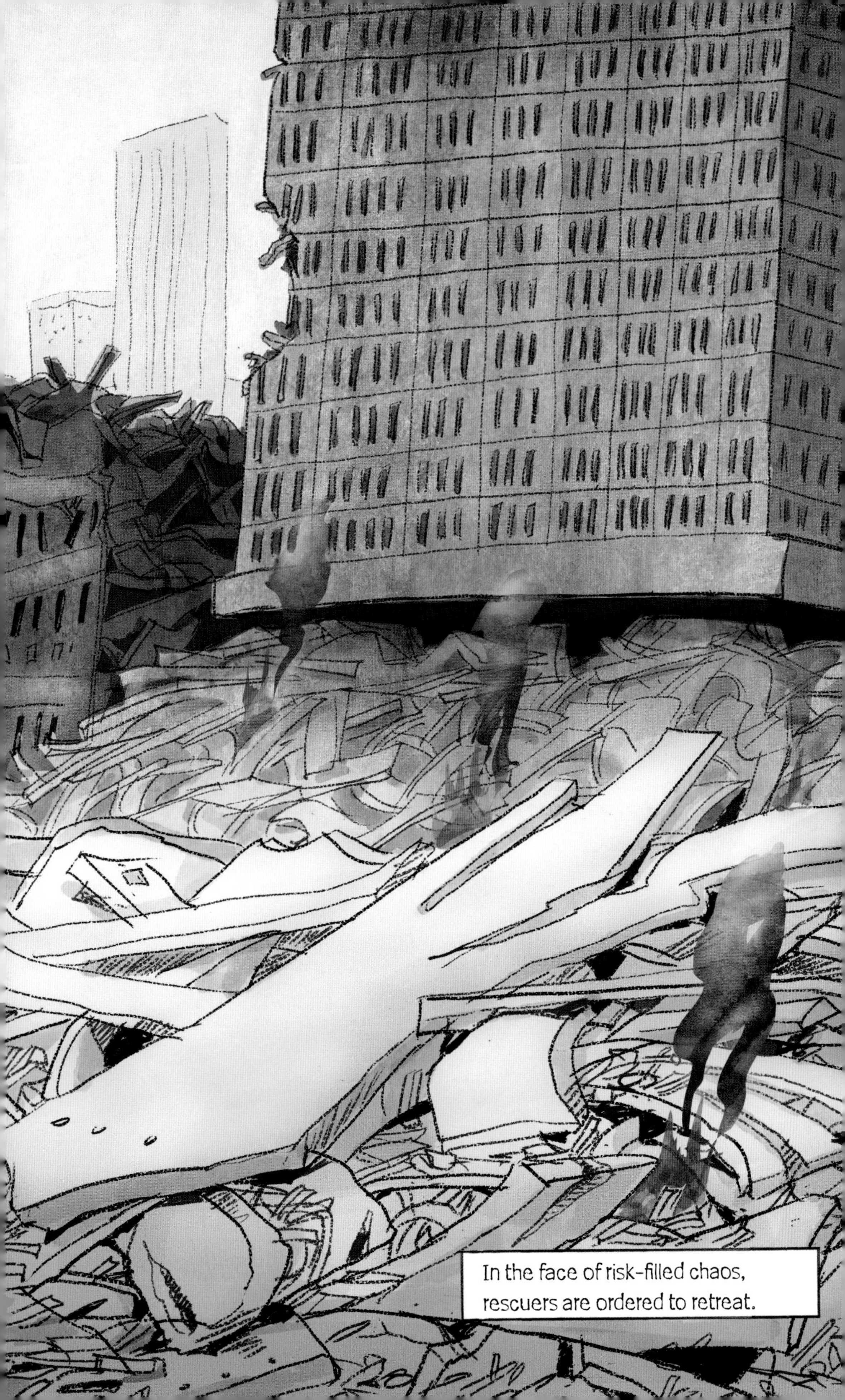
In the face of risk-filled chaos, rescuers are ordered to retreat.

In Connecticut, David Karnes sees the mayhem. The former marine dresses in his uniform, gets a haircut, and speeds to New York. His uniform helps him bluff past roadblocks.

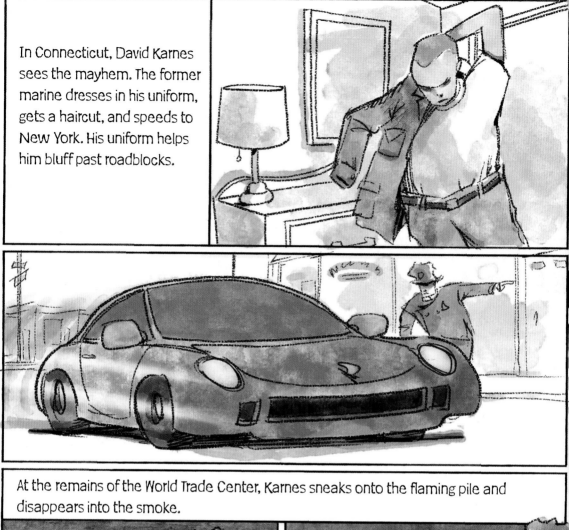

At the remains of the World Trade Center, Karnes sneaks onto the flaming pile and disappears into the smoke.

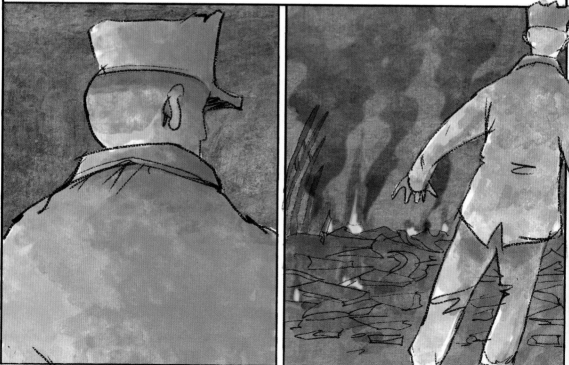

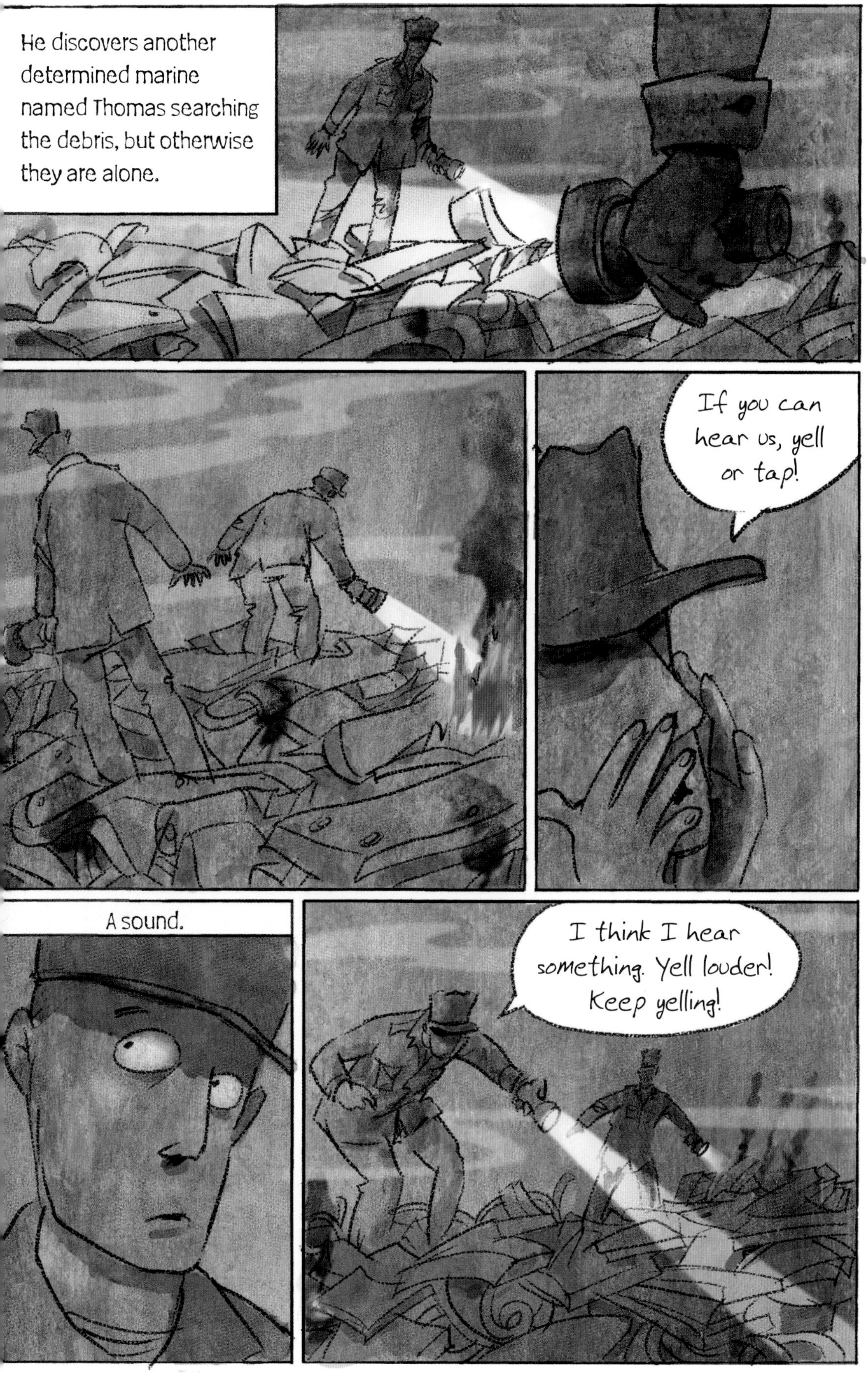
He discovers another determined marine named Thomas searching the debris, but otherwise they are alone.
If you can hear us, yell or tap!
A sound.
I think I hear something. Yell louder! Keep yelling!

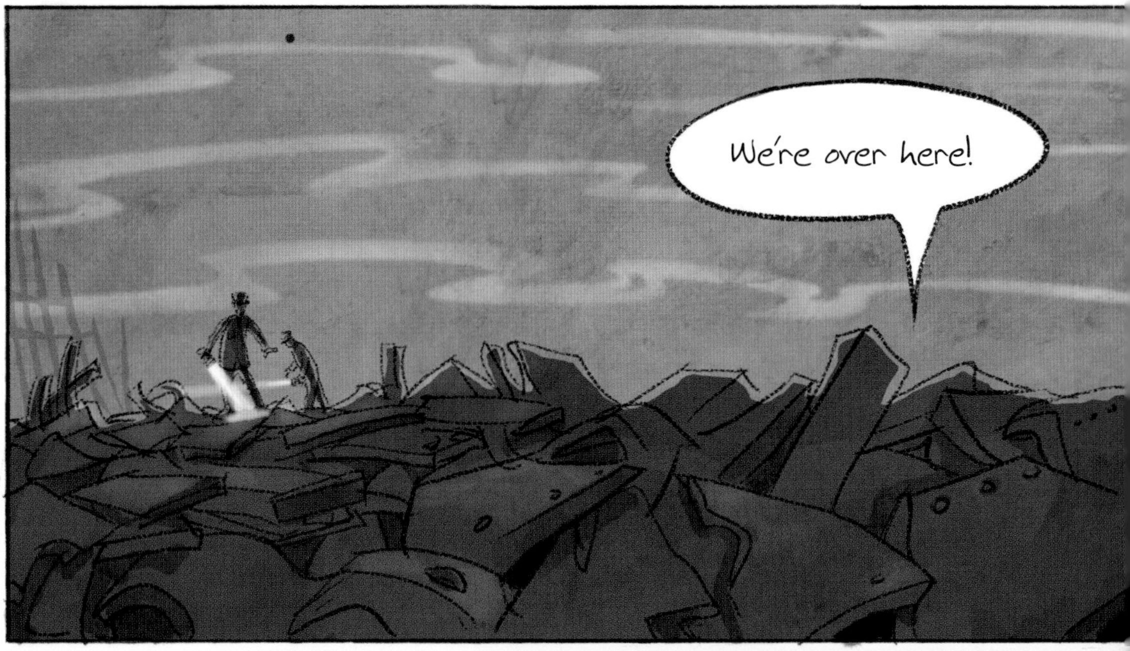
We're over here!

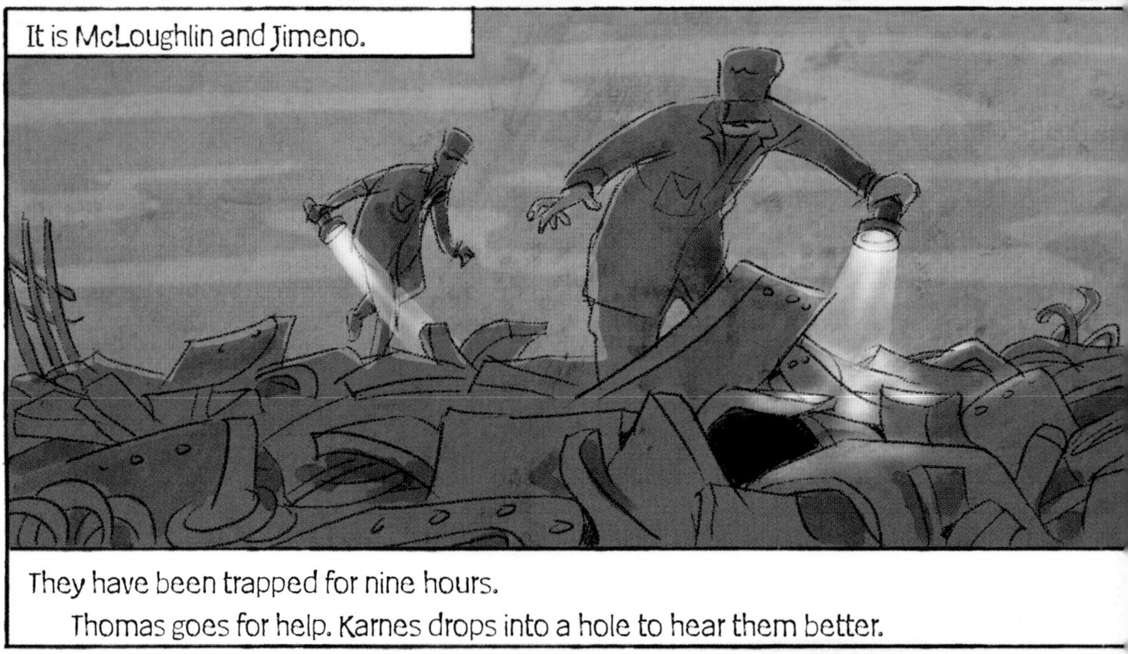
It is McLoughlin and Jimeno.
They have been trapped for nine hours.
Thomas goes for help. Karnes drops into a hole to hear them better.

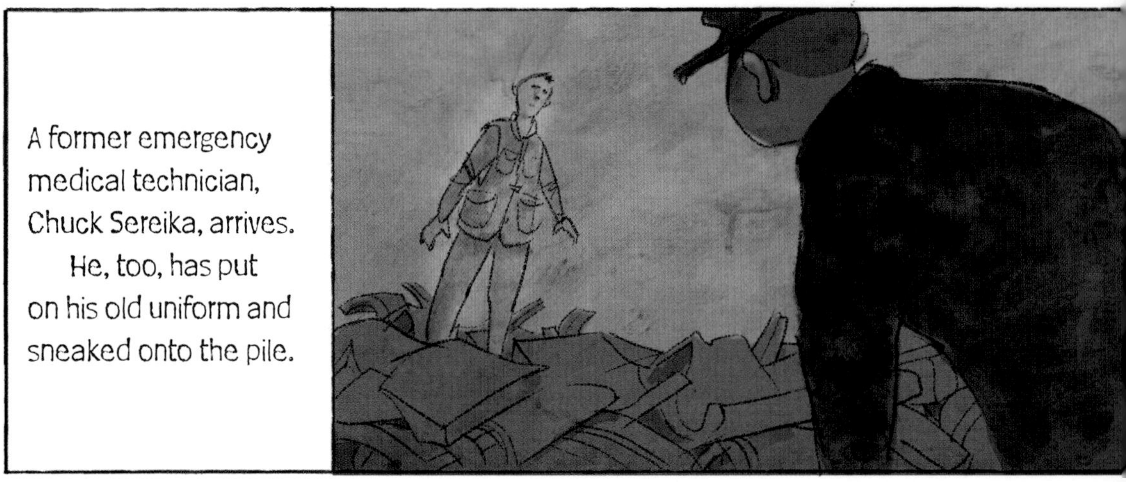
A former emergency medical technician, Chuck Sereika, arrives.
He, too, has put on his old uniform and sneaked onto the pile.

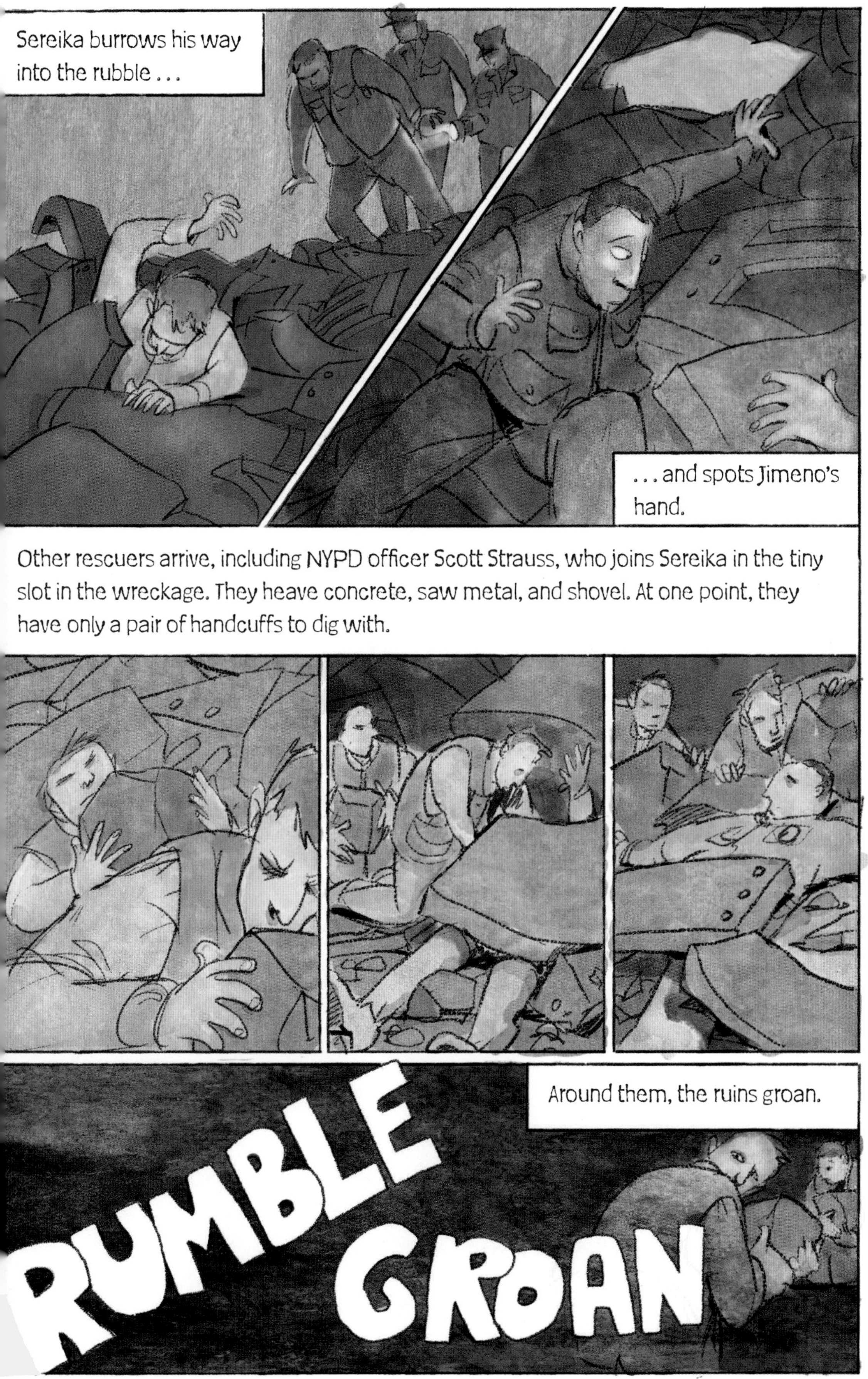
Sereika burrows his way into the rubble . . .
. . . and spots Jimeno's hand.
Other rescuers arrive, including NYPD officer Scott Strauss, who joins Sereika in the tiny slot in the wreckage. They heave concrete, saw metal, and shovel. At one point, they have only a pair of handcuffs to dig with.
Around them, the ruins groan.
RUMBLE
GROAN

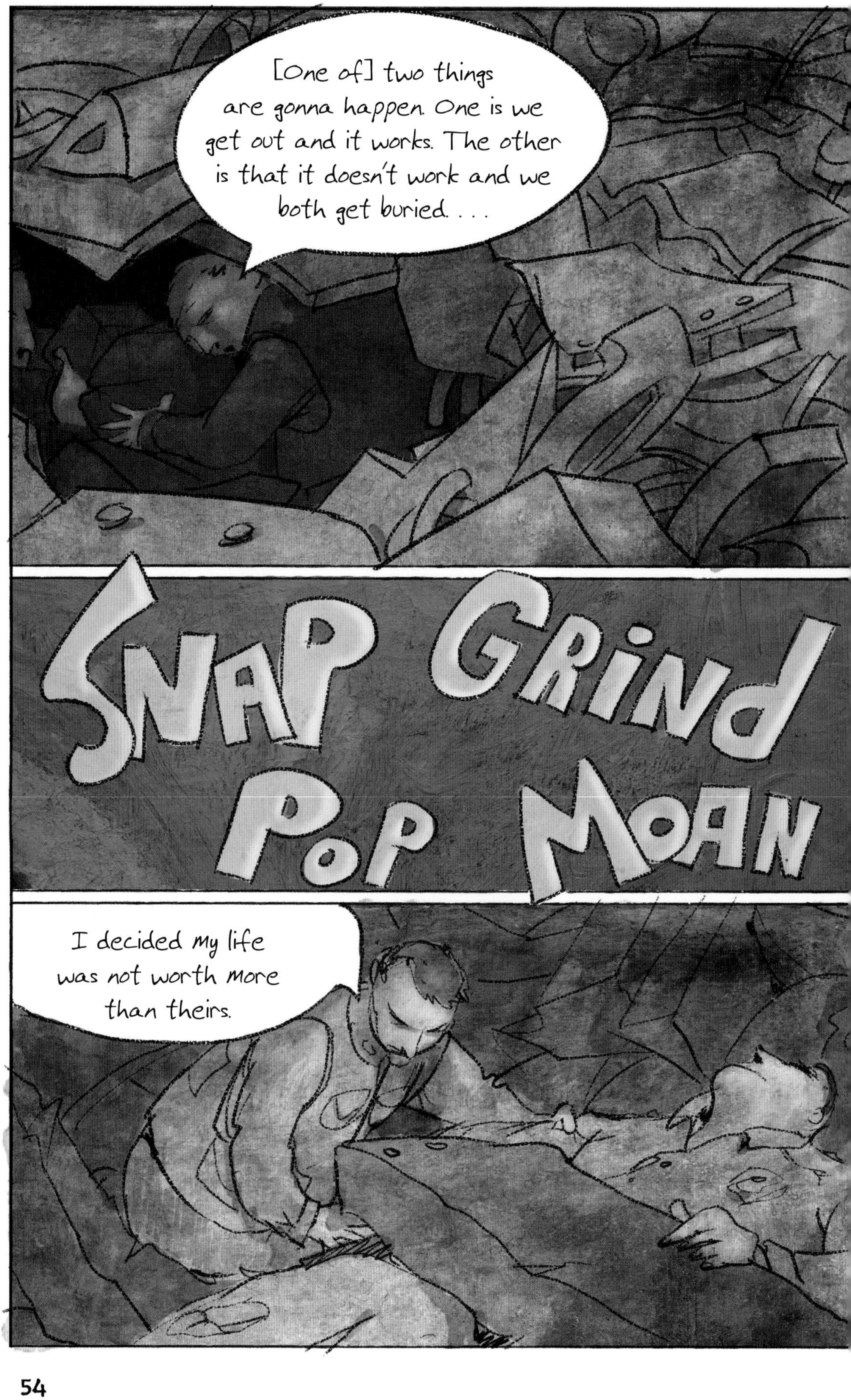
[One of] two things are gonna happen. One is we get out and it works. The other is that it doesn't work and we both get buried. . . .
SNAP GRIND
POP MOAN
I decided my life was not worth more than theirs.

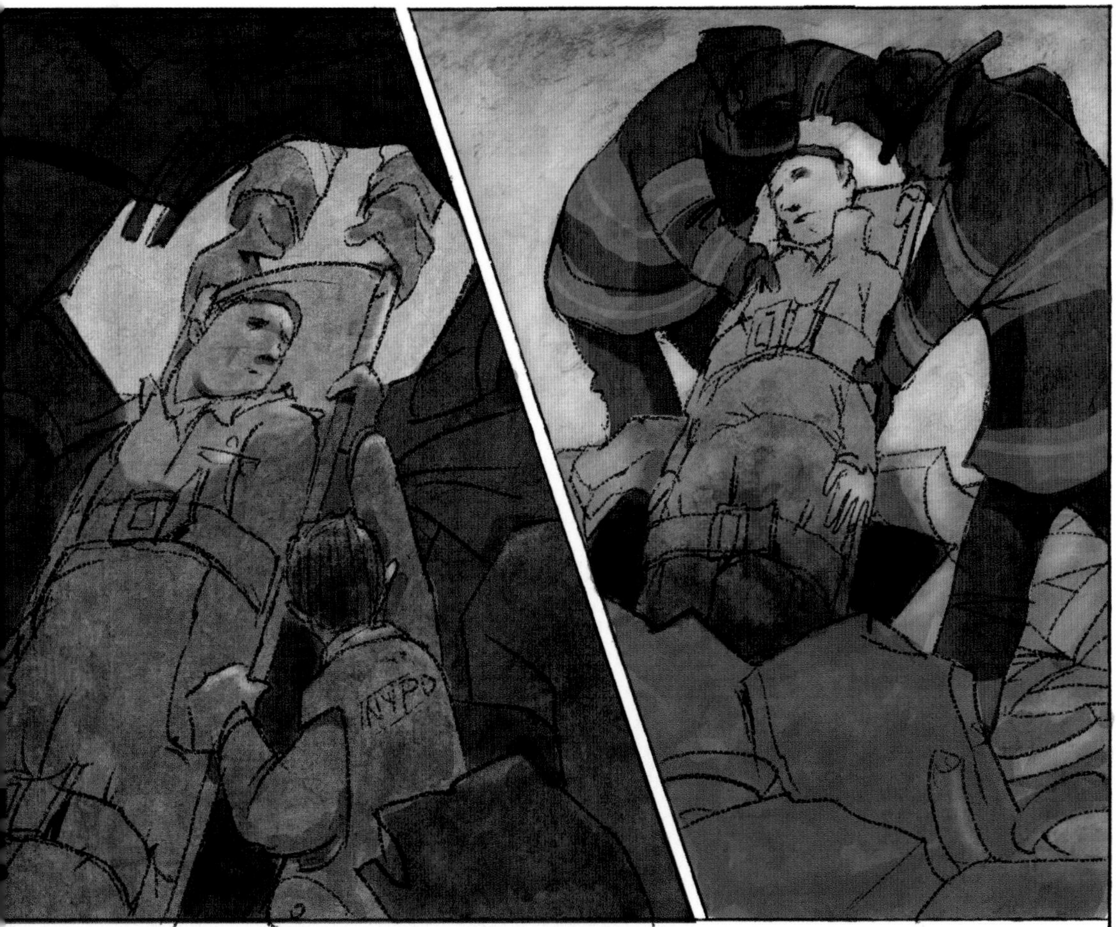
NYPD

They muscle rubble away until Jimeno is free. The steadfast EMT remains in the hole until the cop is pulled clear.

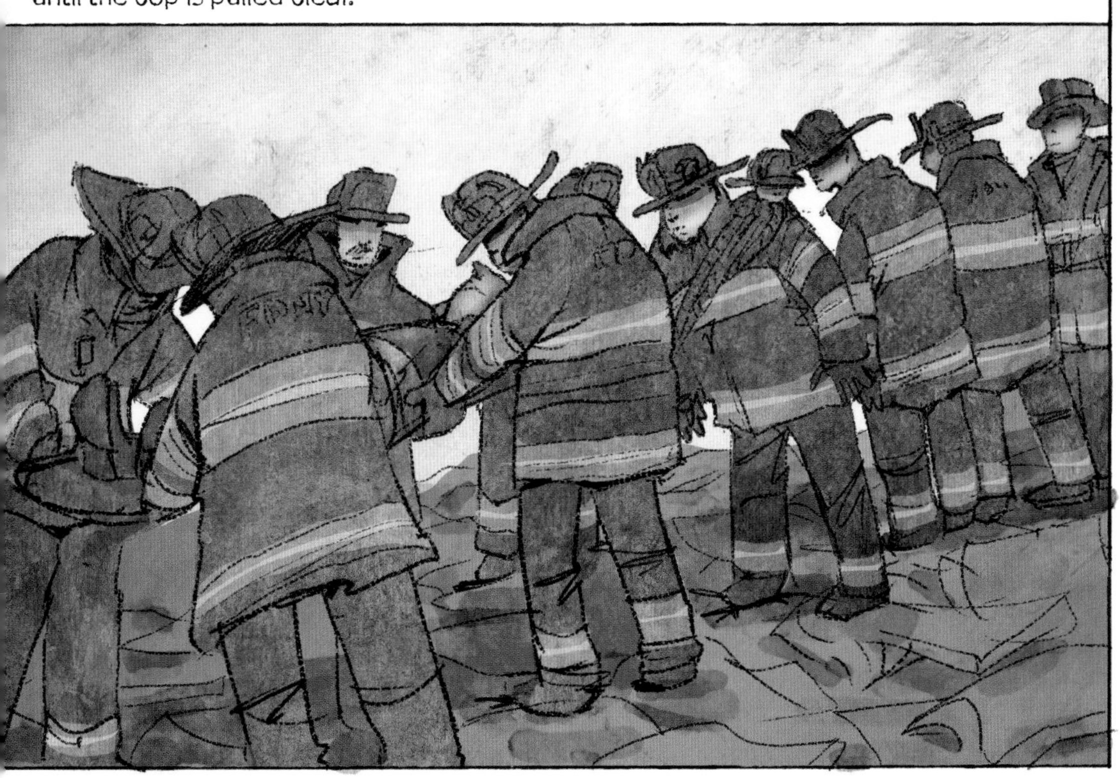

Jimeno's partner McLoughlin remains trapped for another eight hours until he is pulled from his rough tomb . . .

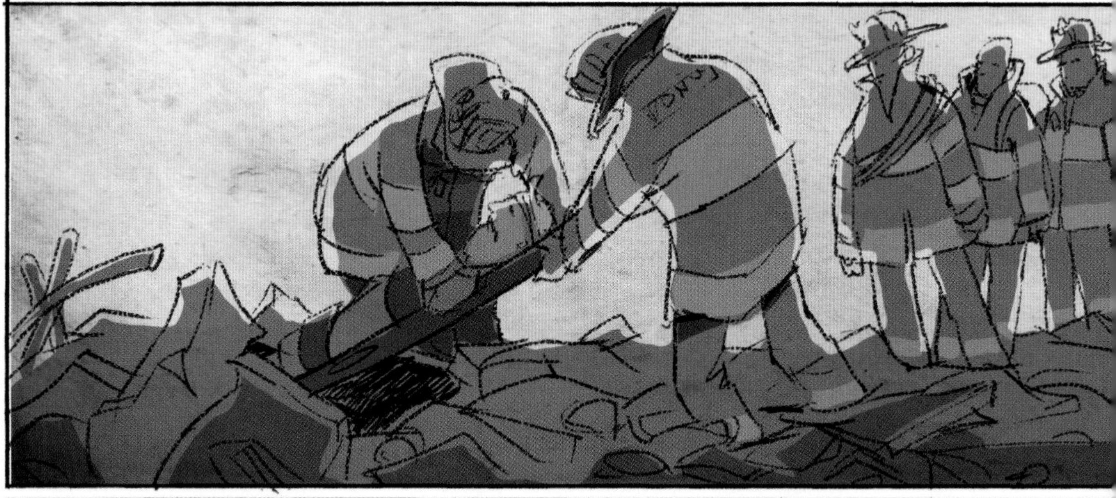

and taken to the hospital . . .

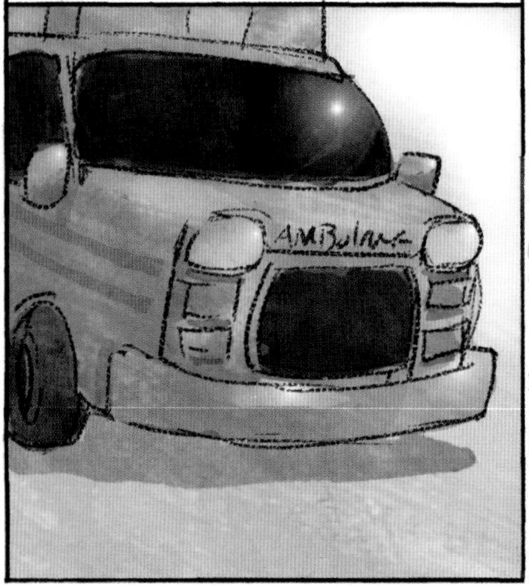

where doctors are sure he is going to die.

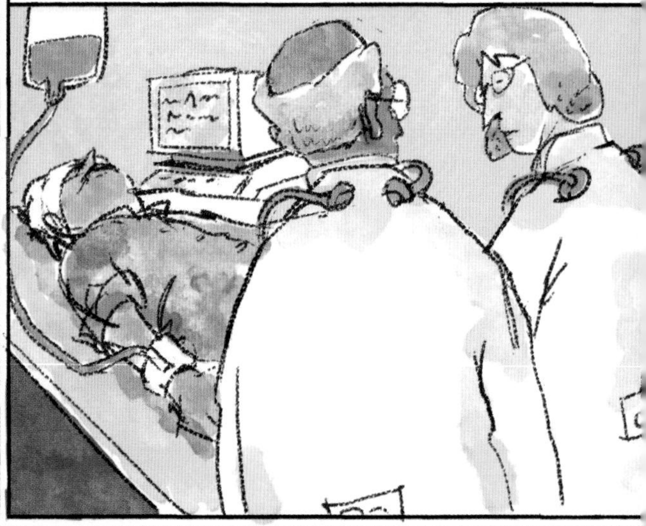

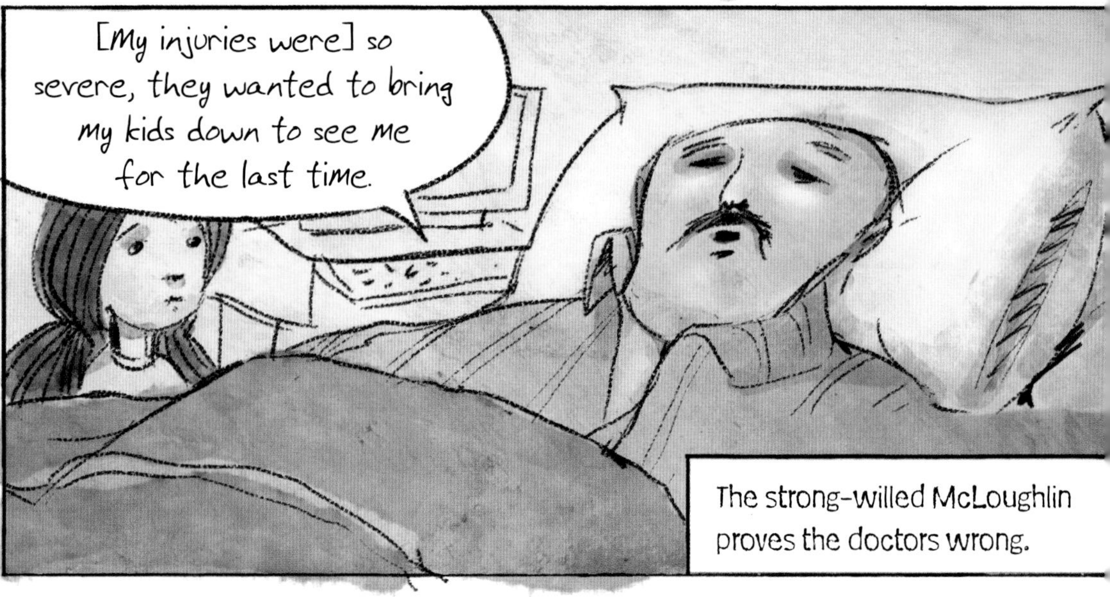
[My injuries were] so severe, they wanted to bring my kids down to see me for the last time.

The strong-willed McLoughlin proves the doctors wrong.

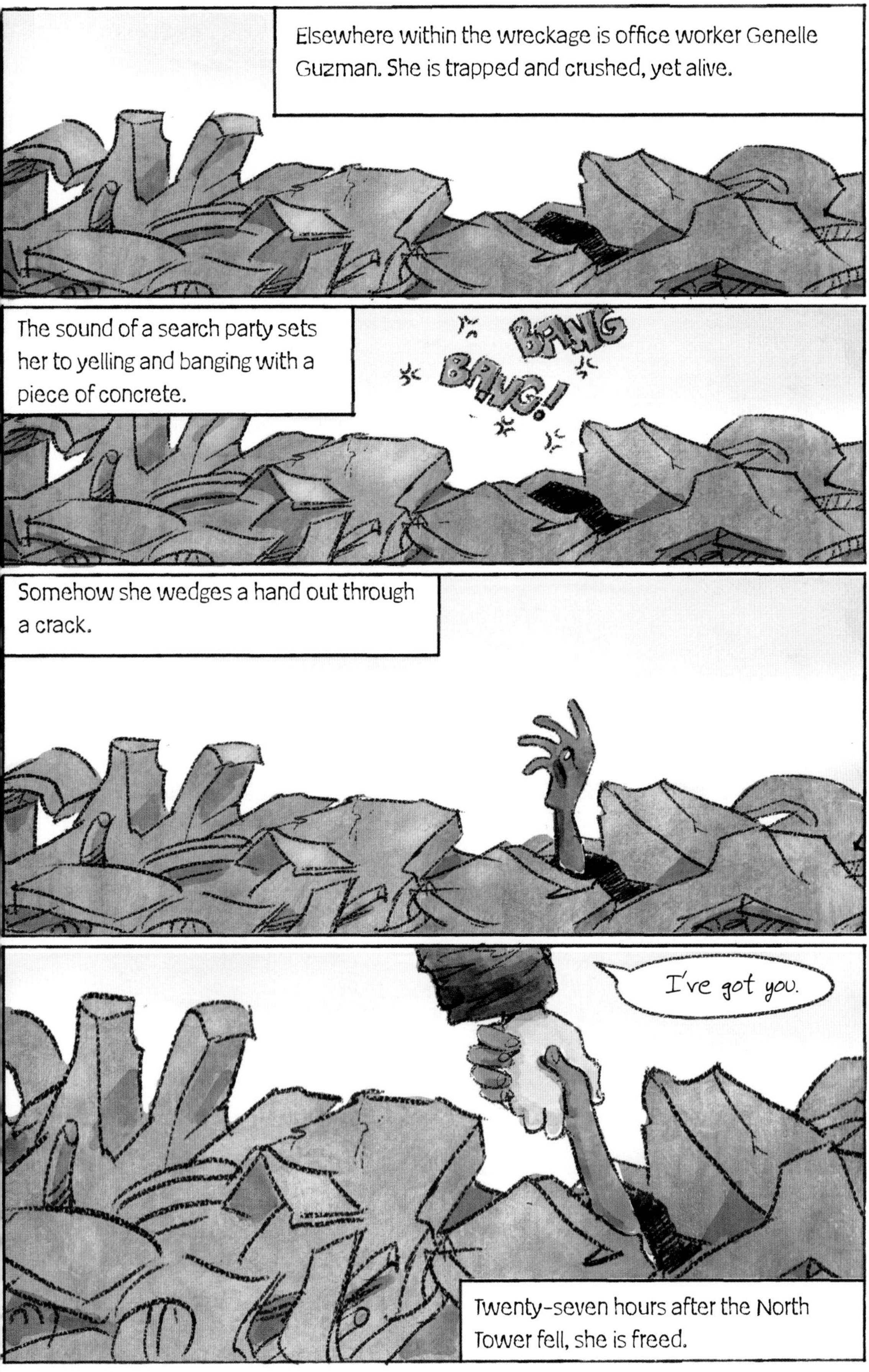
Elsewhere within the wreckage is office worker Genelle Guzman. She is trapped and crushed, yet alive.
The sound of a search party sets her to yelling and banging with a piece of concrete.
BANG
BANG!
Somehow she wedges a hand out through a crack.
I've got you.
Twenty-seven hours after the North Tower fell, she is freed.

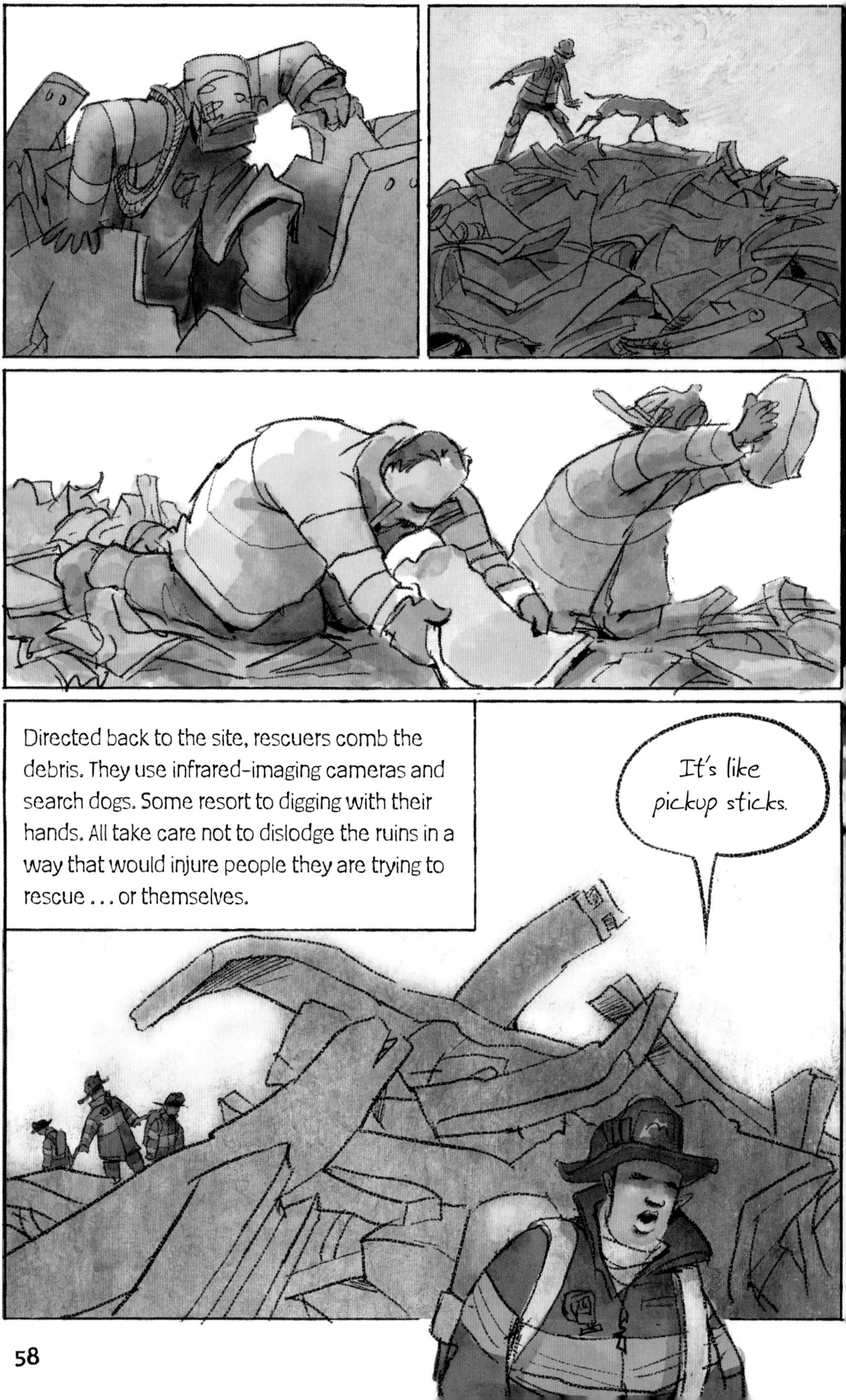
Directed back to the site, rescuers comb the debris. They use infrared-imaging cameras and search dogs. Some resort to digging with their hands. All take care not to dislodge the ruins in a way that would injure people they are trying to rescue . . . or themselves.
It's like pickup sticks.

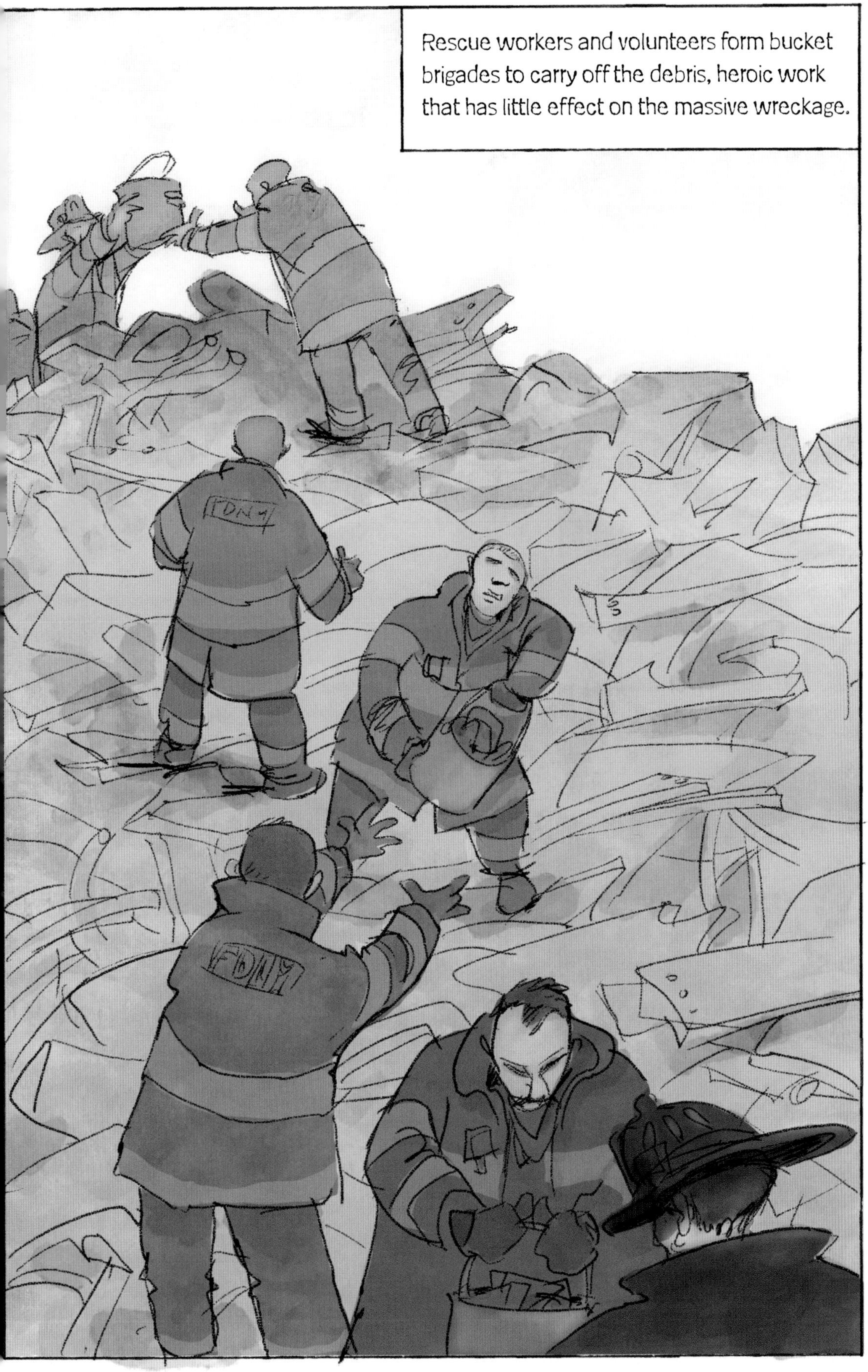
Rescue workers and volunteers form bucket brigades to carry off the debris, heroic work that has little effect on the massive wreckage.
FDNY
FDNY

All around is beeping, the sound from automatic emergency locator devices firefighters wear. But finding the locator doesn't guarantee finding a firefighter.

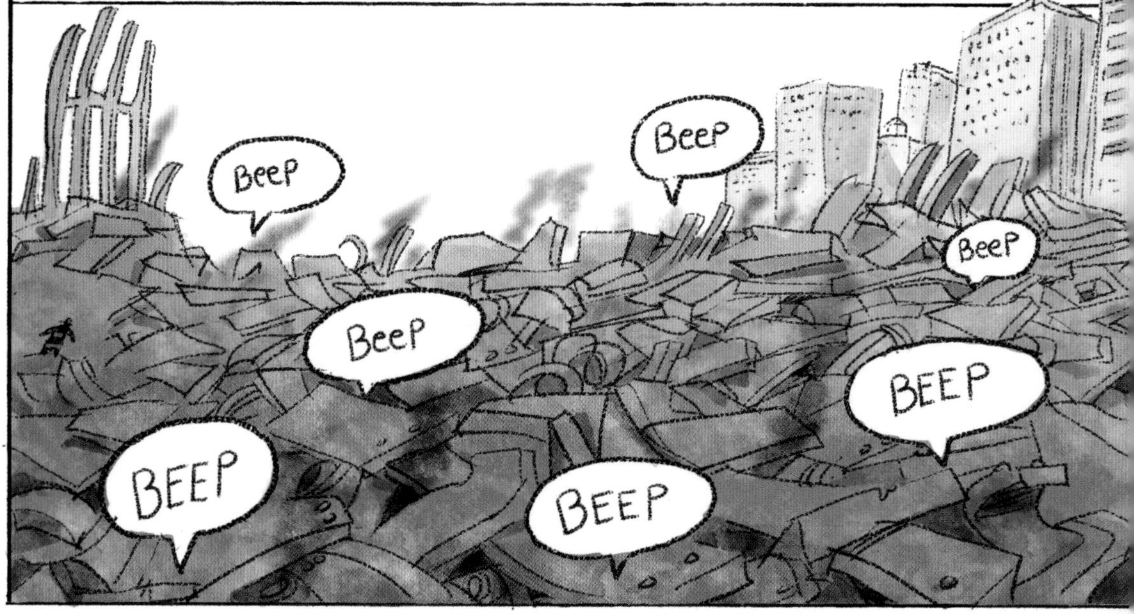
Beep
Beep
Beep
Beep
BEEP
BEEP
BEEP

Fire leaps from the twisted debris, fed by thousands of computers, acres of carpeting, tons of furniture, and untold gallons of hydraulic liquid and different fuels.

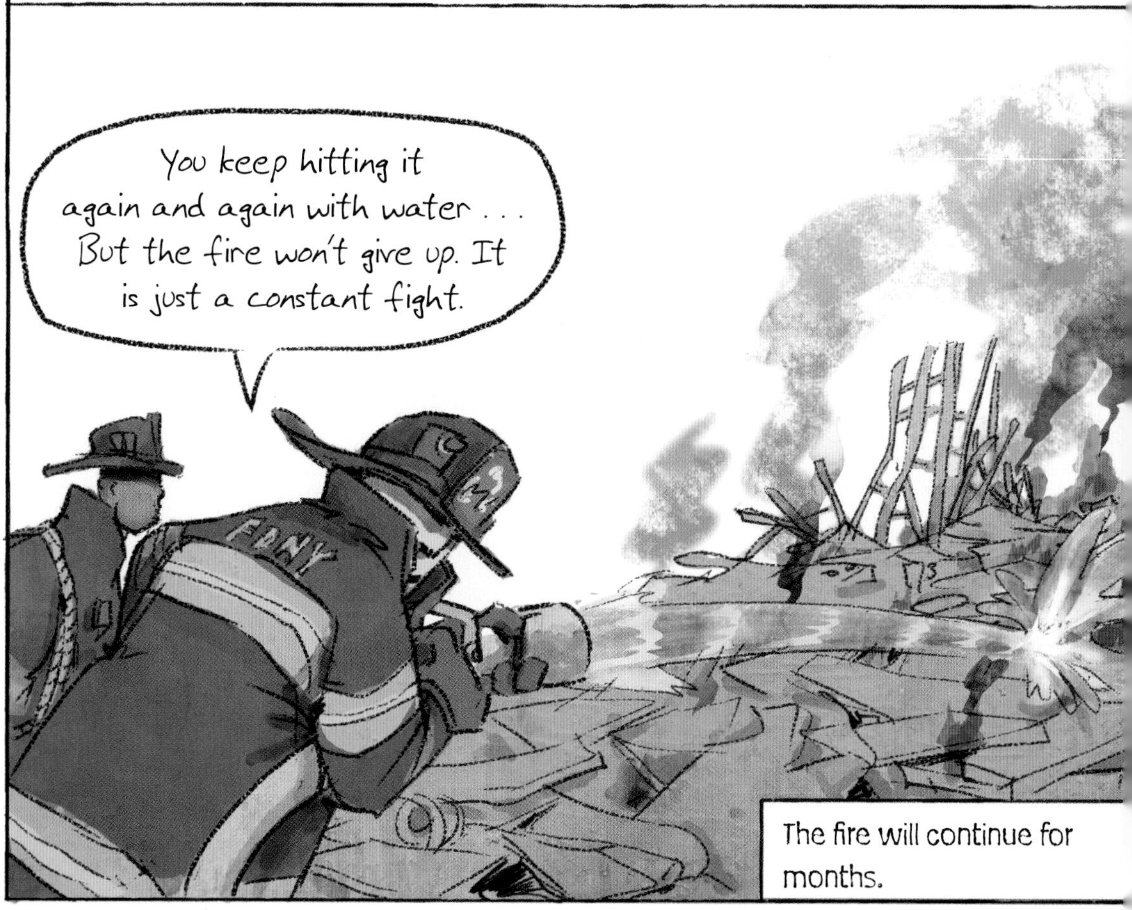
You keep hitting it again and again with water . . . But the fire won't give up. It is just a constant fight.
FDNY
The fire will continue for months.

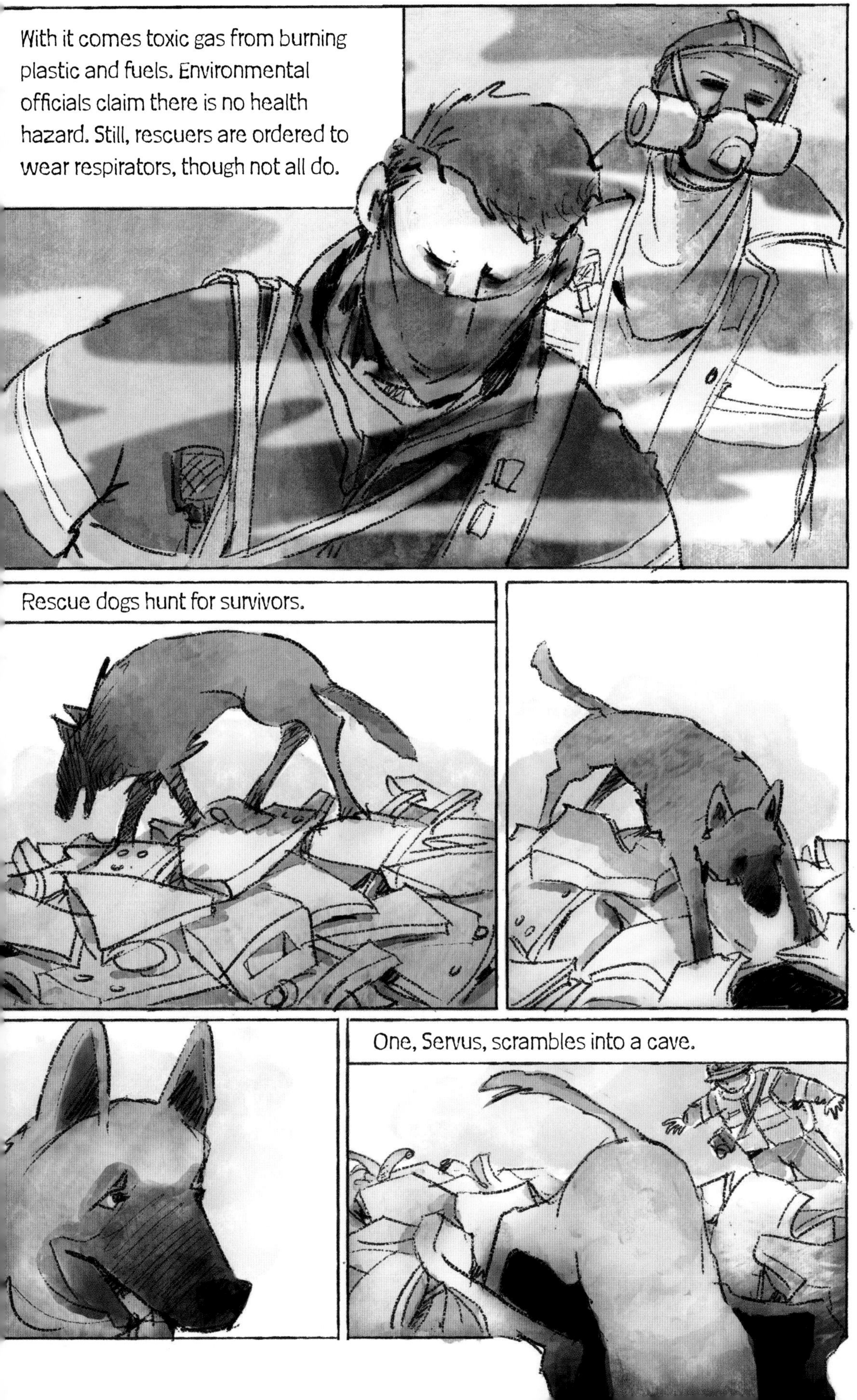
With it comes toxic gas from burning plastic and fuels. Environmental officials claim there is no health hazard. Still, rescuers are ordered to wear respirators, though not all do.
Rescue dogs hunt for survivors.
One, Servus, scrambles into a cave.

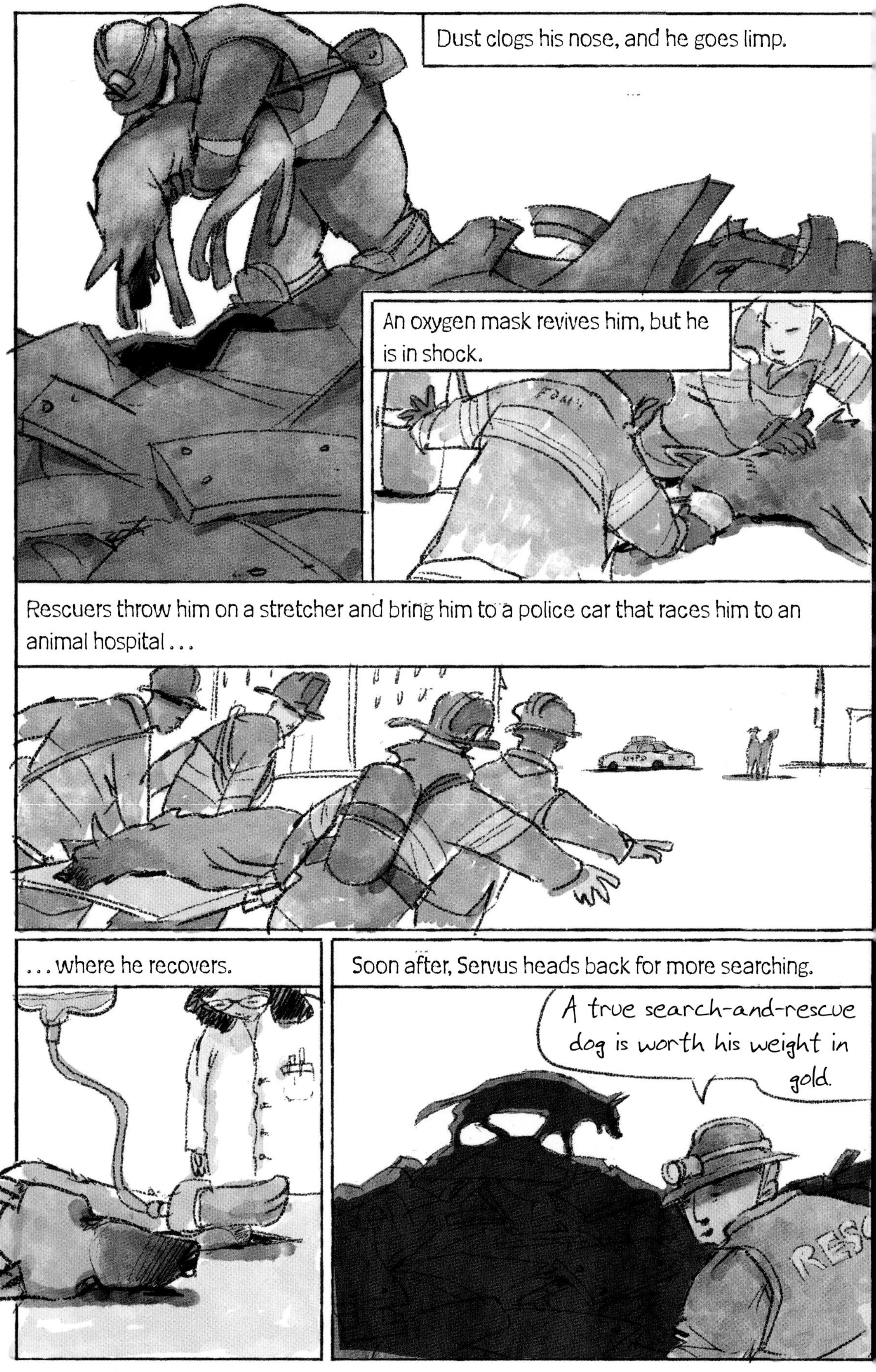
Dust clogs his nose, and he goes limp.
An oxygen mask revives him, but he is in shock.
Rescuers throw him on a stretcher and bring him to a police car that races him to an animal hospital . . .
. . . where he recovers.
Soon after, Servus heads back for more searching.
A true search-and-rescue dog is worth his weight in gold.

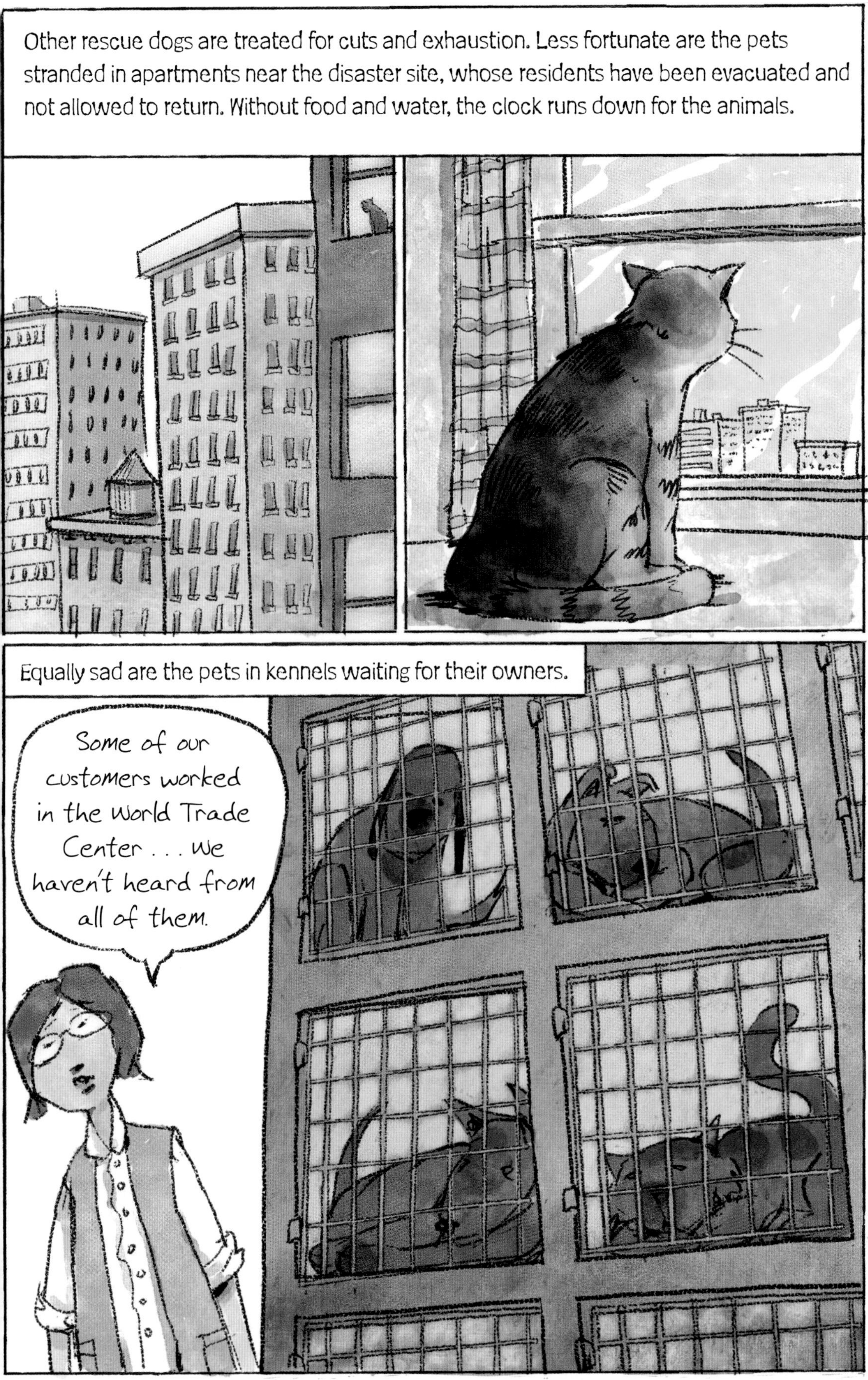
Other rescue dogs are treated for cuts and exhaustion. Less fortunate are the pets stranded in apartments near the disaster site, whose residents have been evacuated and not allowed to return. Without food and water, the clock runs down for the animals.
Equally sad are the pets in kennels waiting for their owners.
Some of our customers worked in the World Trade Center . . . We haven't heard from all of them.

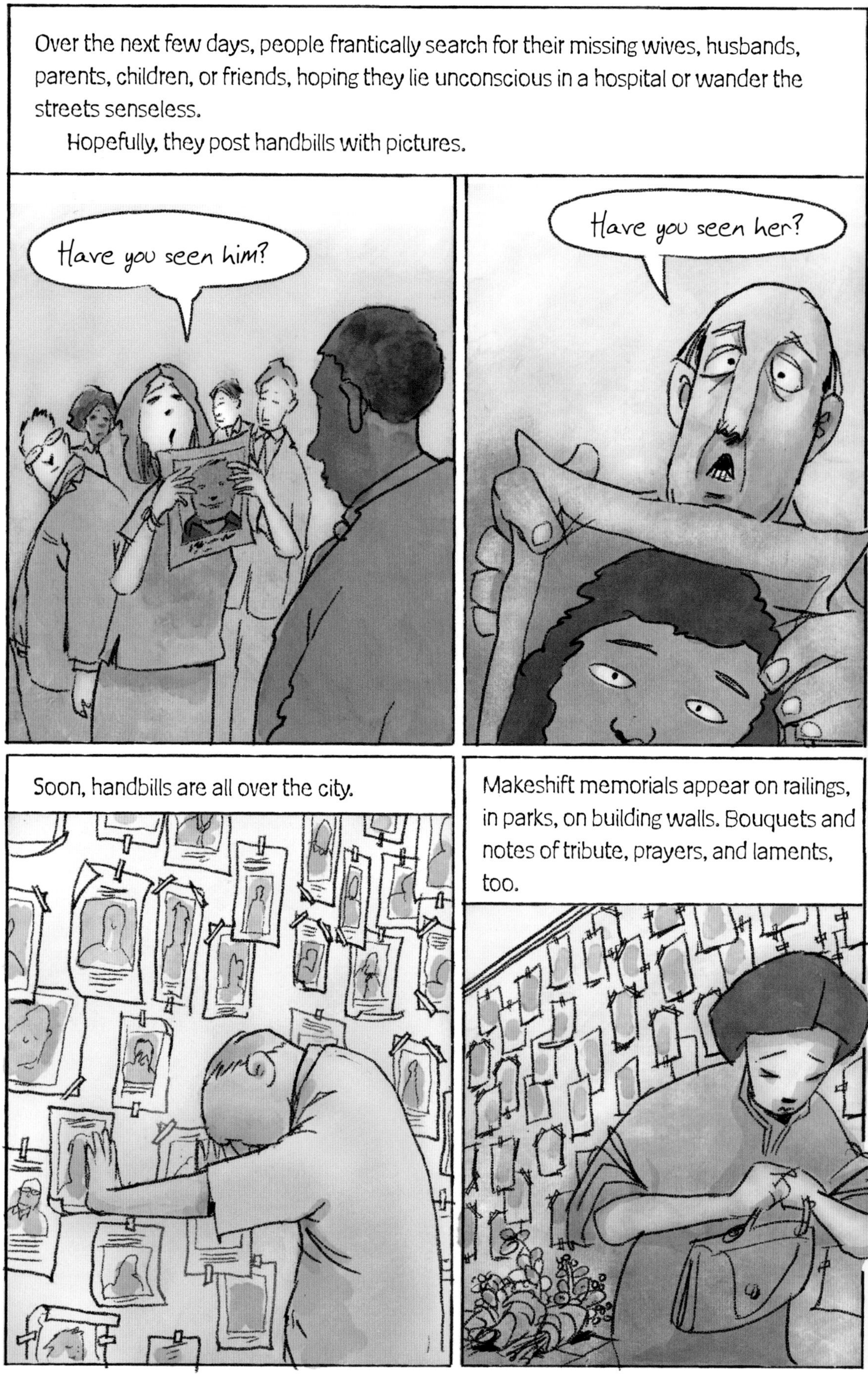
Over the next few days, people frantically search for their missing wives, husbands, parents, children, or friends, hoping they lie unconscious in a hospital or wander the streets senseless.
Hopefully, they post handbills with pictures.
Have you seen him?
Have you seen her?
Soon, handbills are all over the city.
Makeshift memorials appear on railings, in parks, on building walls. Bouquets and notes of tribute, prayers, and laments, too.

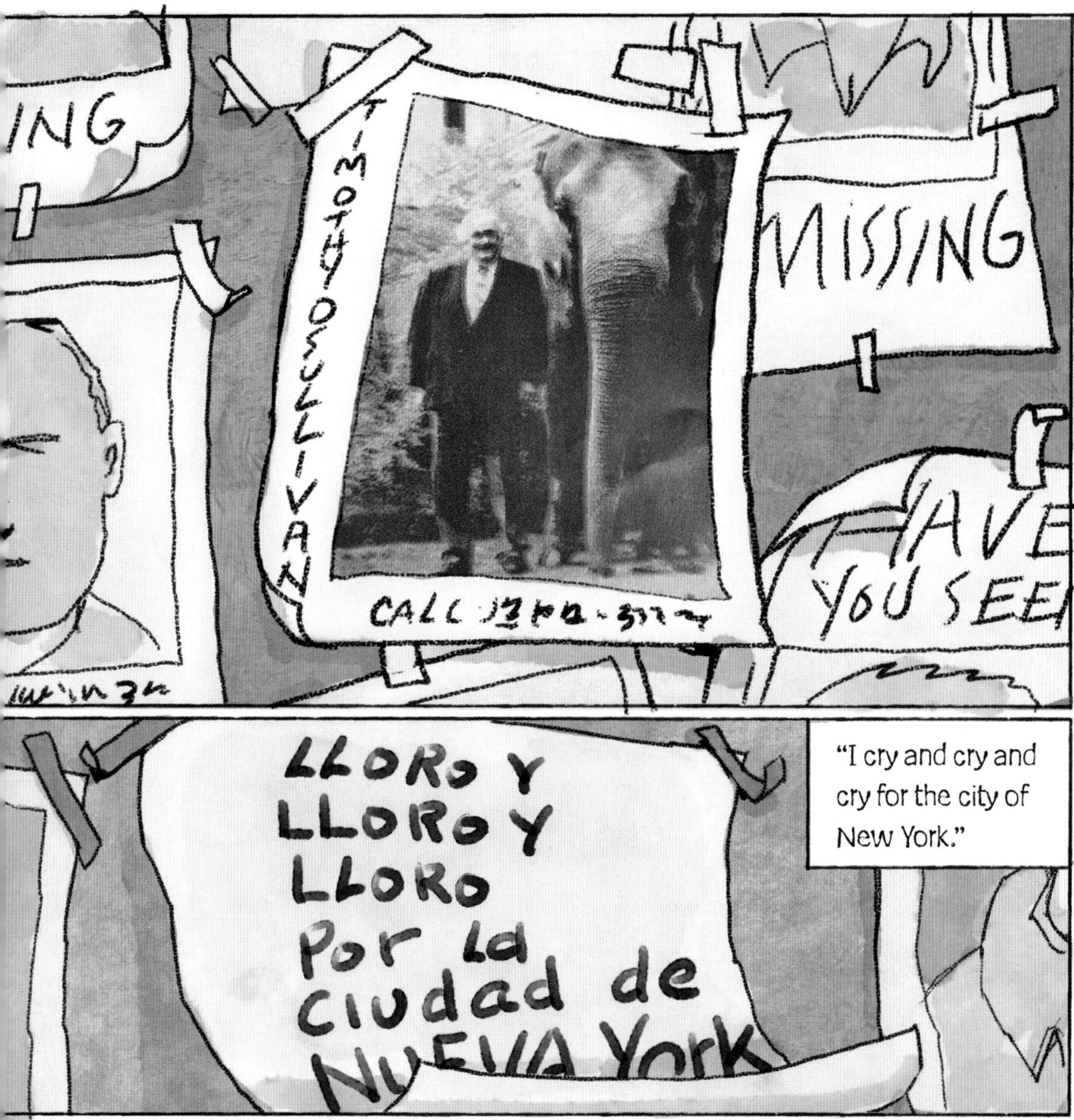
ING
TIMOTHY OSULLIVAN
MISSING
LLORO Y
LLORO Y
LLORO
Por la
ciudad de
NUEVA York
"I cry and cry and cry for the city of New York."

A central processing center for information on missing people is set up. Distraught people form long lines to enter.

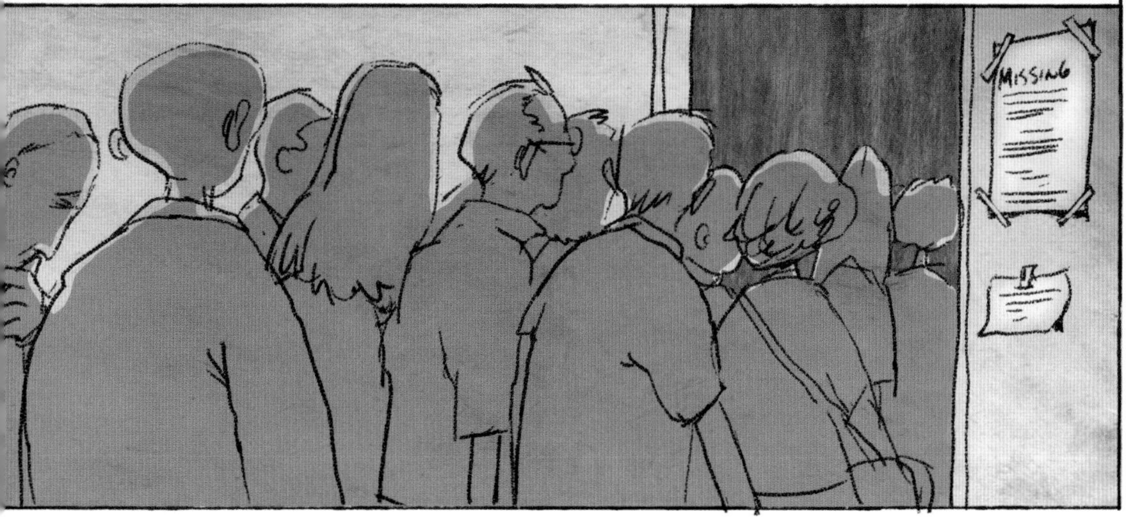
MISSING

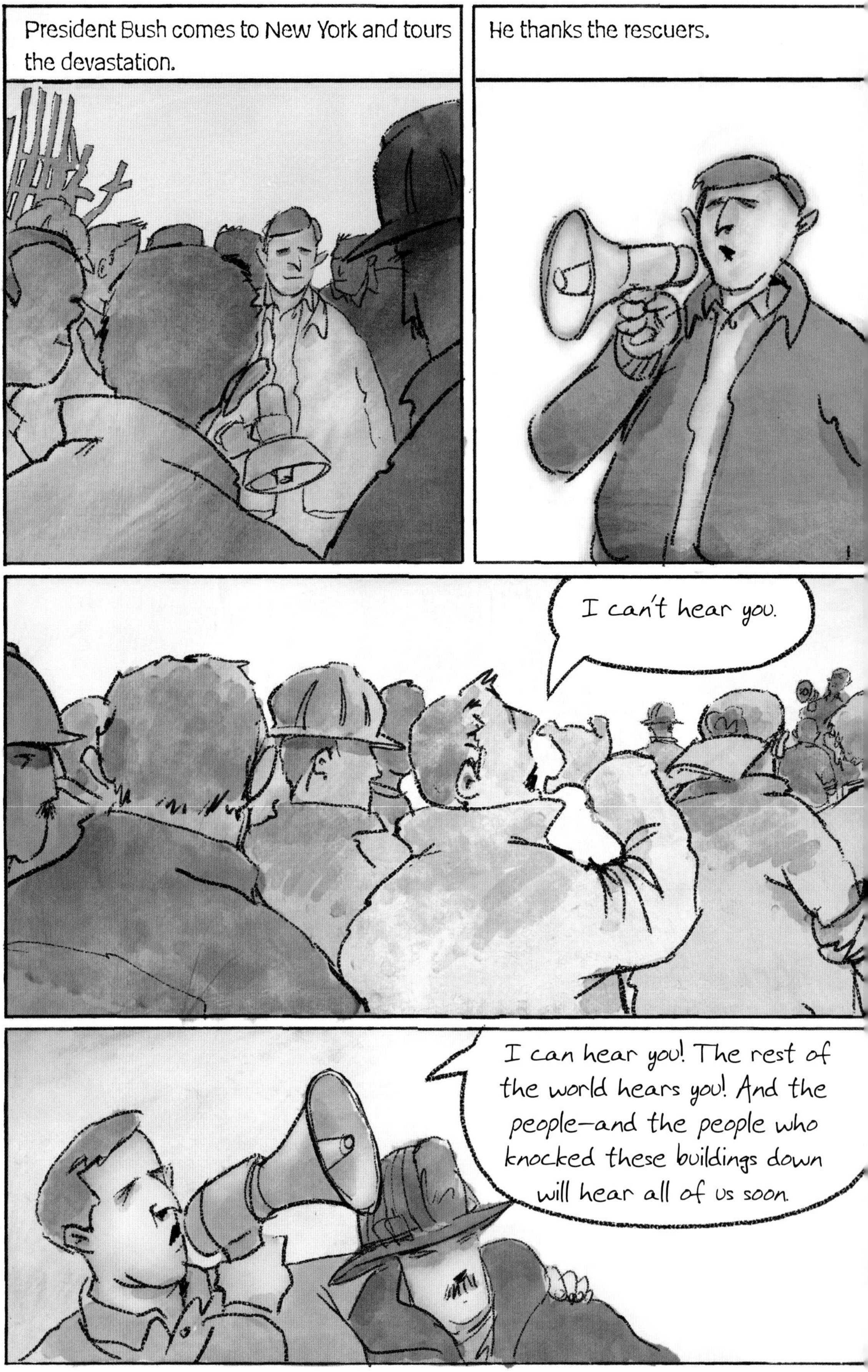
President Bush comes to New York and tours the devastation.
He thanks the rescuers.
I can't hear you.
I can hear you! The rest of the world hears you! And the people—and the people who knocked these buildings down will hear all of us soon.

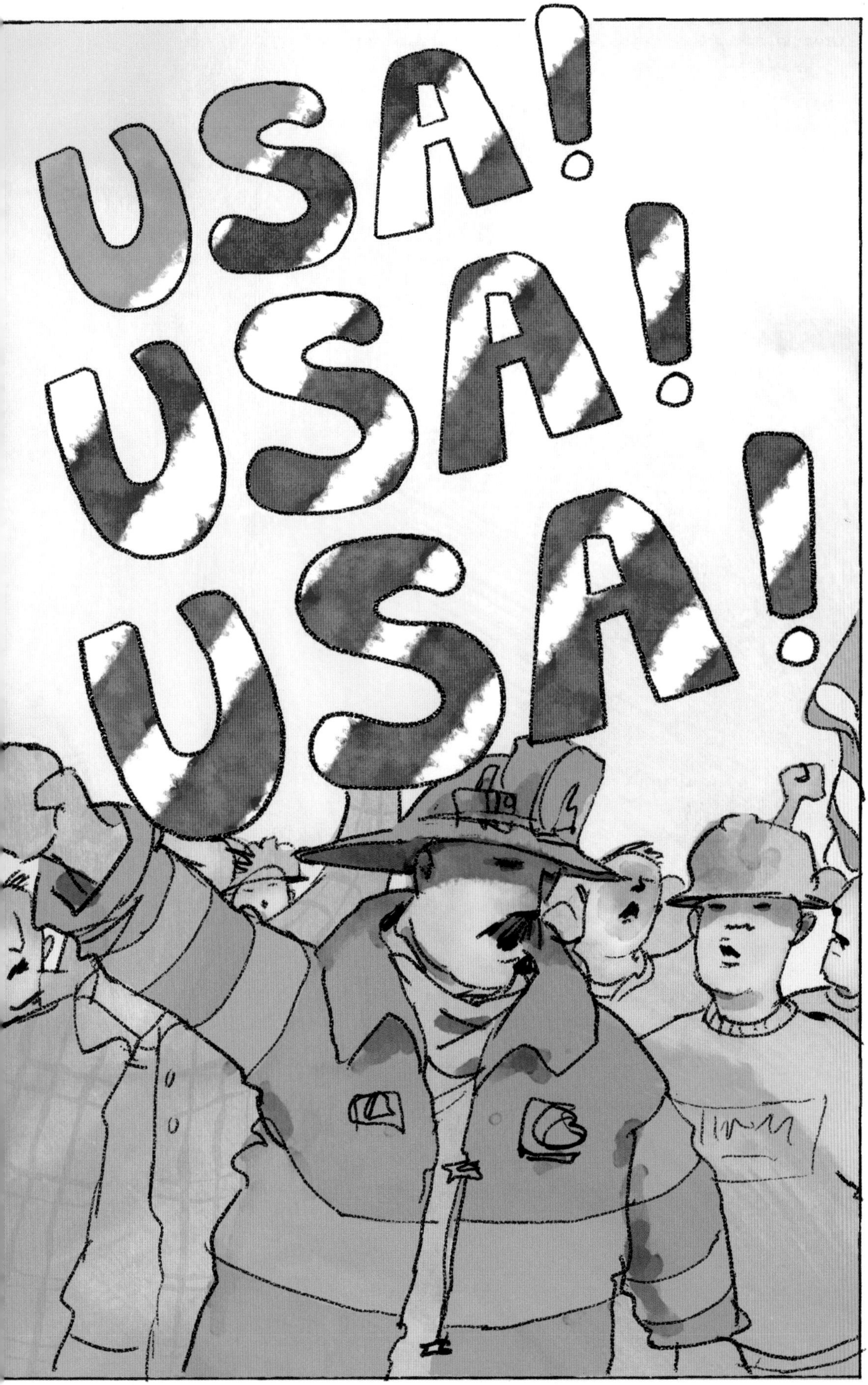
USA!
USA!
USA!

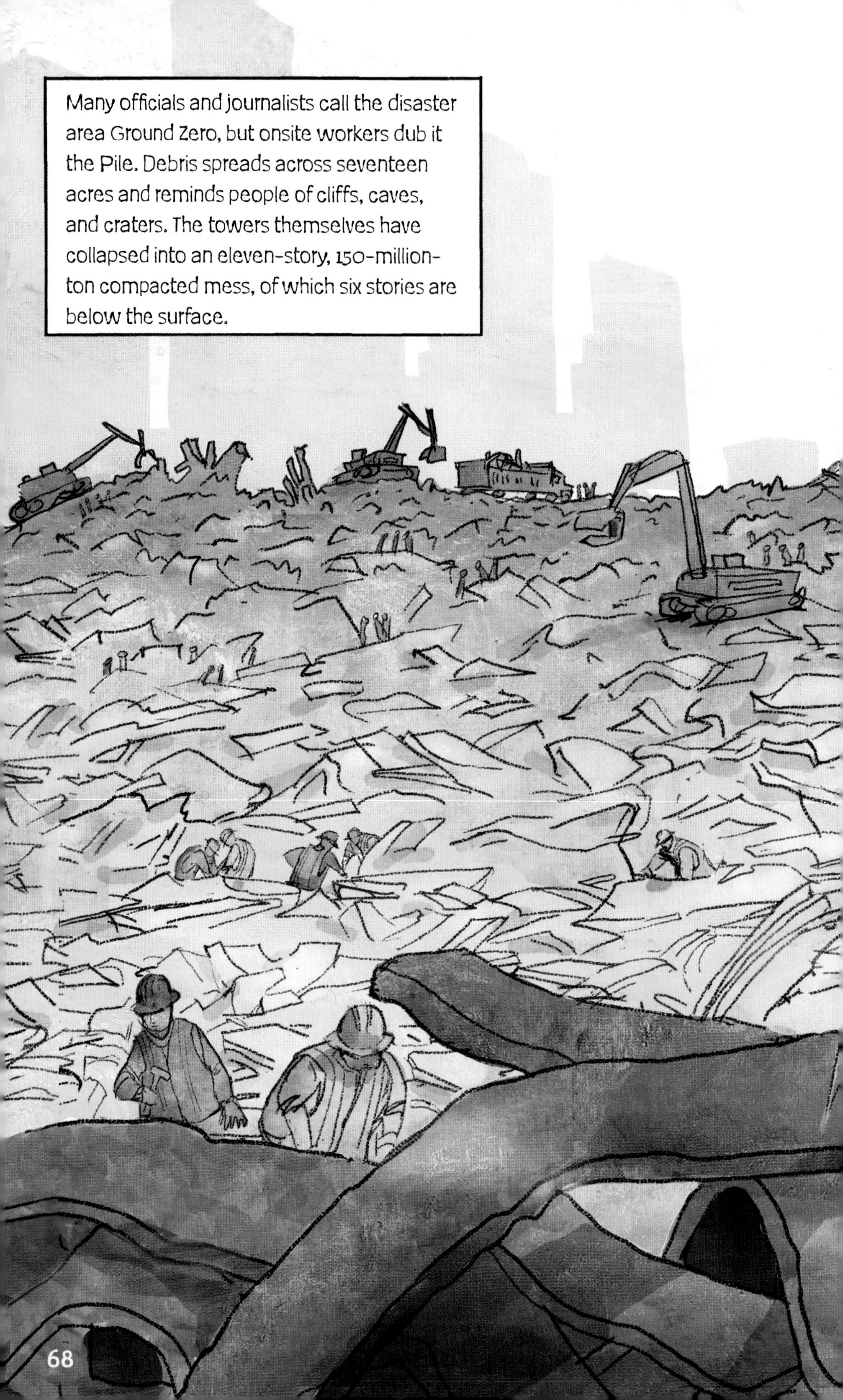
Many officials and journalists call the disaster area Ground Zero, but onsite workers dub it the Pile. Debris spreads across seventeen acres and reminds people of cliffs, caves, and craters. The towers themselves have collapsed into an eleven-story, 150-million-ton compacted mess, of which six stories are below the surface.

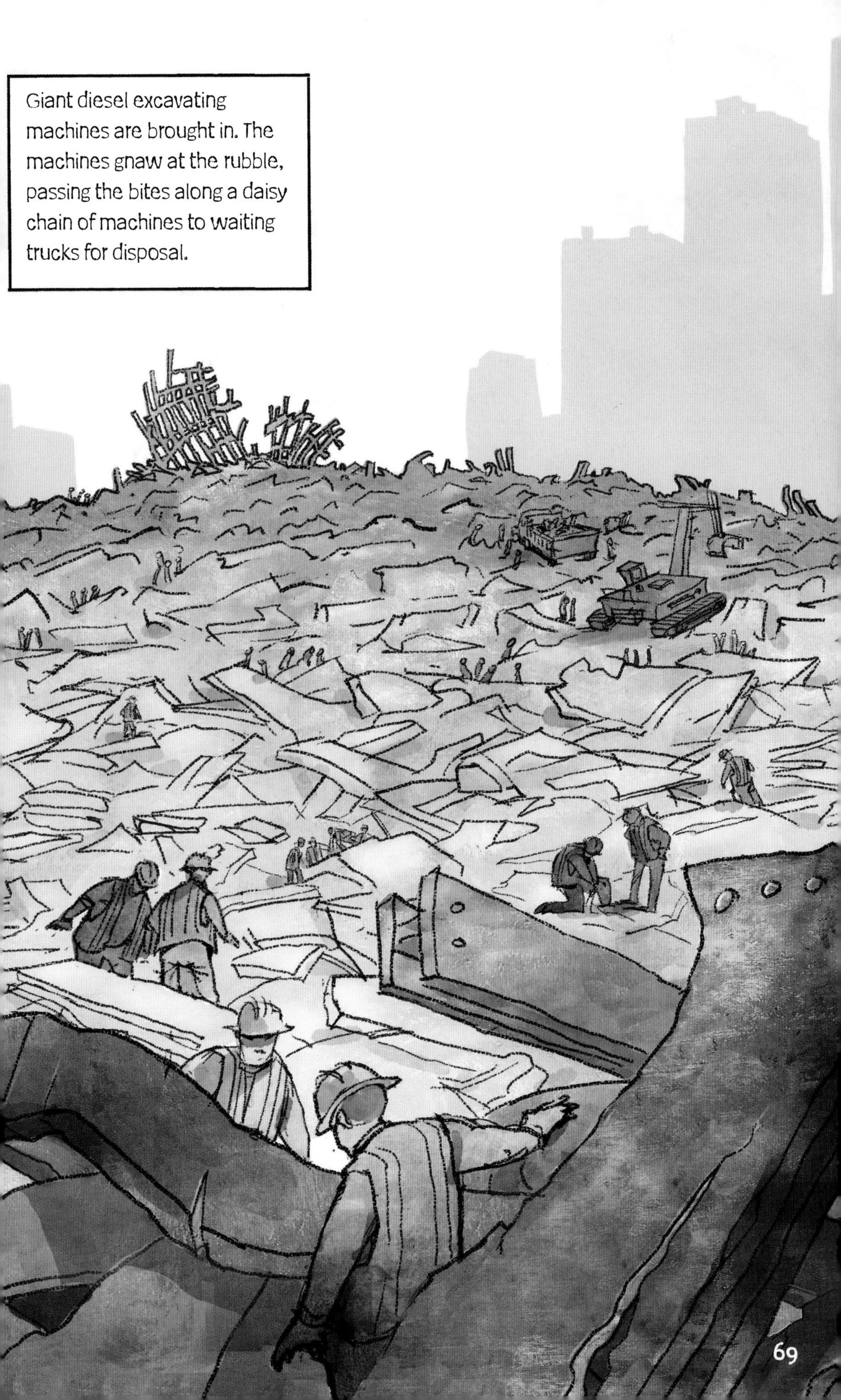
Giant diesel excavating machines are brought in. The machines gnaw at the rubble, passing the bites along a daisy chain of machines to waiting trucks for disposal.

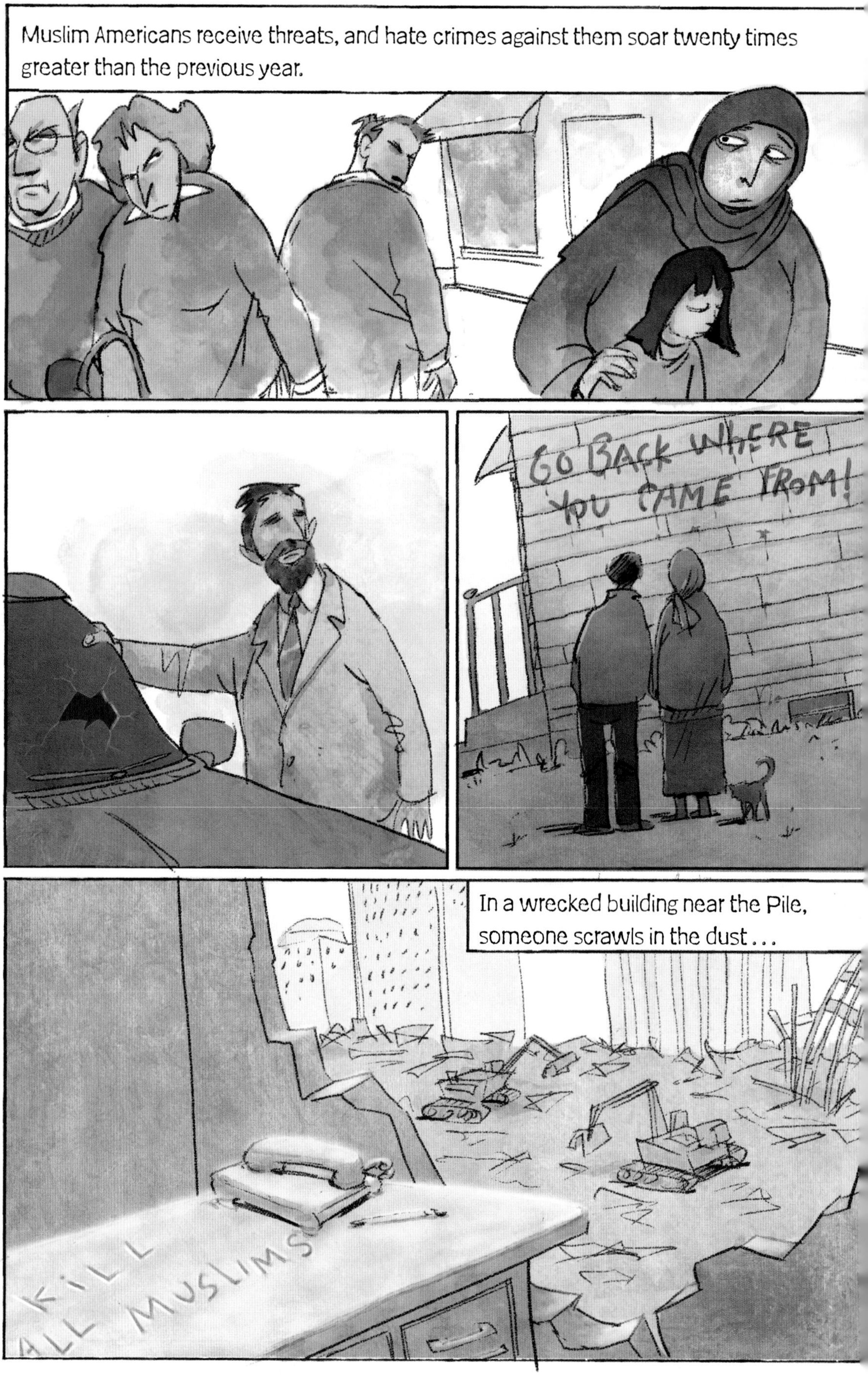
Muslim Americans receive threats, and hate crimes against them soar twenty times greater than the previous year.
GO BACK WHERE YOU CAME FROM!
In a wrecked building near the Pile, someone scrawls in the dust . . .
KILL ALL MUSLIMS

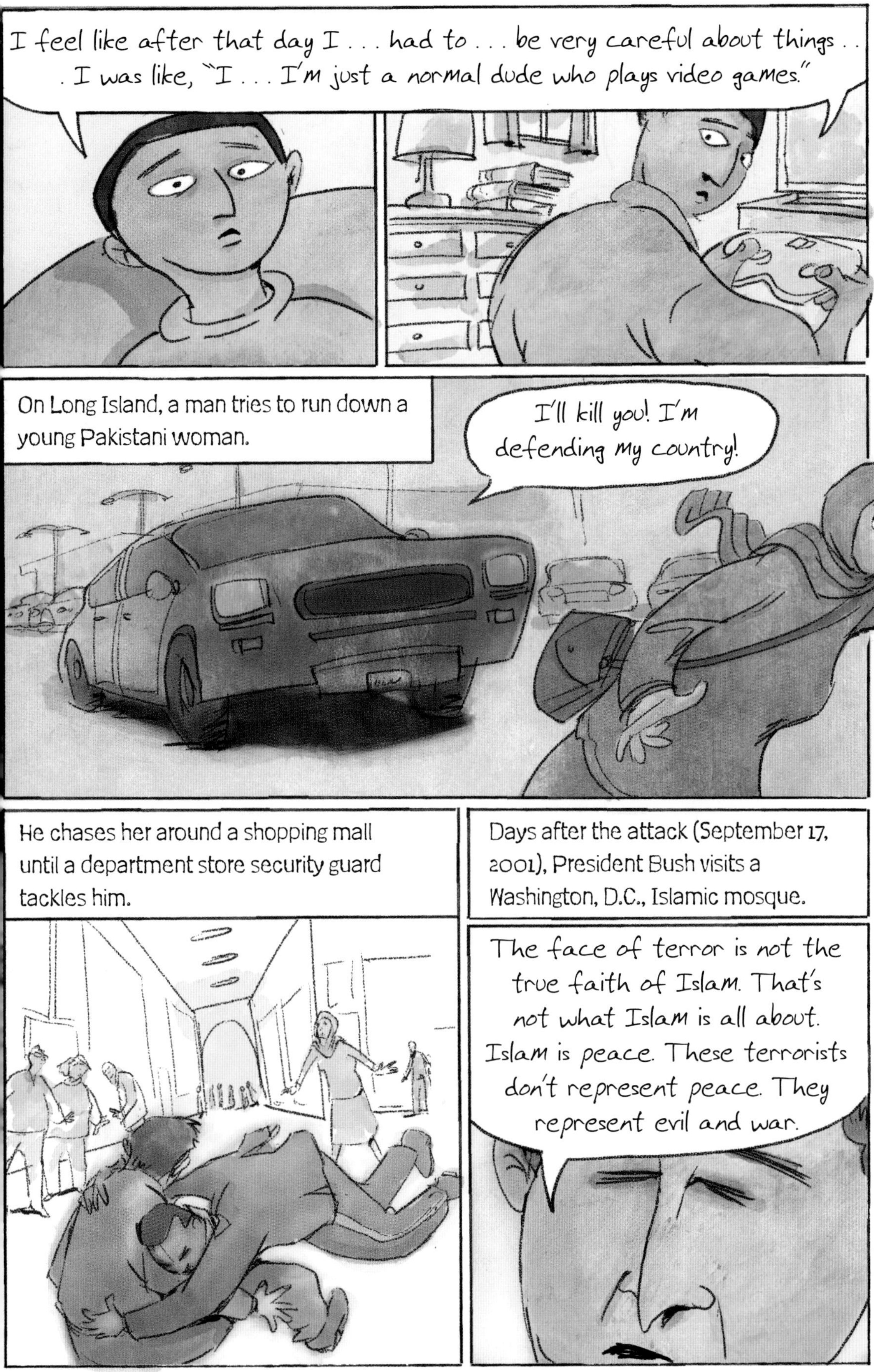
I feel like after that day I . . . had to . . . be very careful about things . . . I was like, "I . . . I'm just a normal dude who plays video games."
On Long Island, a man tries to run down a young Pakistani woman.
I'll kill you! I'm defending my country!
He chases her around a shopping mall until a department store security guard tackles him.
Days after the attack (September 17, 2001), President Bush visits a Washington, D.C., Islamic mosque.
The face of terror is not the true faith of Islam. That's not what Islam is all about. Islam is *peace*. These terrorists don't represent *peace*. They represent evil and war.

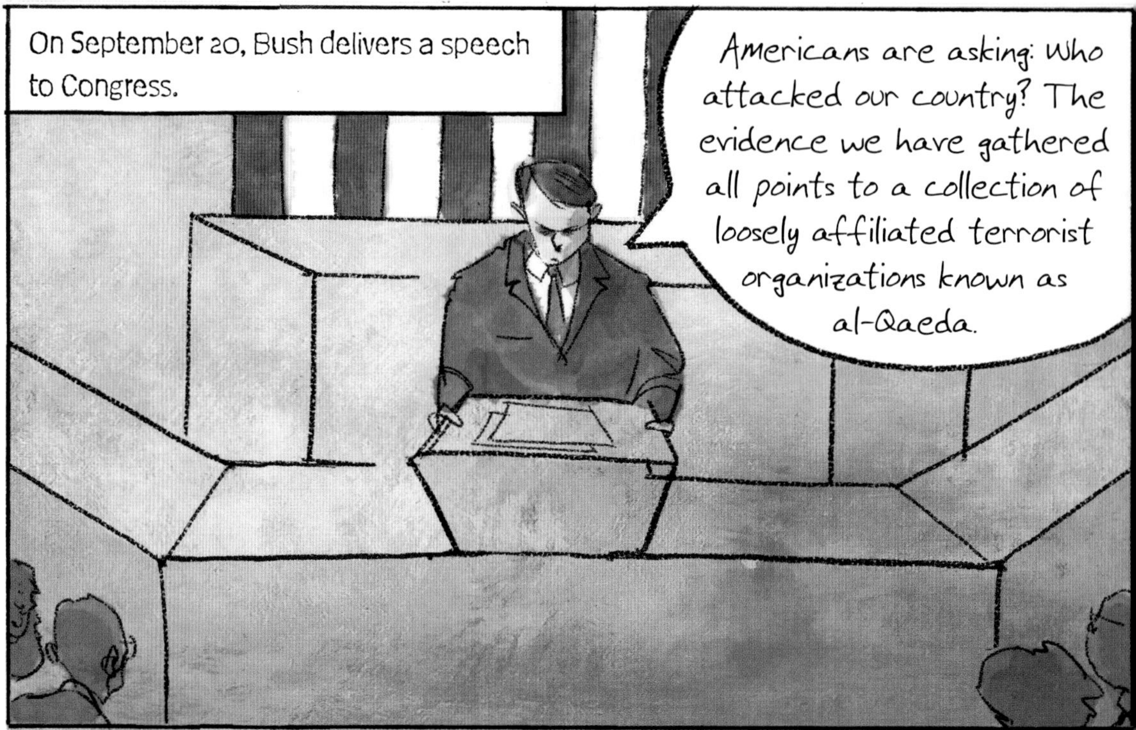
On September 20, Bush delivers a speech to Congress.
Americans are asking: Who attacked our country? The evidence we have gathered all points to a collection of loosely affiliated terrorist organizations known as al-Qaeda.

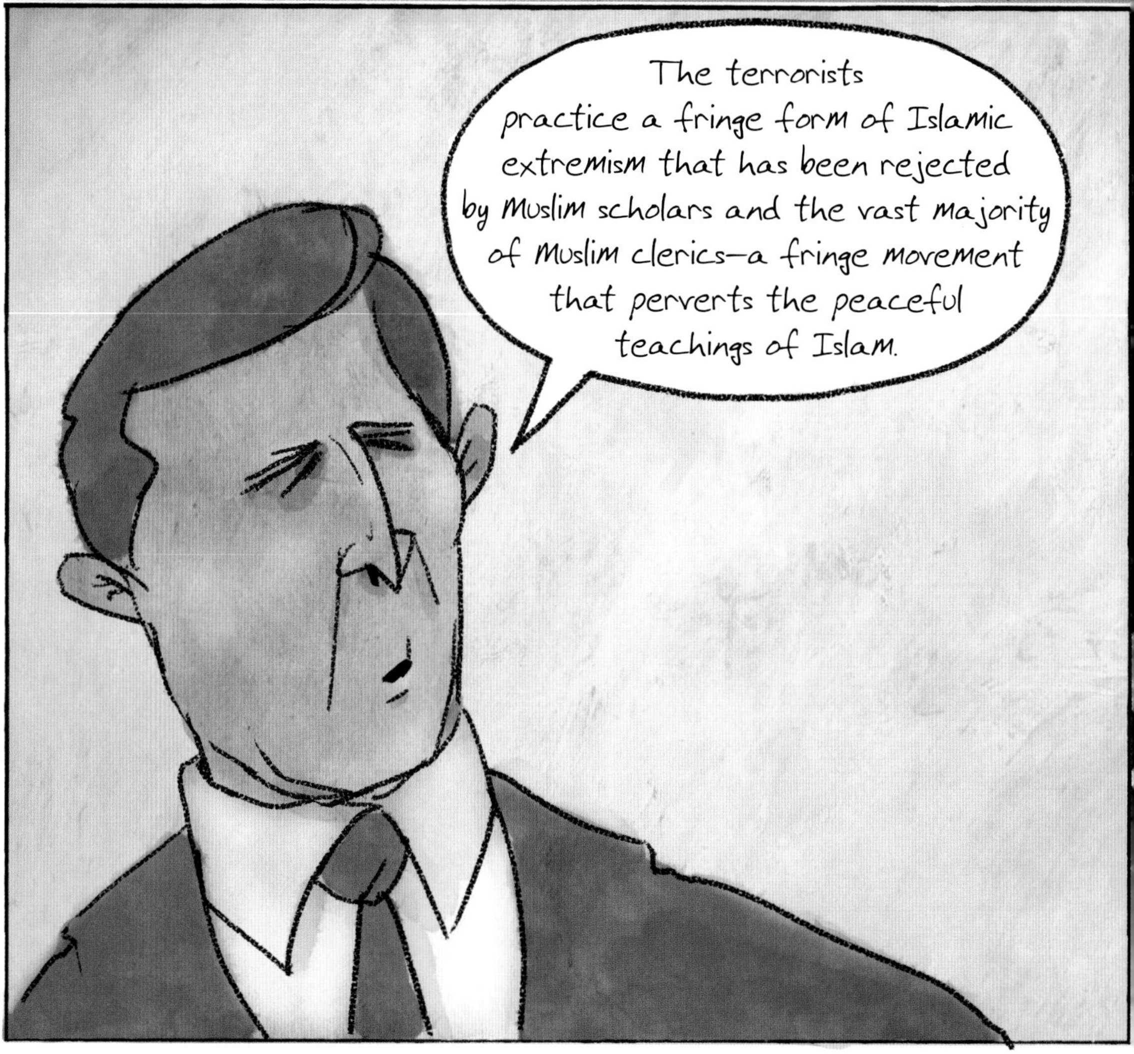
The terrorists practice a fringe form of Islamic extremism that has been rejected by Muslim scholars and the vast majority of Muslim clerics—a fringe movement that perverts the peaceful teachings of Islam.

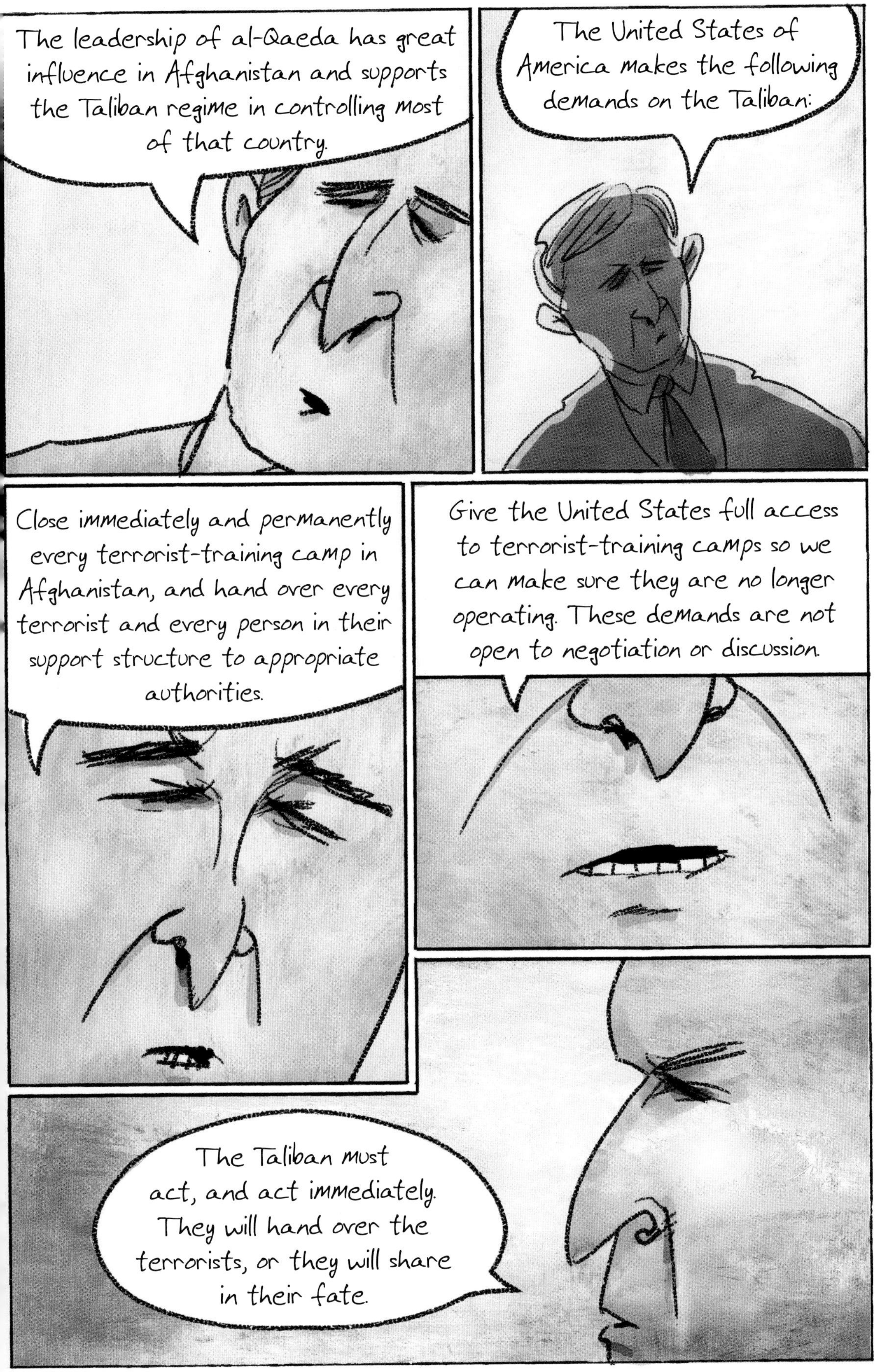
The leadership of al-Qaeda has great influence in Afghanistan and supports the Taliban regime in controlling most of that country.
The United States of America makes the following demands on the Taliban:
Close immediately and permanently every terrorist-training camp in Afghanistan, and hand over every terrorist and every person in their support structure to appropriate authorities.
Give the United States full access to terrorist-training camps so we can make sure they are no longer operating. These demands are not open to negotiation or discussion.
The Taliban must act, and act immediately. They will hand over the terrorists, or they will share in their fate.

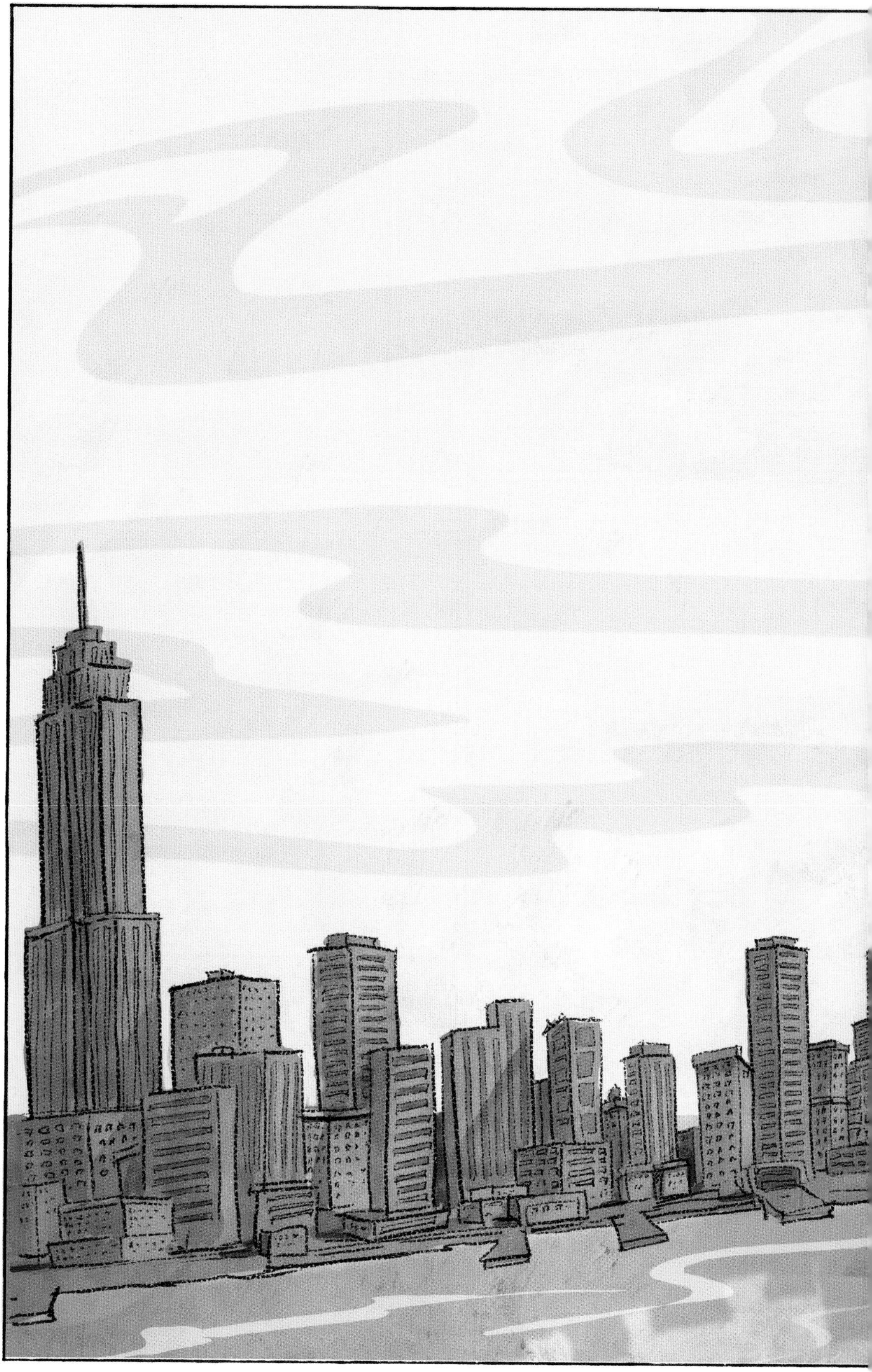

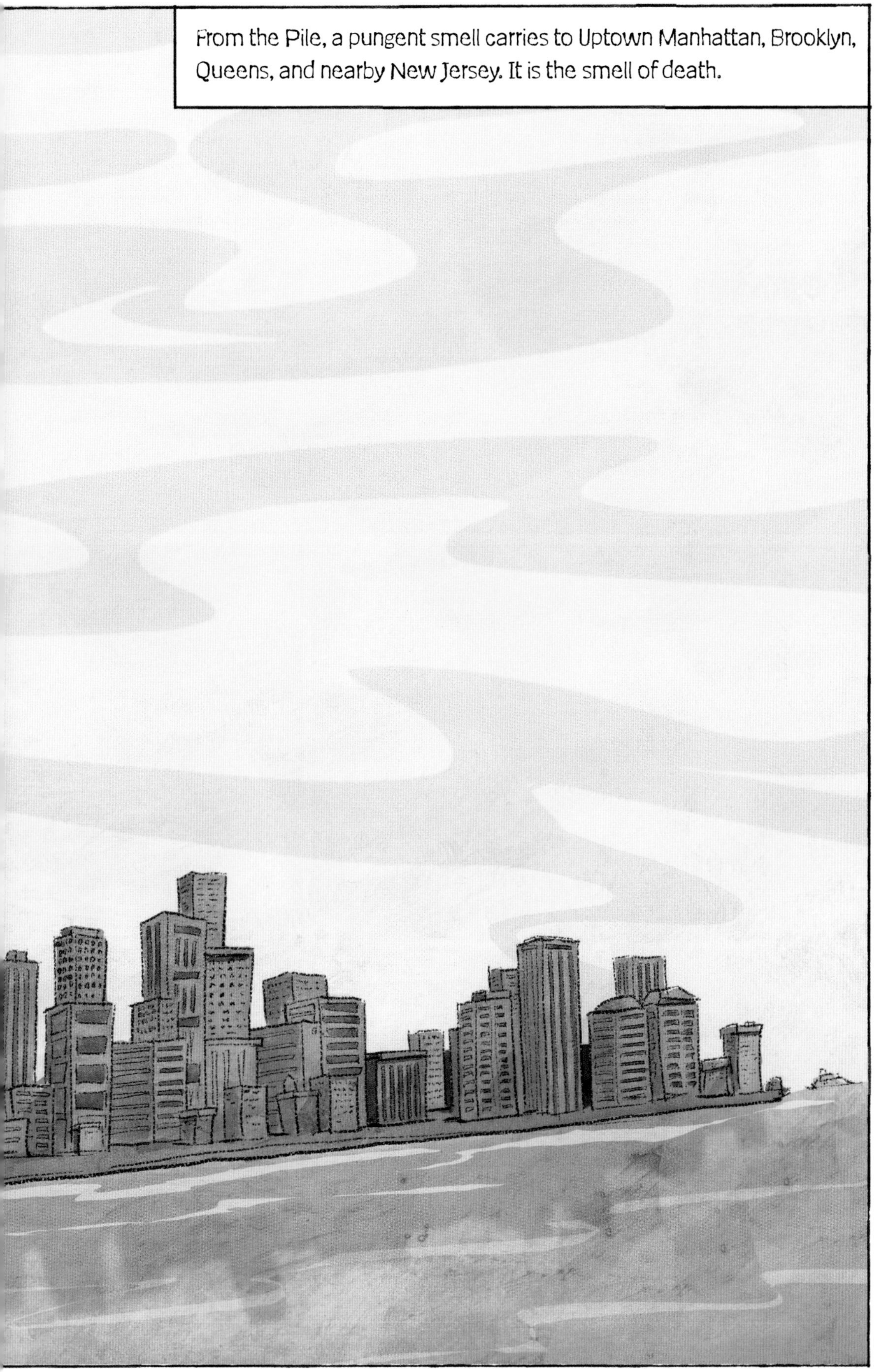
From the Pile, a pungent smell carries to Uptown Manhattan, Brooklyn, Queens, and nearby New Jersey. It is the smell of death.

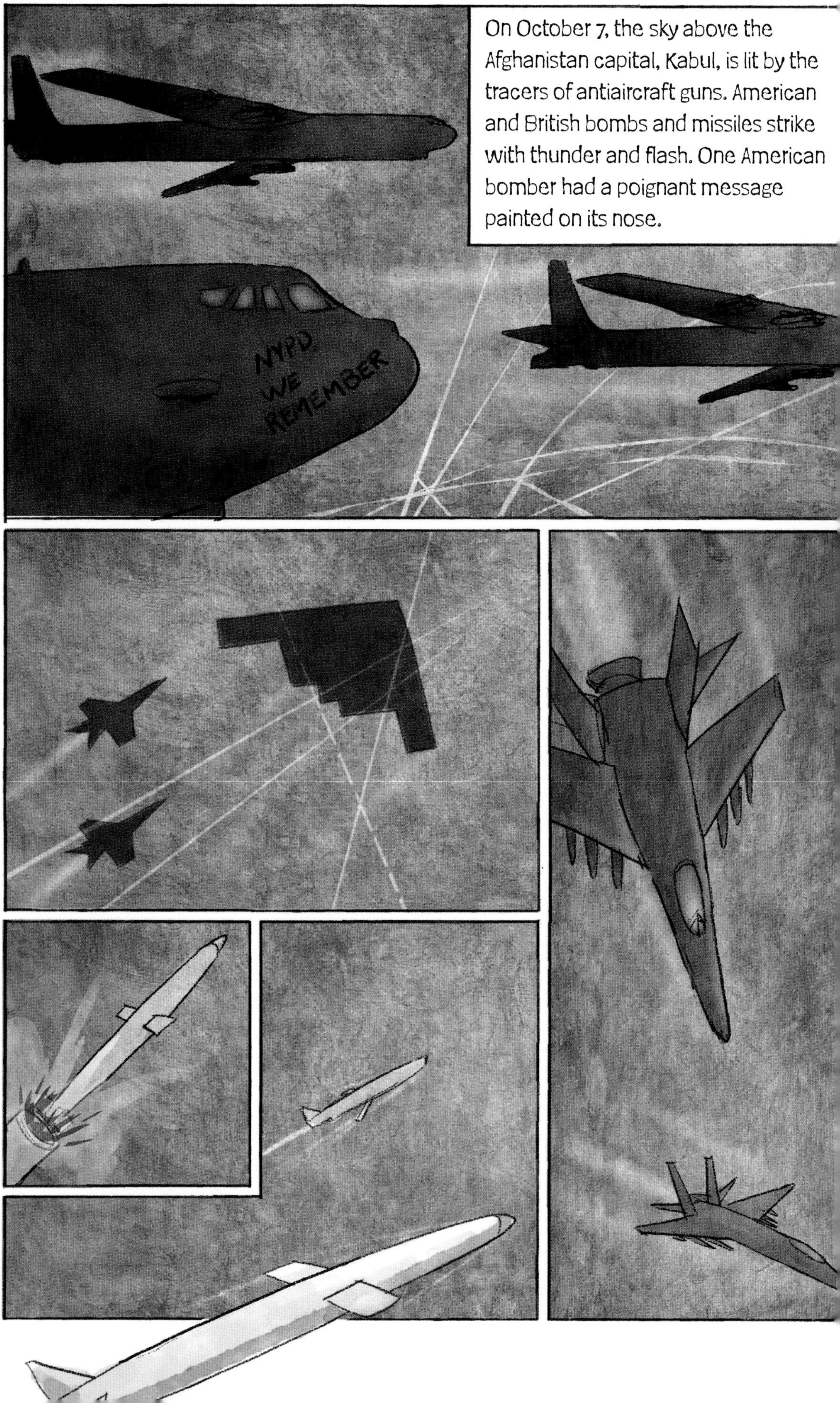
On October 7, the sky above the Afghanistan capital, Kabul, is lit by the tracers of antiaircraft guns. American and British bombs and missiles strike with thunder and flash. One American bomber had a poignant message painted on its nose.
NYPD WE REMEMBER

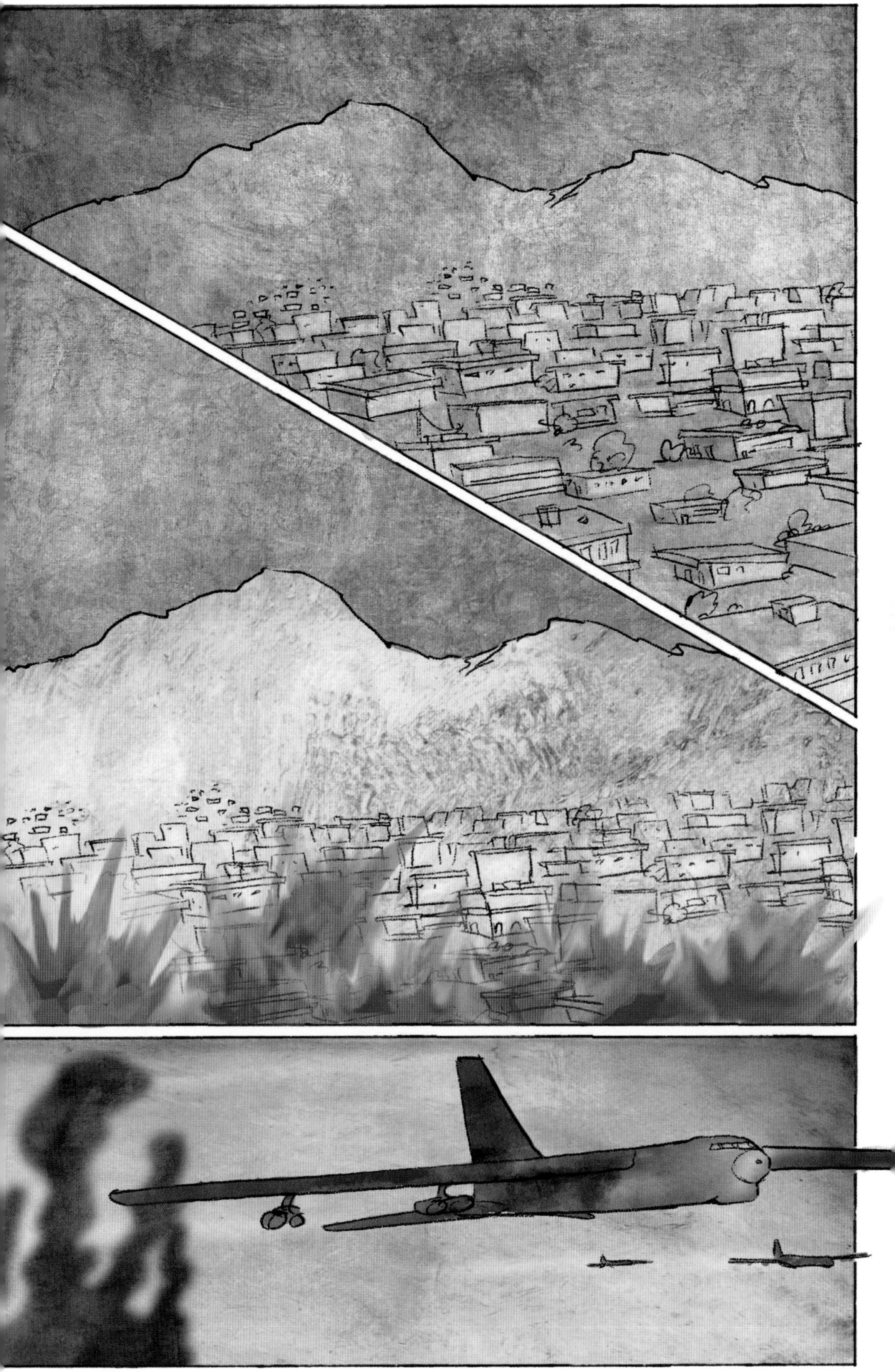

The Central Intelligence Agency orders some of its agents into Afghanistan to gain the support of anti-Taliban Afghans.

To that end, they bring three cardboard boxes, each packed with three million dollars in one-hundred-dollar bills.

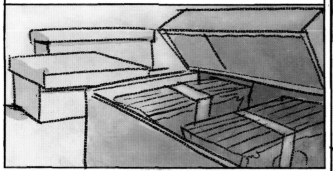

They also receive another directive.

[The team should] exert all efforts to find Osama bin Laden . . . and kill him . . . I want bin Laden's head shipped in a box . . . I want to . . . show bin Laden's head to the President.

Helicopters deliver the CIA team and American special forces into Afghanistan.

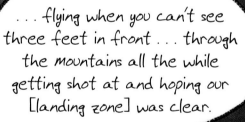

... flying when you can't see three feet in front ... through the mountains all the while getting shot at and hoping our [landing zone] was clear.

Afghan allies meet them.

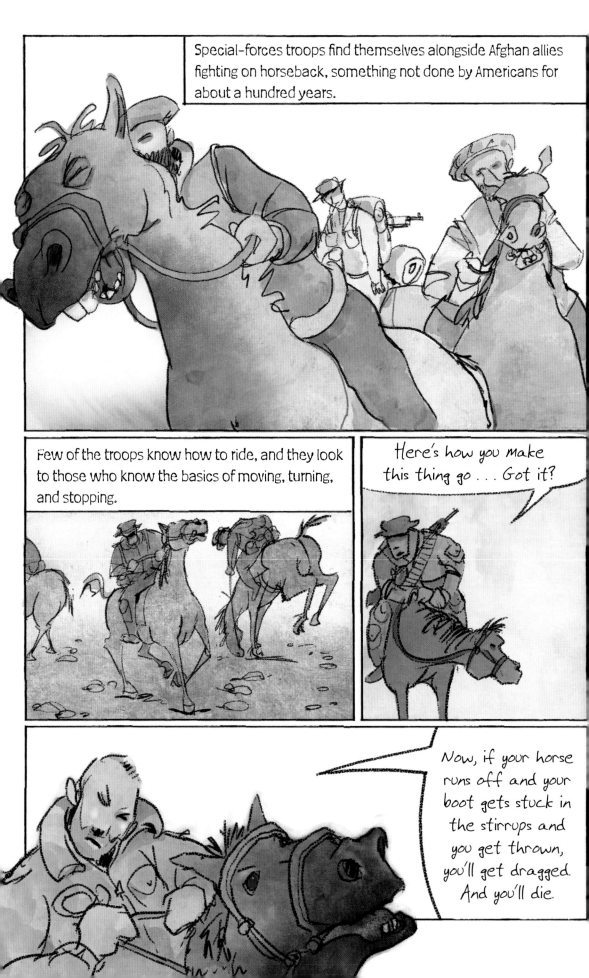

Special-forces troops find themselves alongside Afghan allies fighting on horseback, something not done by Americans for about a hundred years.

Few of the troops know how to ride, and they look to those who know the basics of moving, turning, and stopping.

Here's how you make this thing go . . . Got it?

Now, if your horse runs off and your boot gets stuck in the stirrups and you get thrown, you'll get dragged. And you'll die.

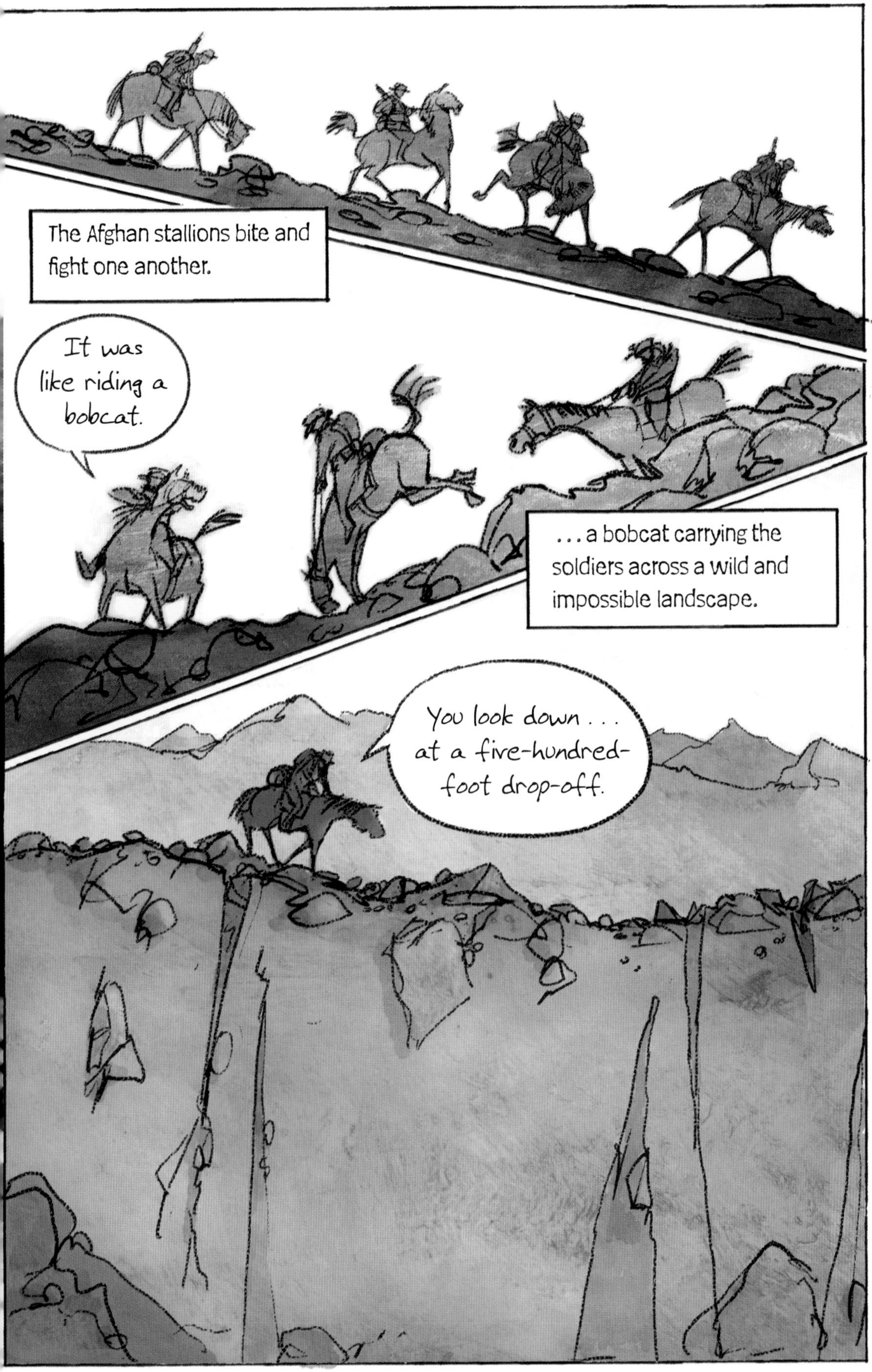
The Afghan stallions bite and fight one another.
It was like riding a bobcat.
. . . a bobcat carrying the soldiers across a wild and impossible landscape.
You look down . . . at a five-hundred-foot drop-off.

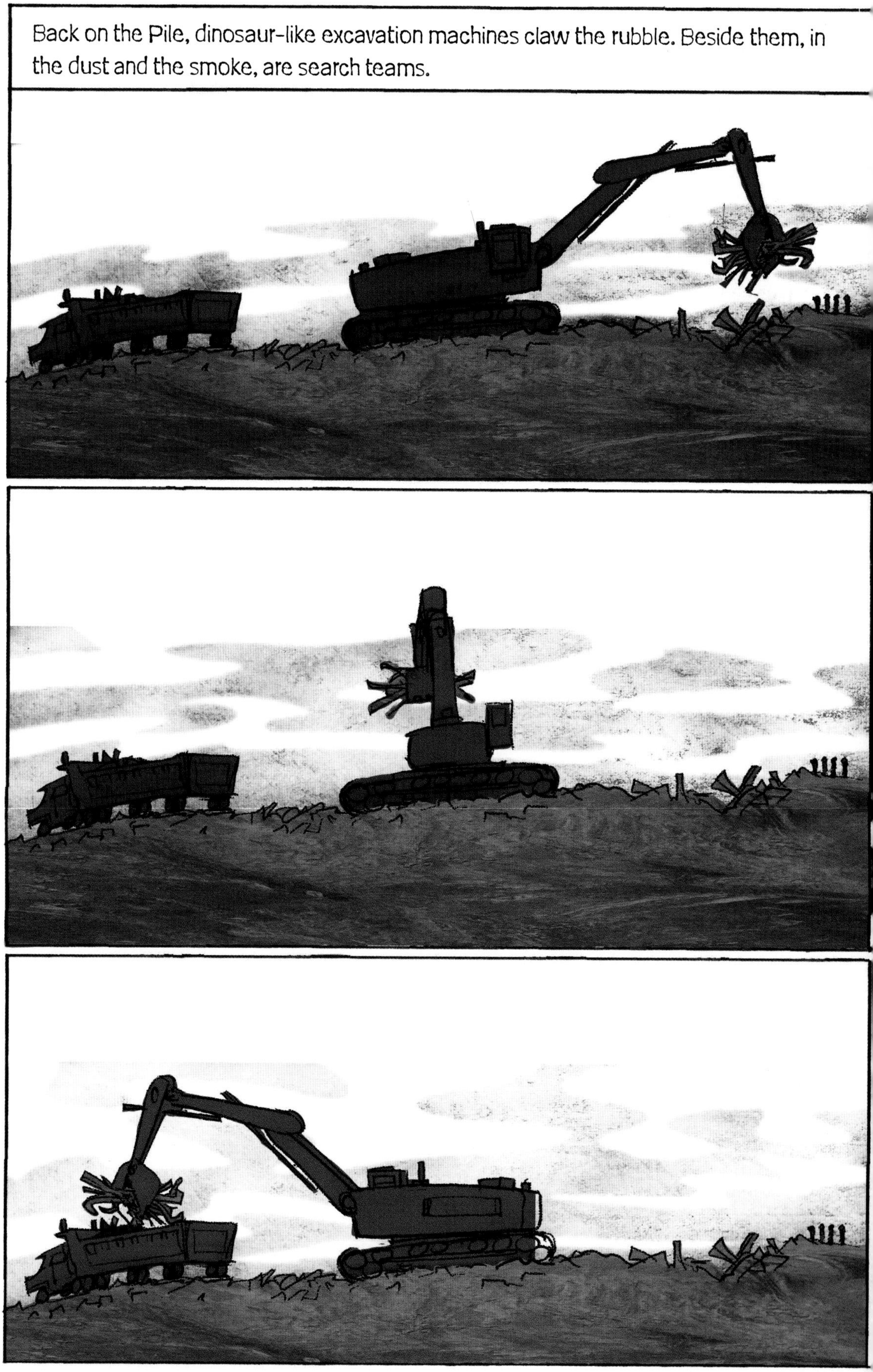
Back on the Pile, dinosaur-like excavation machines claw the rubble. Beside them, in the dust and the smoke, are search teams.

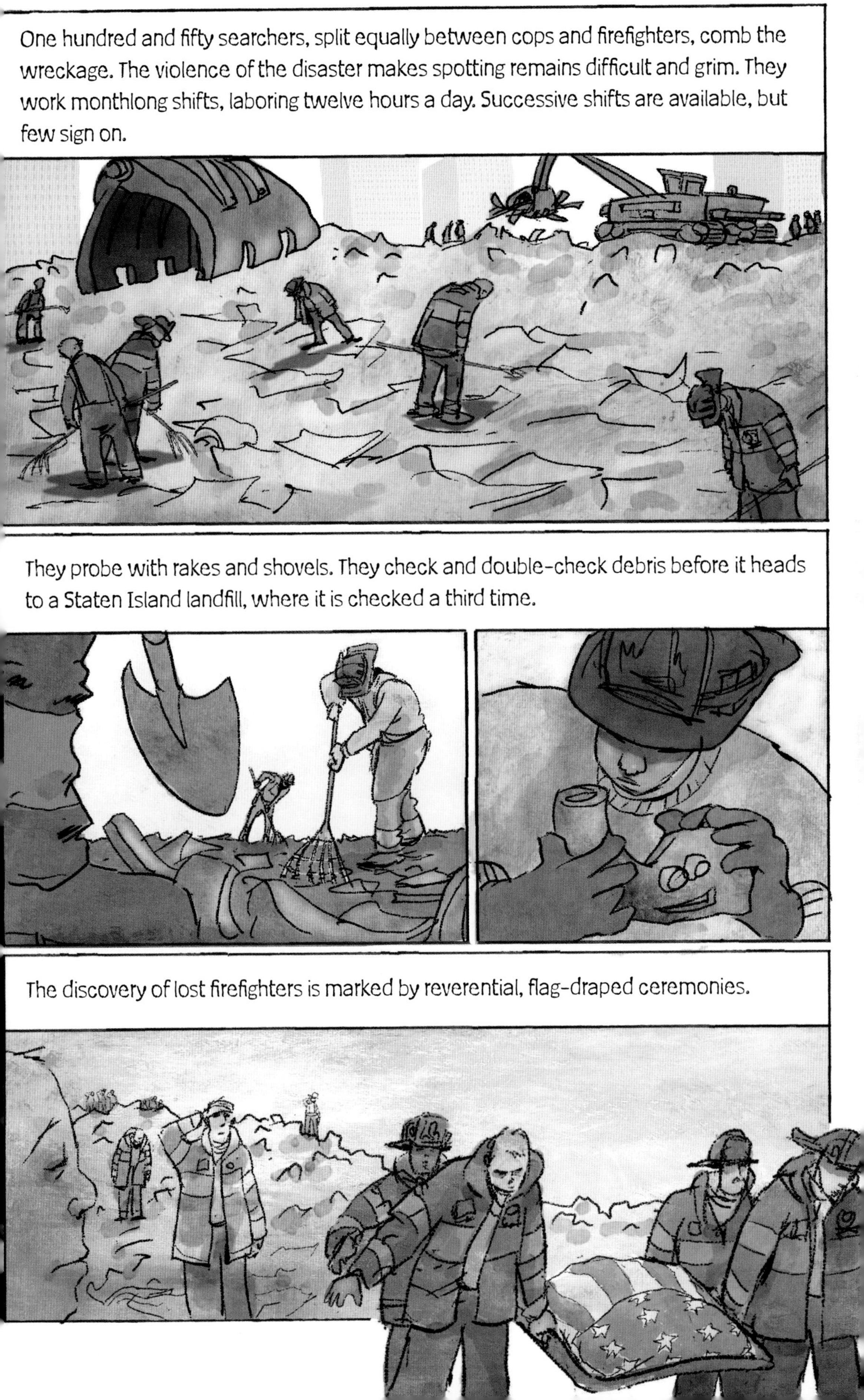
One hundred and fifty searchers, split equally between cops and firefighters, comb the wreckage. The violence of the disaster makes spotting remains difficult and grim. They work monthlong shifts, laboring twelve hours a day. Successive shifts are available, but few sign on.
They probe with rakes and shovels. They check and double-check debris before it heads to a Staten Island landfill, where it is checked a third time.
The discovery of lost firefighters is marked by reverential, flag-draped ceremonies.

Remains are taken to an uptown building to be identified. Teams of doctors work to match the ghastly findings to victims.

Sometimes they use DNA, the biological marker unique to each of us, to discover the identity. Other times, they use fingerprints, personal effects, and photos.

Dental records are important too. Volunteer dentists can sometimes identify a victim from a single tooth.

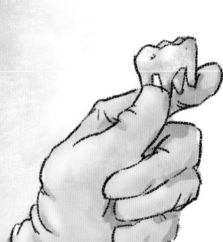

It represents the person we knew, the person we love.

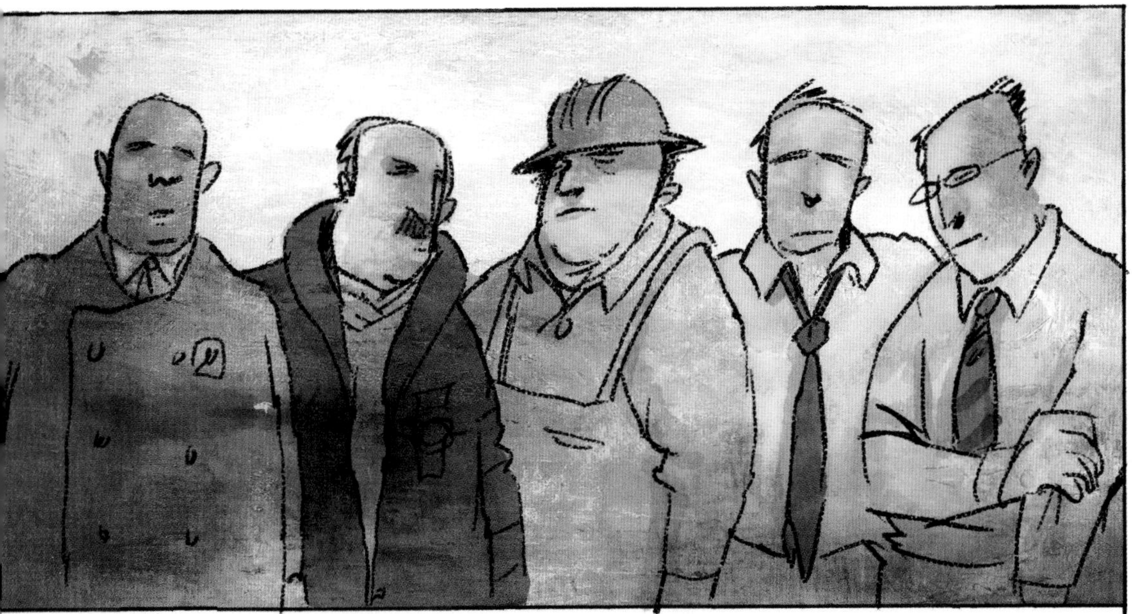

The City of New York manages the disaster. Fire and police leaders, construction bosses, engineers, and government officials crowd into a kindergarten room at a nearby school and decide the tactics of recovery.

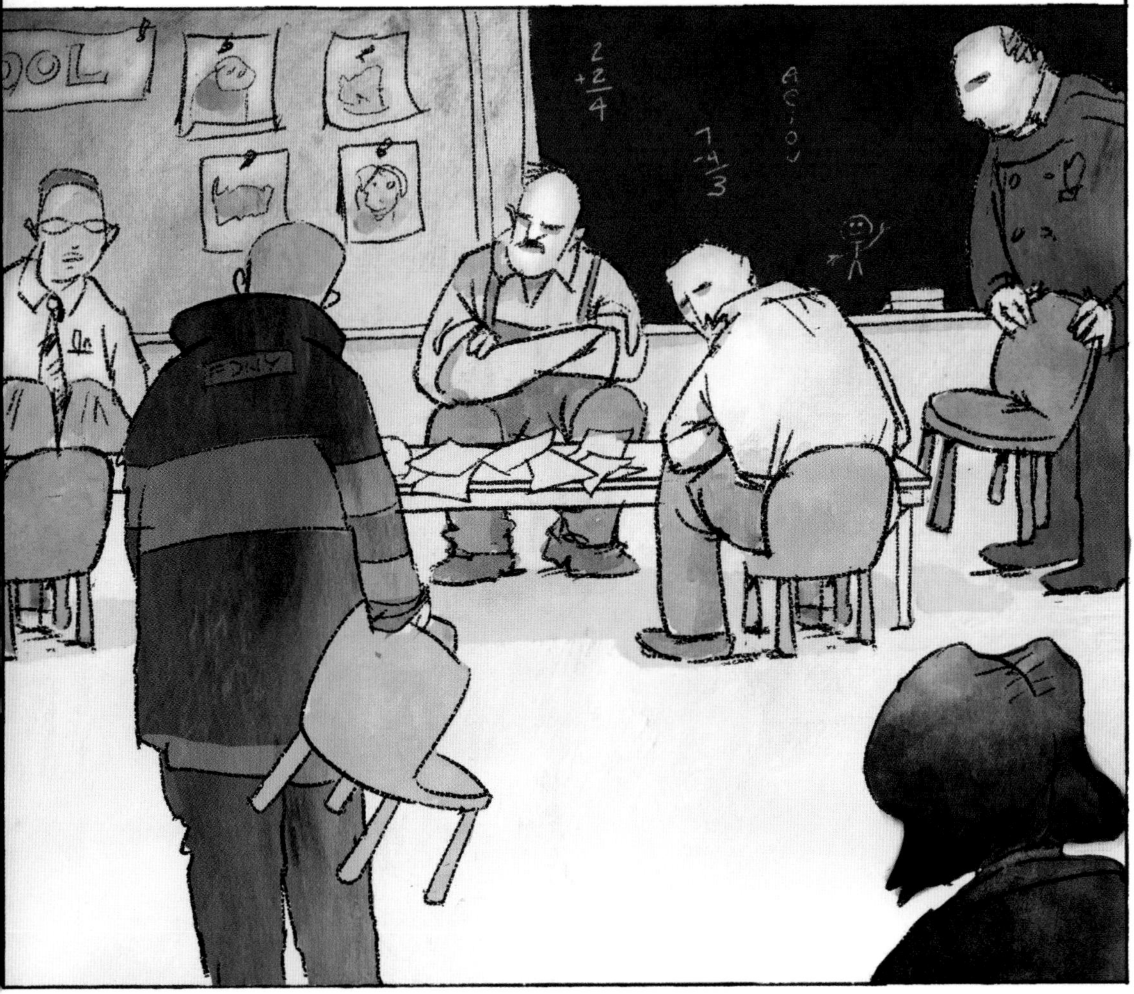
FDNY

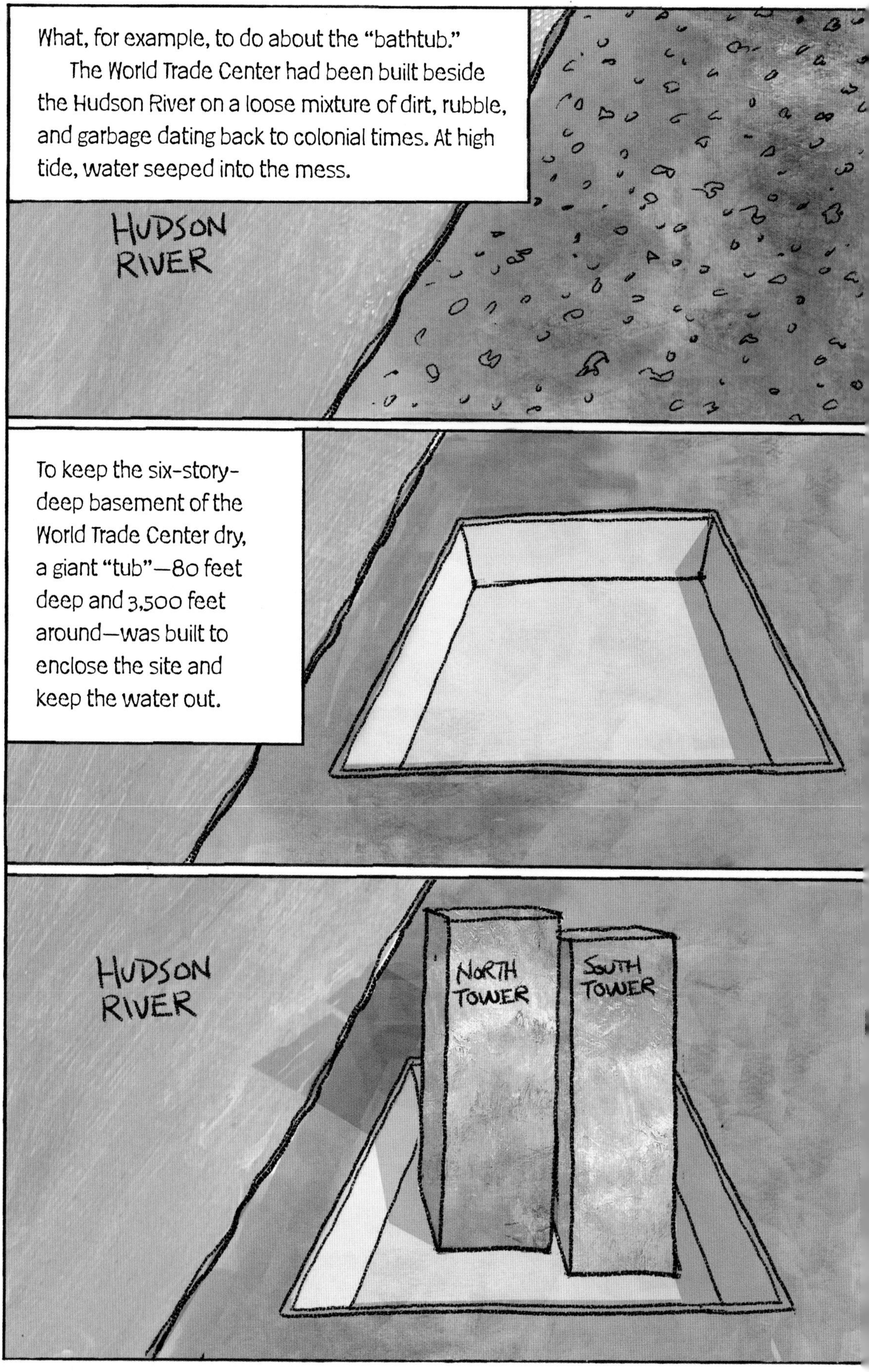
What, for example, to do about the "bathtub."
The World Trade Center had been built beside the Hudson River on a loose mixture of dirt, rubble, and garbage dating back to colonial times. At high tide, water seeped into the mess.
HUDSON RIVER
To keep the six-story-deep basement of the World Trade Center dry, a giant "tub"—80 feet deep and 3,500 feet around—was built to enclose the site and keep the water out.
HUDSON RIVER
NORTH TOWER
SOUTH TOWER

Now, part of the tub wall is bowing.
If it breaks, water will flood subway lines and submerge much of the Pile.

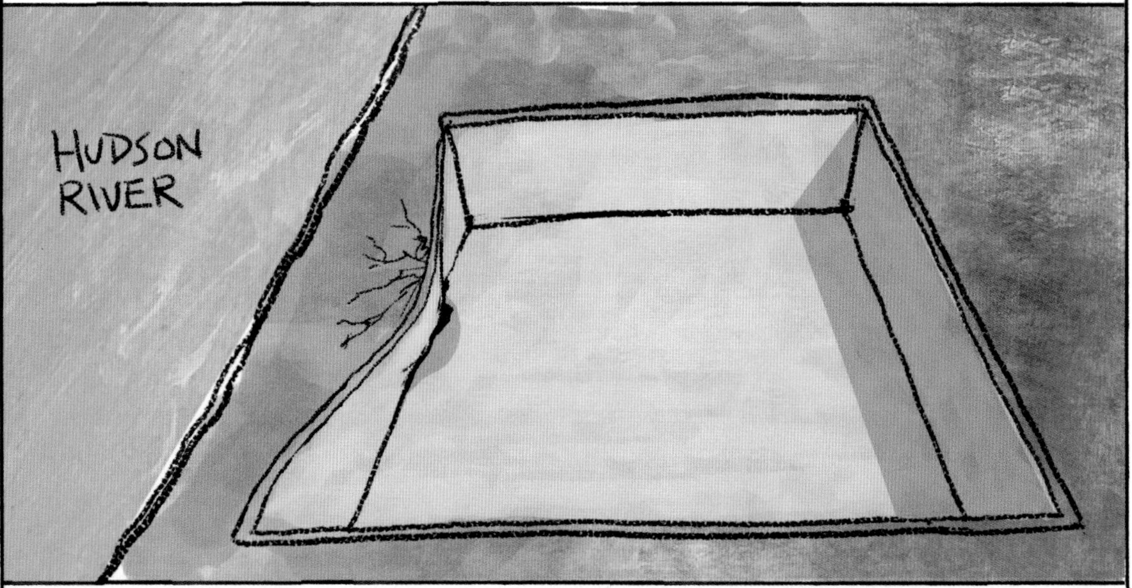
HUDSON RIVER

Engineers race to drain water surrounding the tub and pile reinforcing dirt beside it.
After much worry, the wall holds.

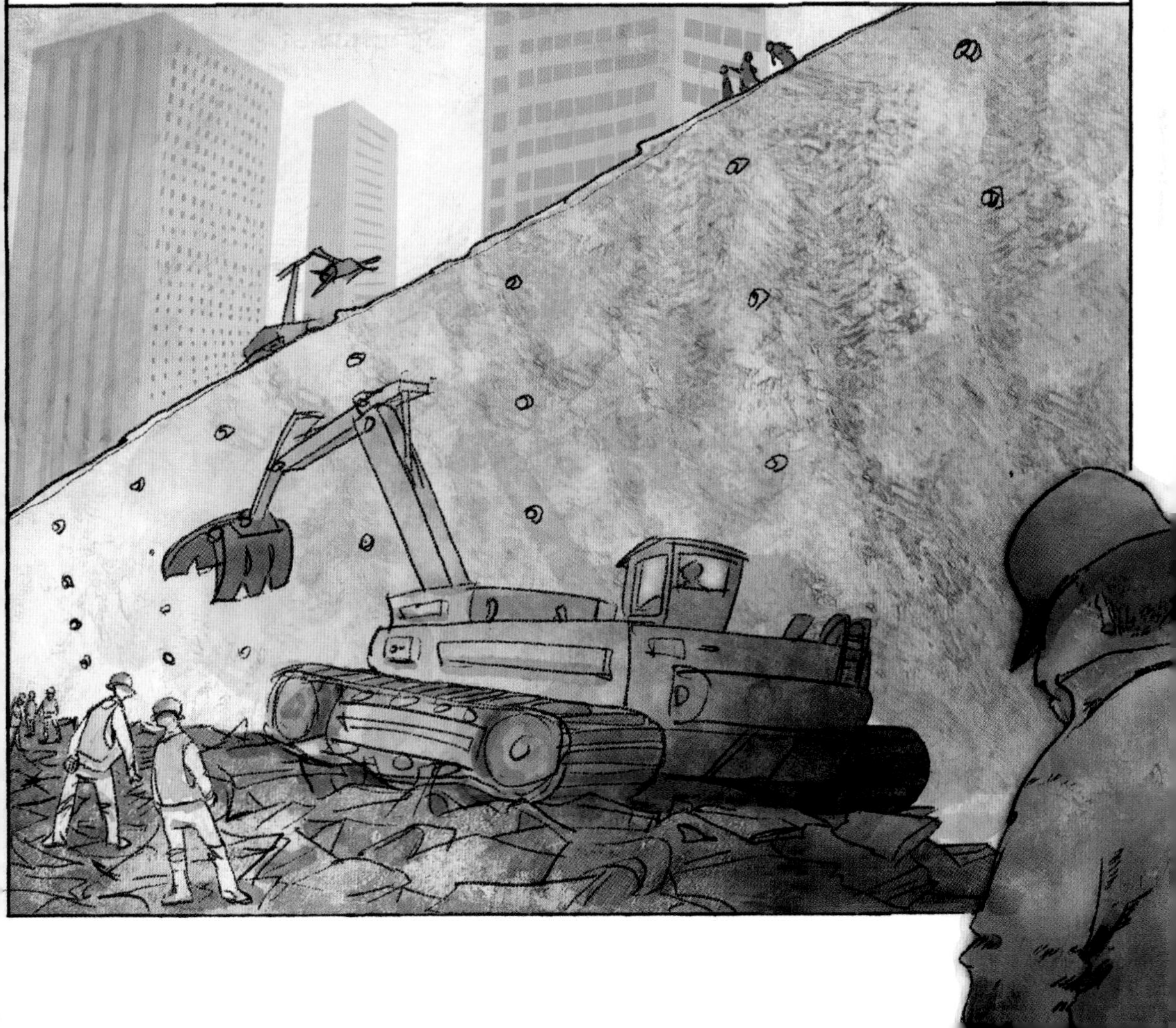

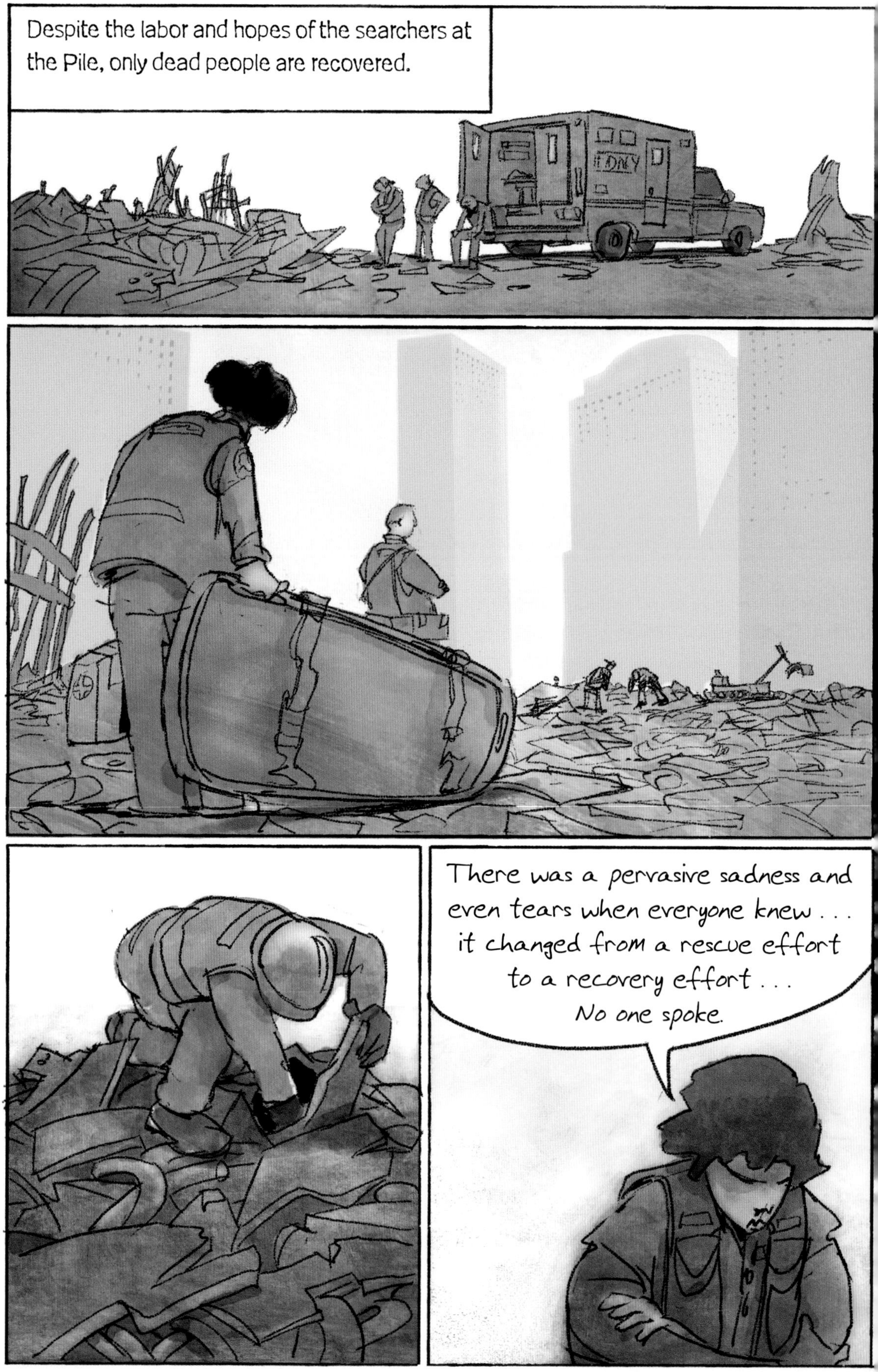
Despite the labor and hopes of the searchers at the Pile, only dead people are recovered.
FDNY
There was a pervasive sadness and even tears when everyone knew . . . it changed from a rescue effort to a recovery effort . . . No one spoke.

In November, city leaders try to speed cleanup at the Pile and direct search teams to be reduced. Angry firefighters see this as callous to fallen firefighters who have yet to be recovered.

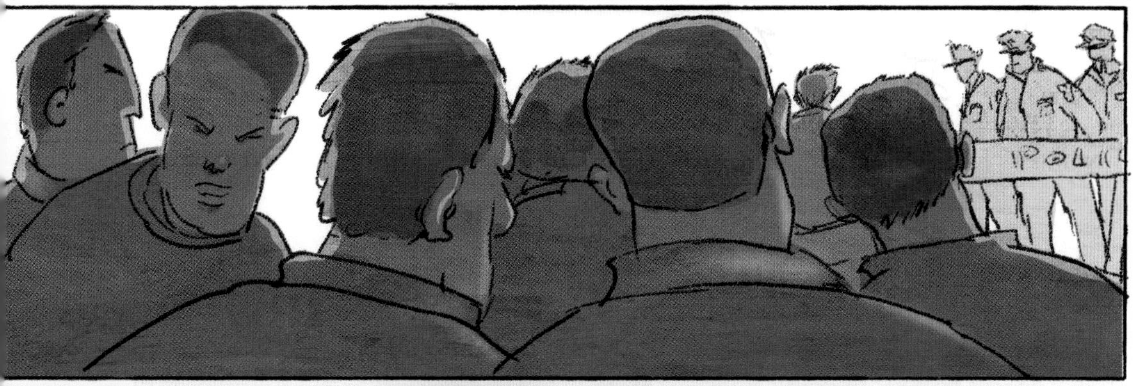

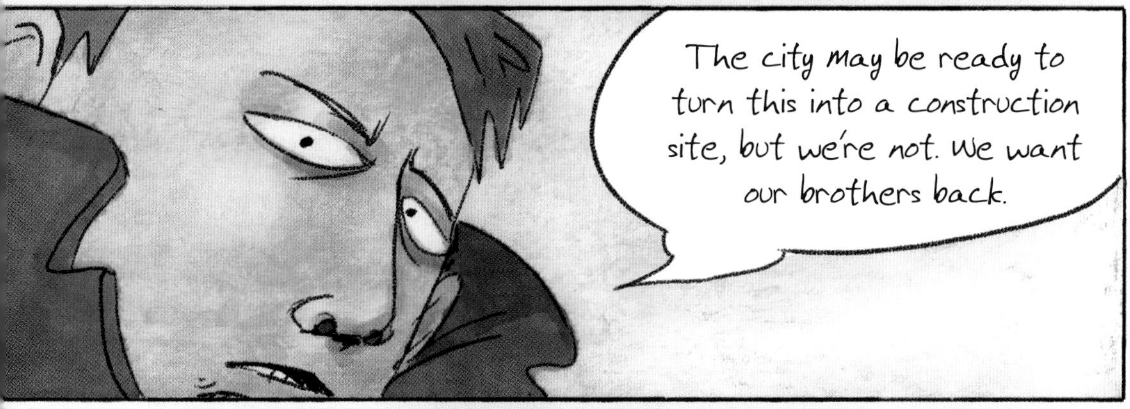
The city may be ready to turn this into a construction site, but we're not. We want our brothers back.

About a thousand firefighters gather outside the Pile. Fighting breaks out when police try to maintain order.

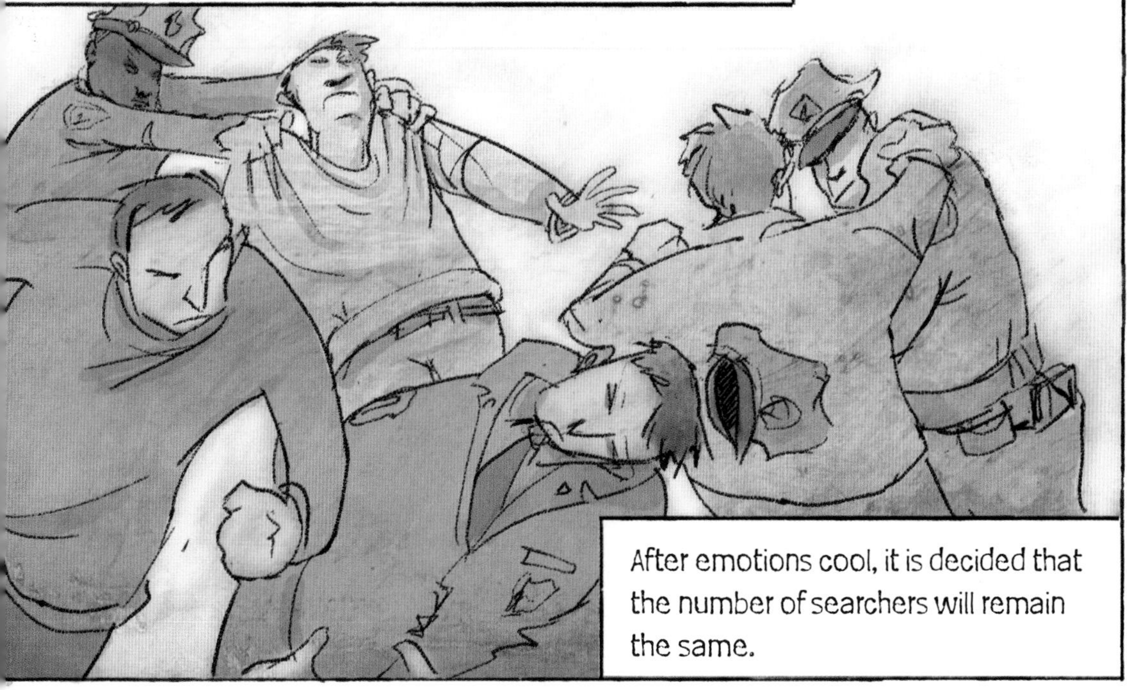
After emotions cool, it is decided that the number of searchers will remain the same.

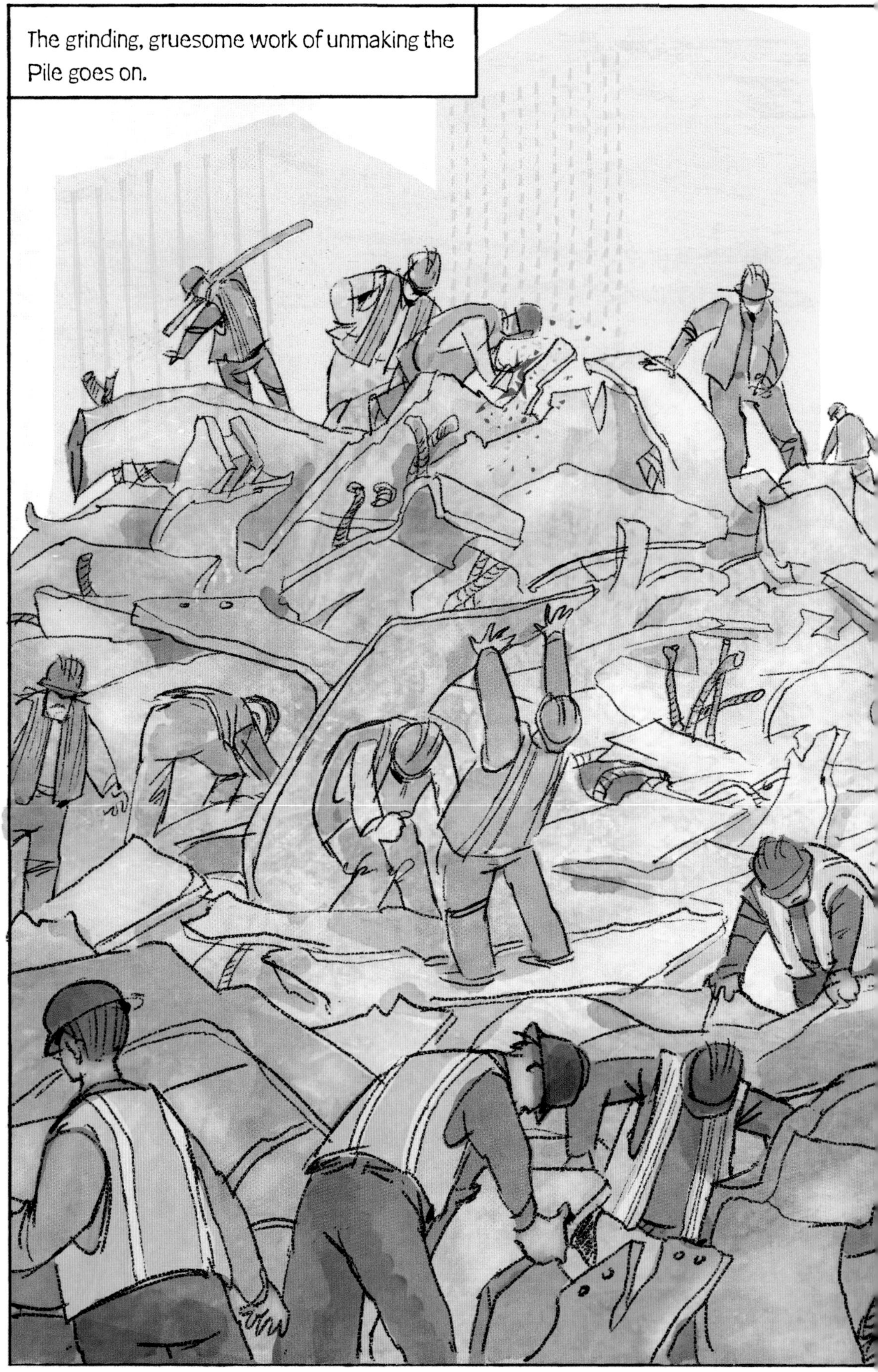
The grinding, gruesome work of unmaking the Pile goes on.

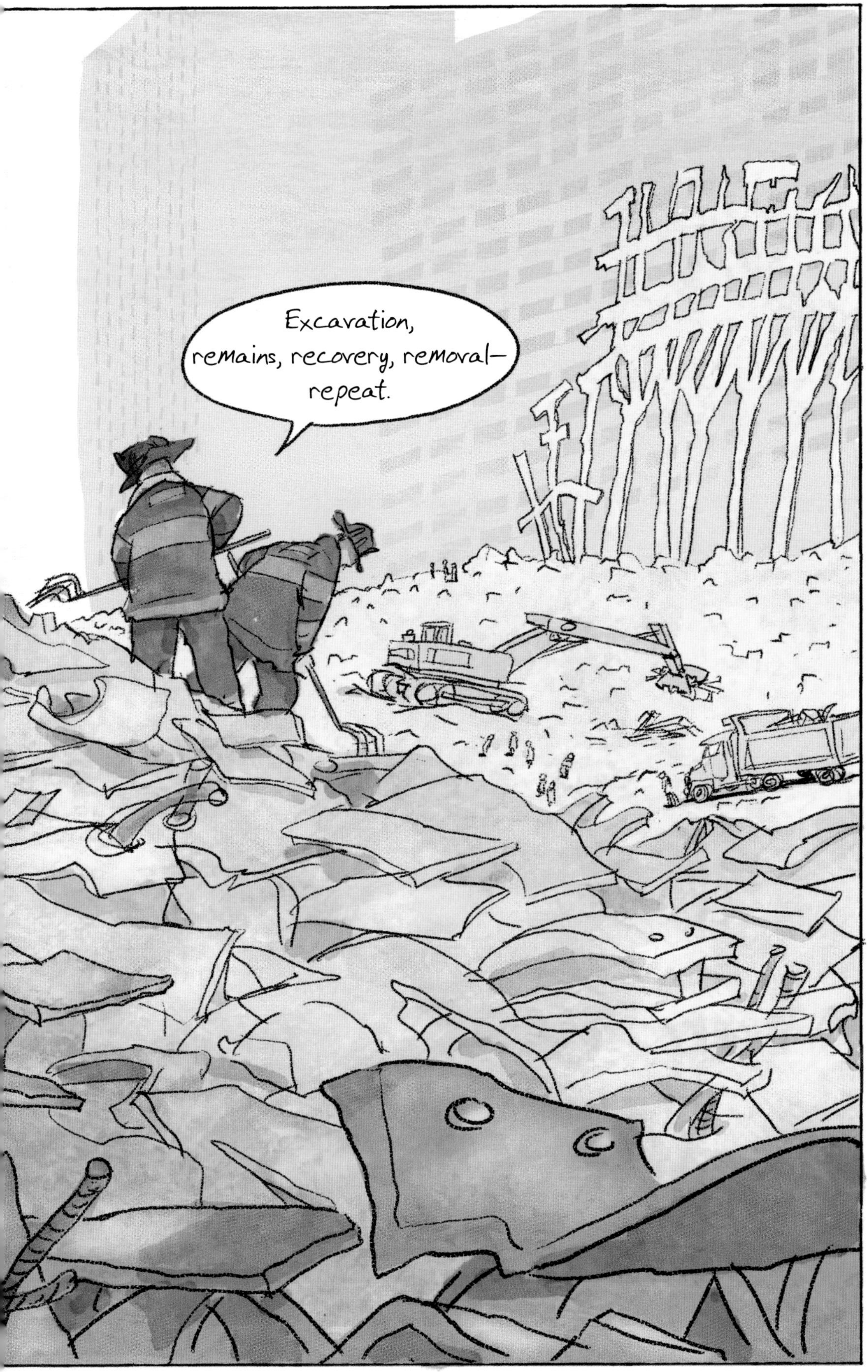
Excavation,
remains, recovery, removal—
repeat.

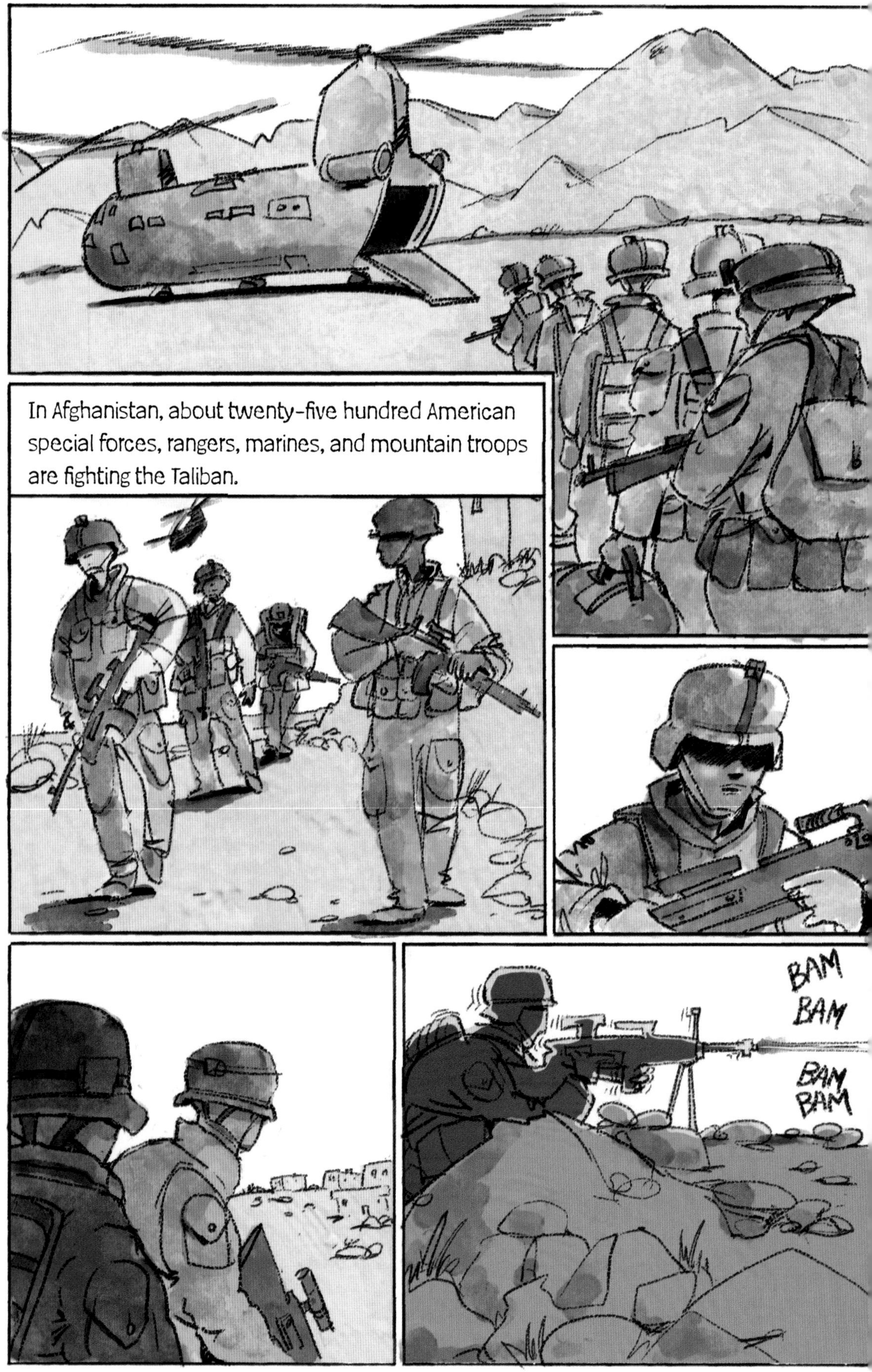
In Afghanistan, about twenty-five hundred American special forces, rangers, marines, and mountain troops are fighting the Taliban.
BAM
BAM
BAM
BAM

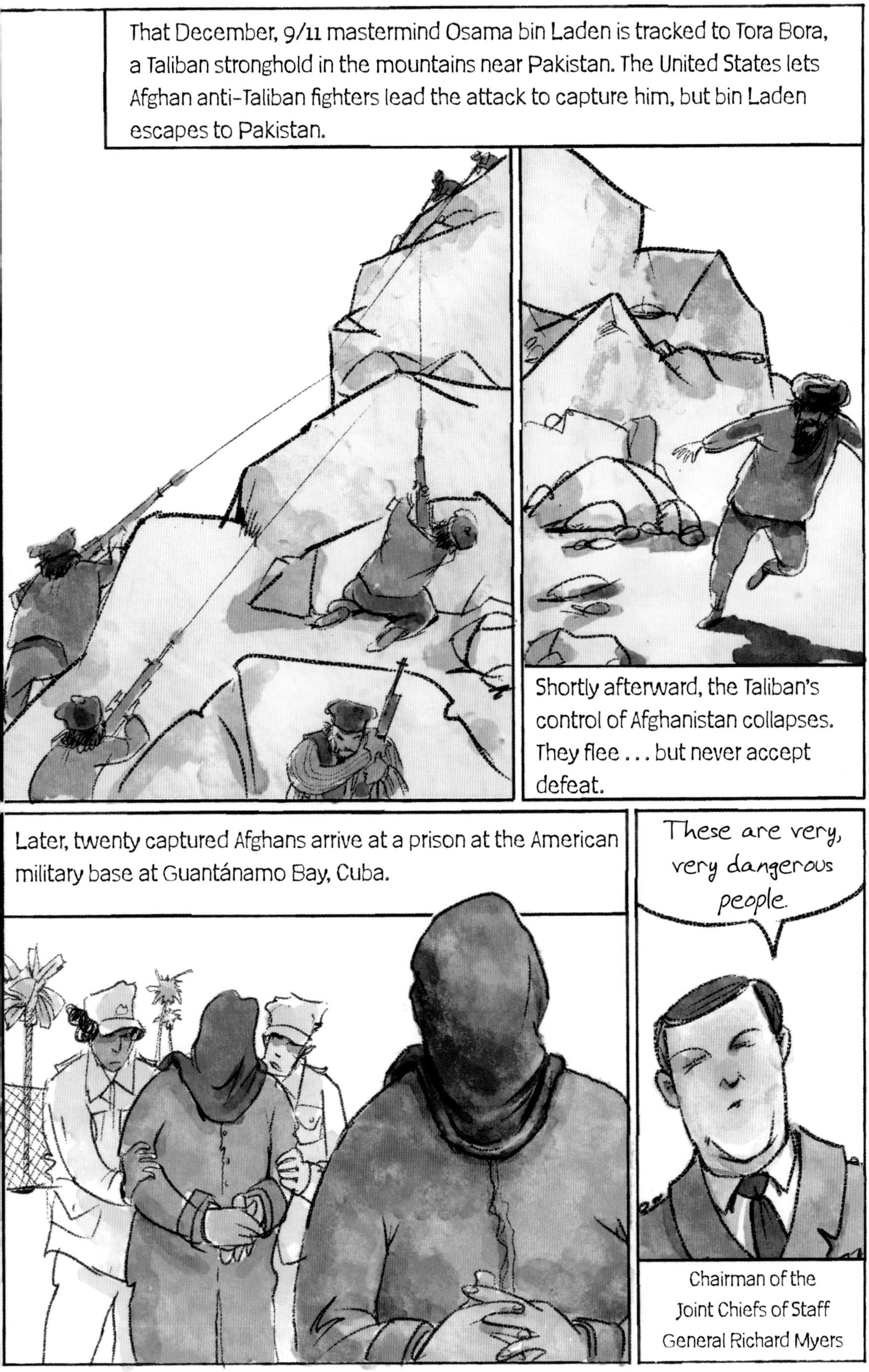
That December, 9/11 mastermind Osama bin Laden is tracked to Tora Bora, a Taliban stronghold in the mountains near Pakistan. The United States lets Afghan anti-Taliban fighters lead the attack to capture him, but bin Laden escapes to Pakistan.
Shortly afterward, the Taliban's control of Afghanistan collapses. They flee . . . but never accept defeat.
Later, twenty captured Afghans arrive at a prison at the American military base at Guantánamo Bay, Cuba.
These are very, very dangerous people.
Chairman of the Joint Chiefs of Staff General Richard Myers

In March 2002, remembrances of the 9/11 tragedy are held in New York City, Washington, D.C., and Shanksville, Pennsylvania. Though sorrowful, the bravery of first responders and ordinary civilians is celebrated, including the passengers of Flight 93, who died at Shanksville. It was discovered they had fought the hijackers, preventing another building from being attacked . . . but at the cost of their own lives.

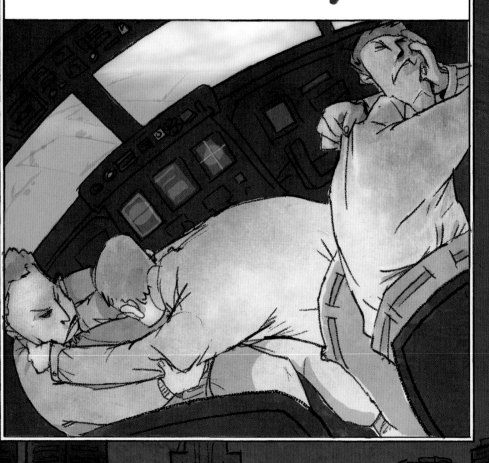

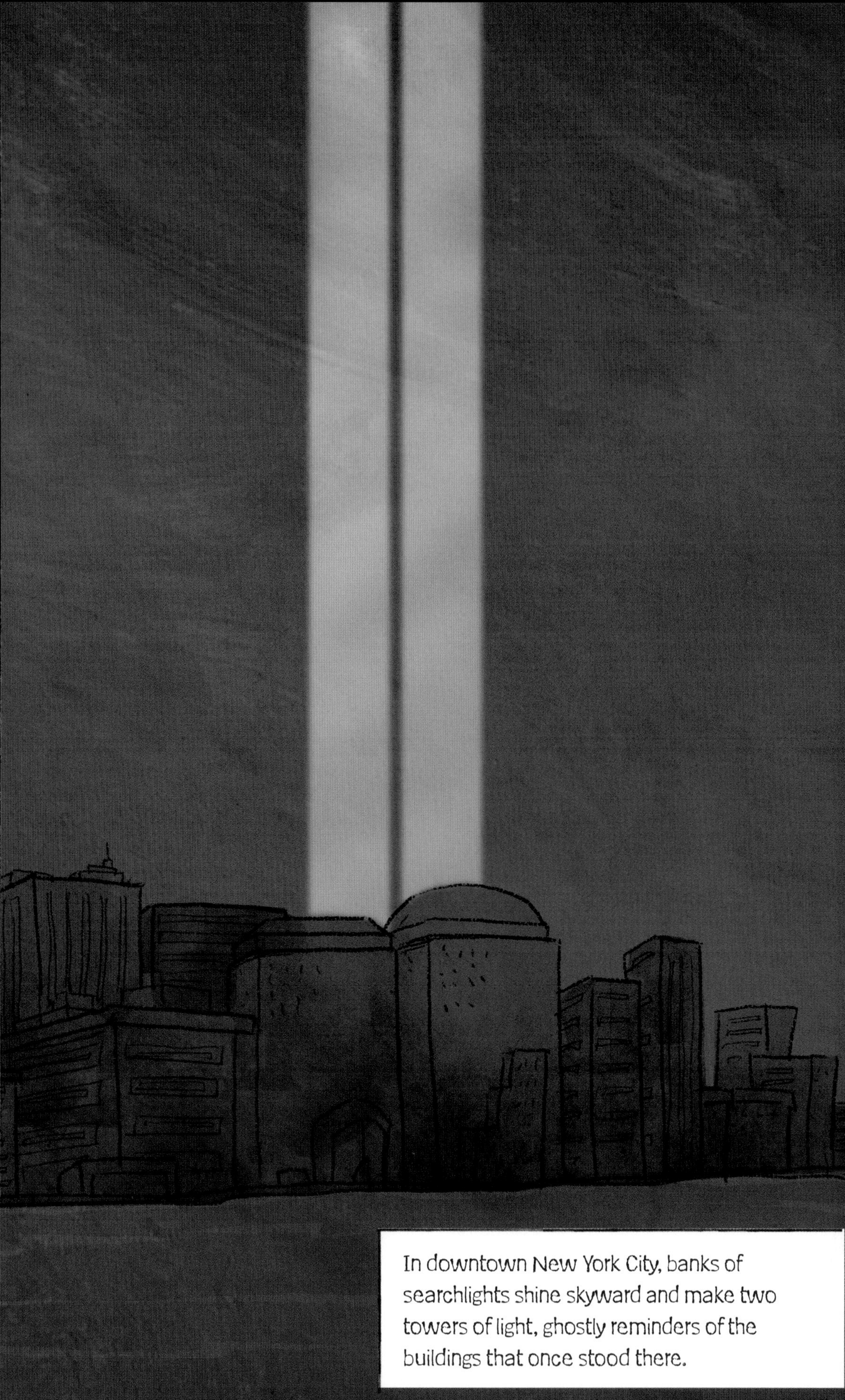
In downtown New York City, banks of searchlights shine skyward and make two towers of light, ghostly reminders of the buildings that once stood there.

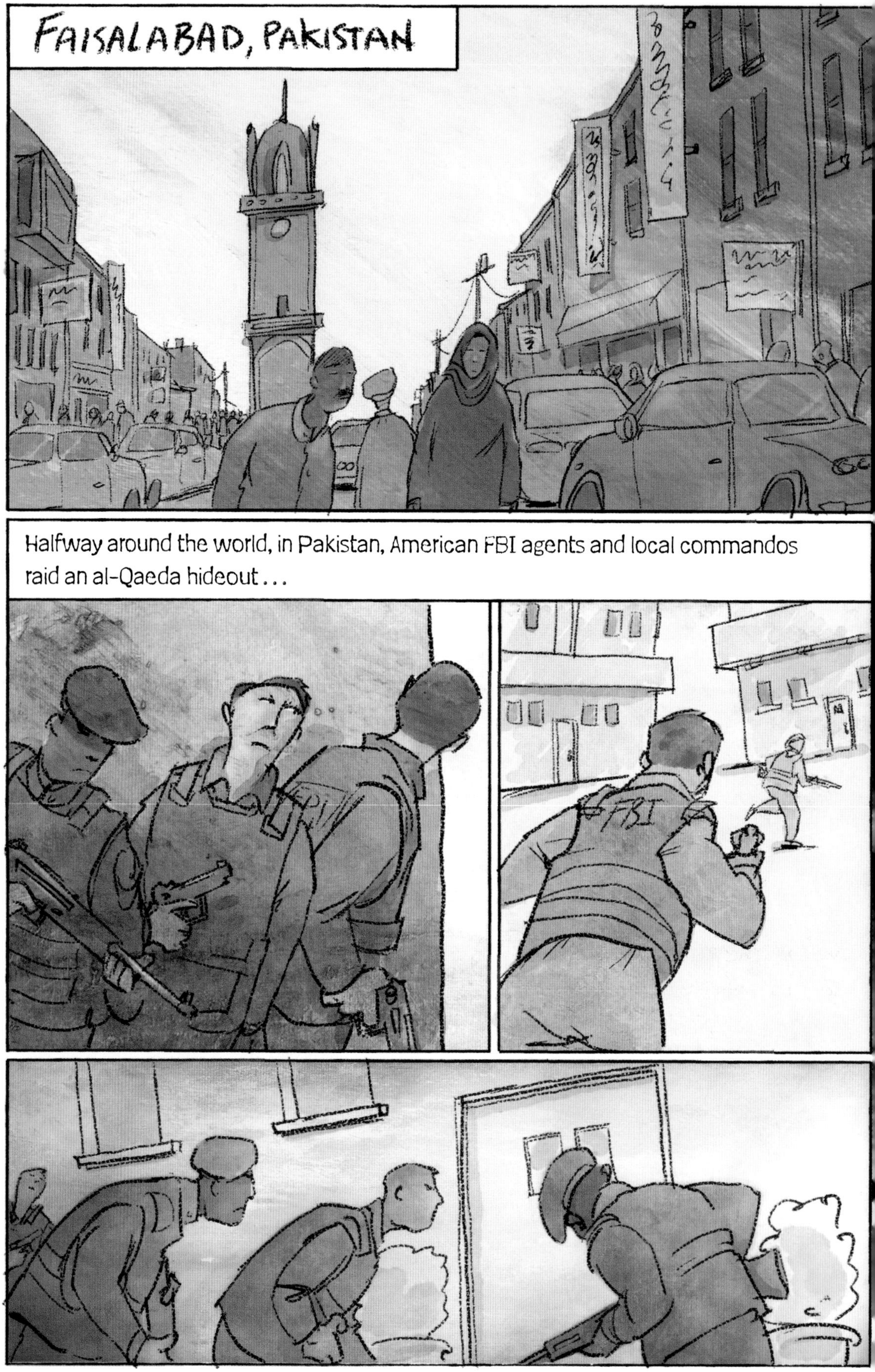
FAISALABAD, PAKISTAN
Halfway around the world, in Pakistan, American FBI agents and local commandos raid an al-Qaeda hideout...
FBI

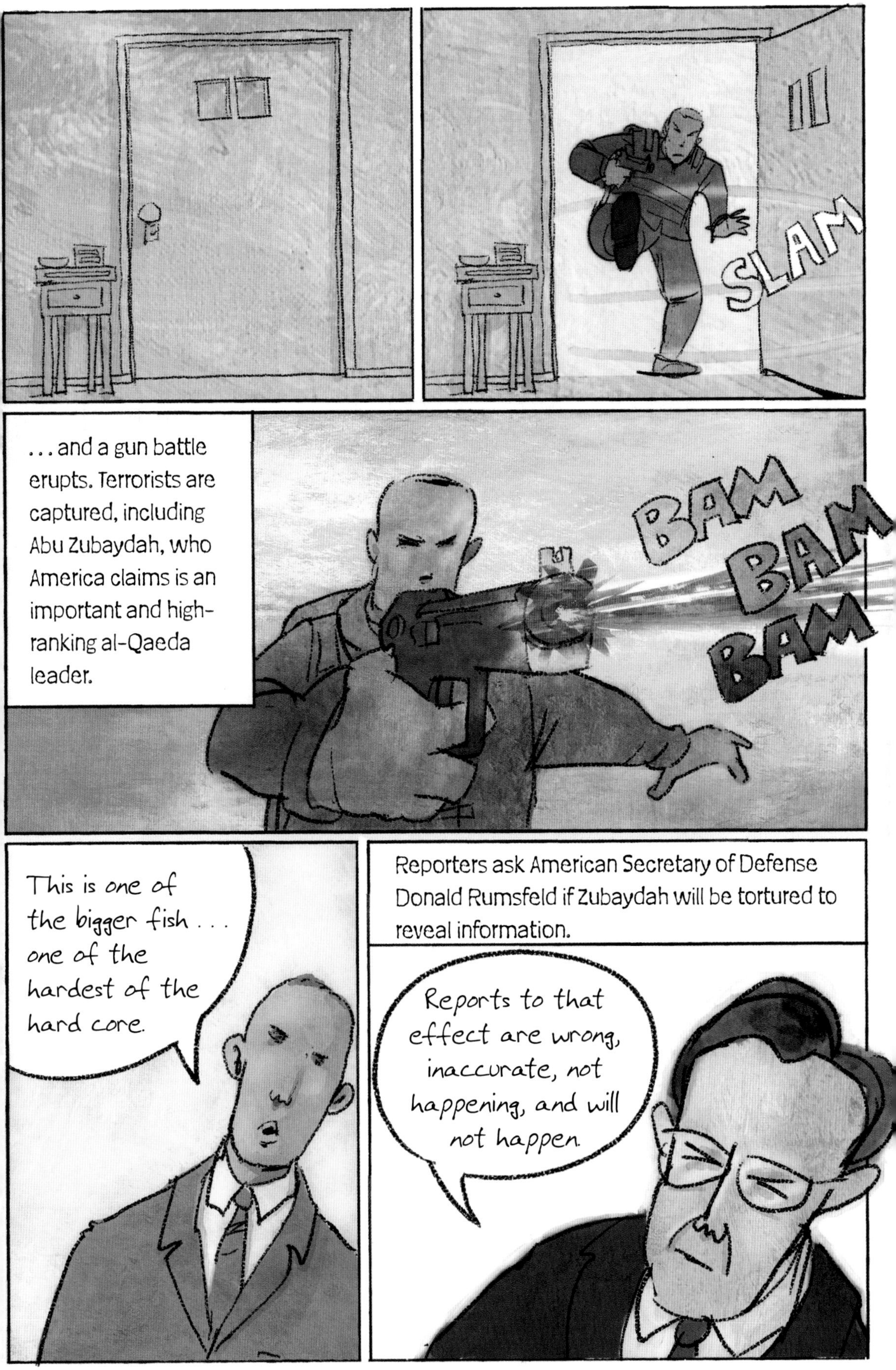

SLAM
. . . and a gun battle erupts. Terrorists are captured, including Abu Zubaydah, who America claims is an important and high-ranking al-Qaeda leader.
BAM BAM BAM
This is one of the bigger fish . . . one of the hardest of the hard core.
Reporters ask American Secretary of Defense Donald Rumsfeld if Zubaydah will be tortured to reveal information.
Reports to that effect are wrong, inaccurate, not happening, and will not happen.

Zubaydah is shuttled among secret prisons in Thailand, Poland, and Lithuania.

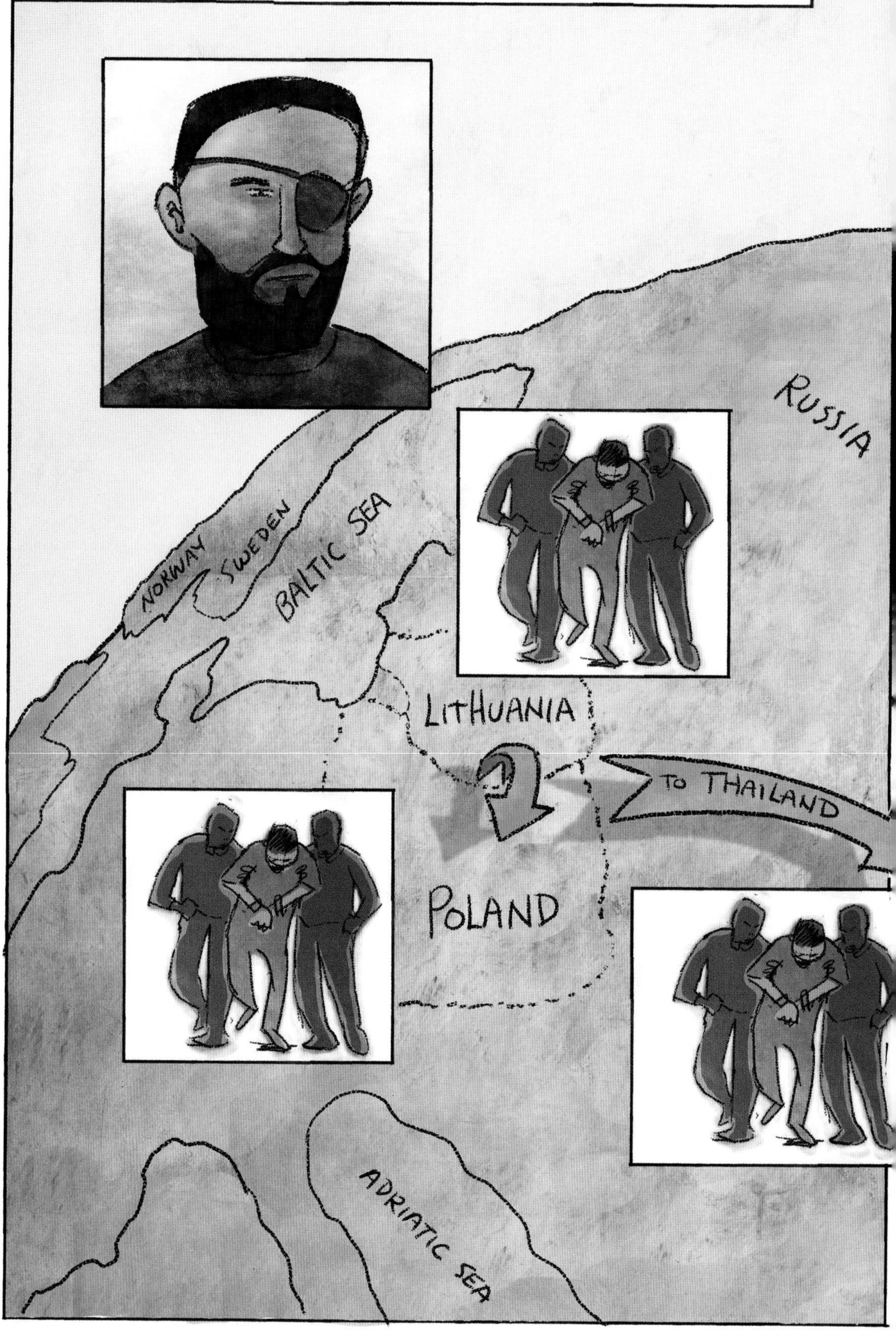
RUSSIA
NORWAY
SWEDEN
BALTIC SEA
LITHUANIA
TO THAILAND
POLAND
ADRIATIC SEA

Less than six months after his capture, government agents confine Zubaydah in small boxes for hours and hours at a time and "waterboard" him two to four times a day, that is, mimic the feeling of drowning by placing a water-soaked cloth over his face.

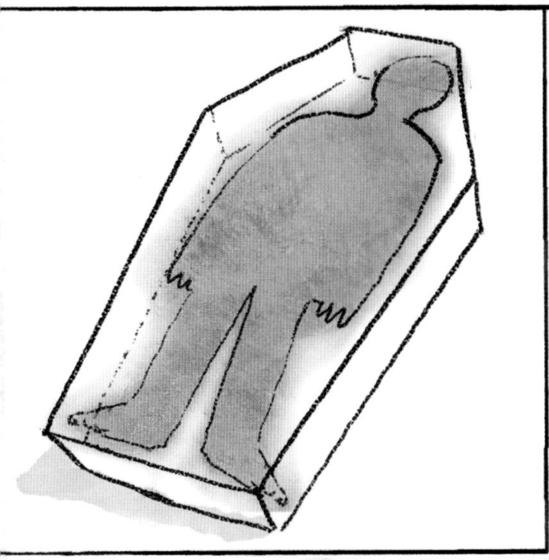

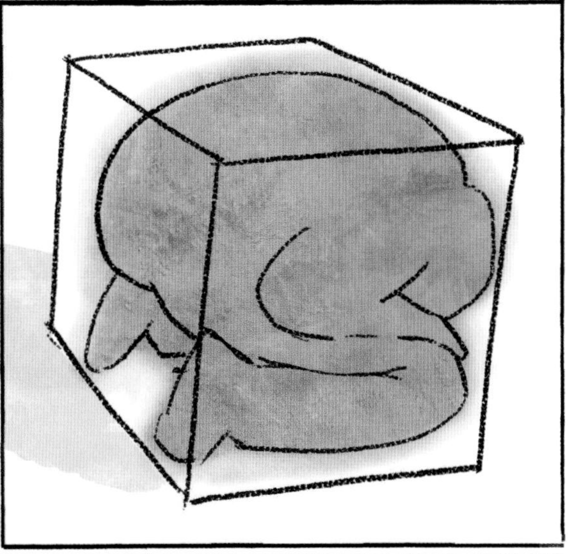

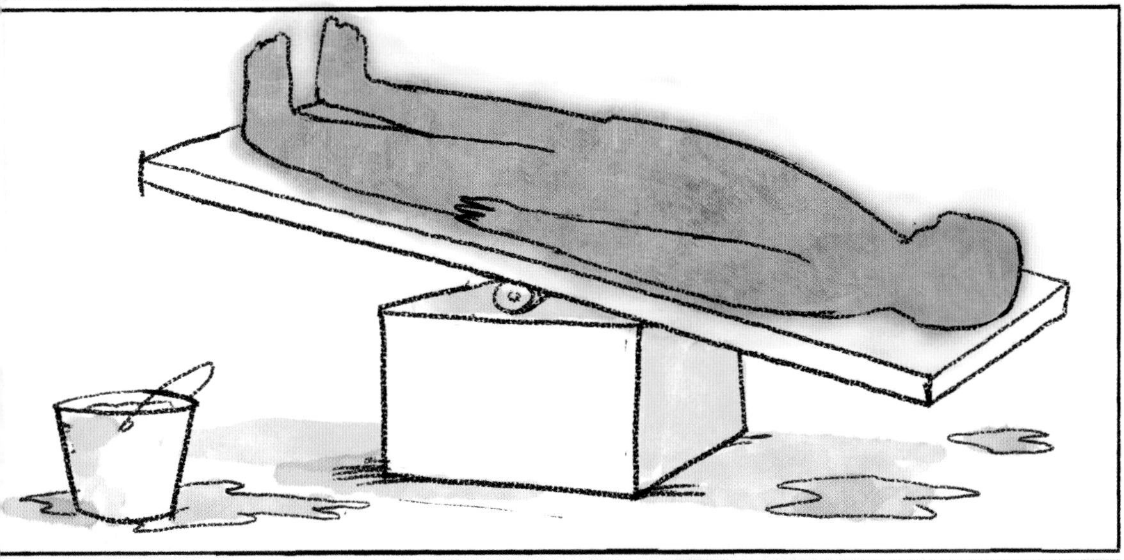

Though the government had in prior years described this as torture, it now insists that it is just "aggressive interrogation." And, they swear, it wrings valuable information from Zubaydah.

Other prisoners will receive aggressive and enhanced interrogation.

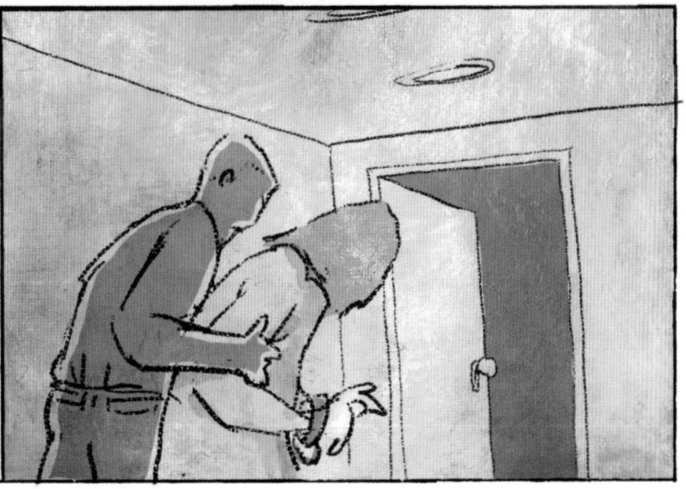

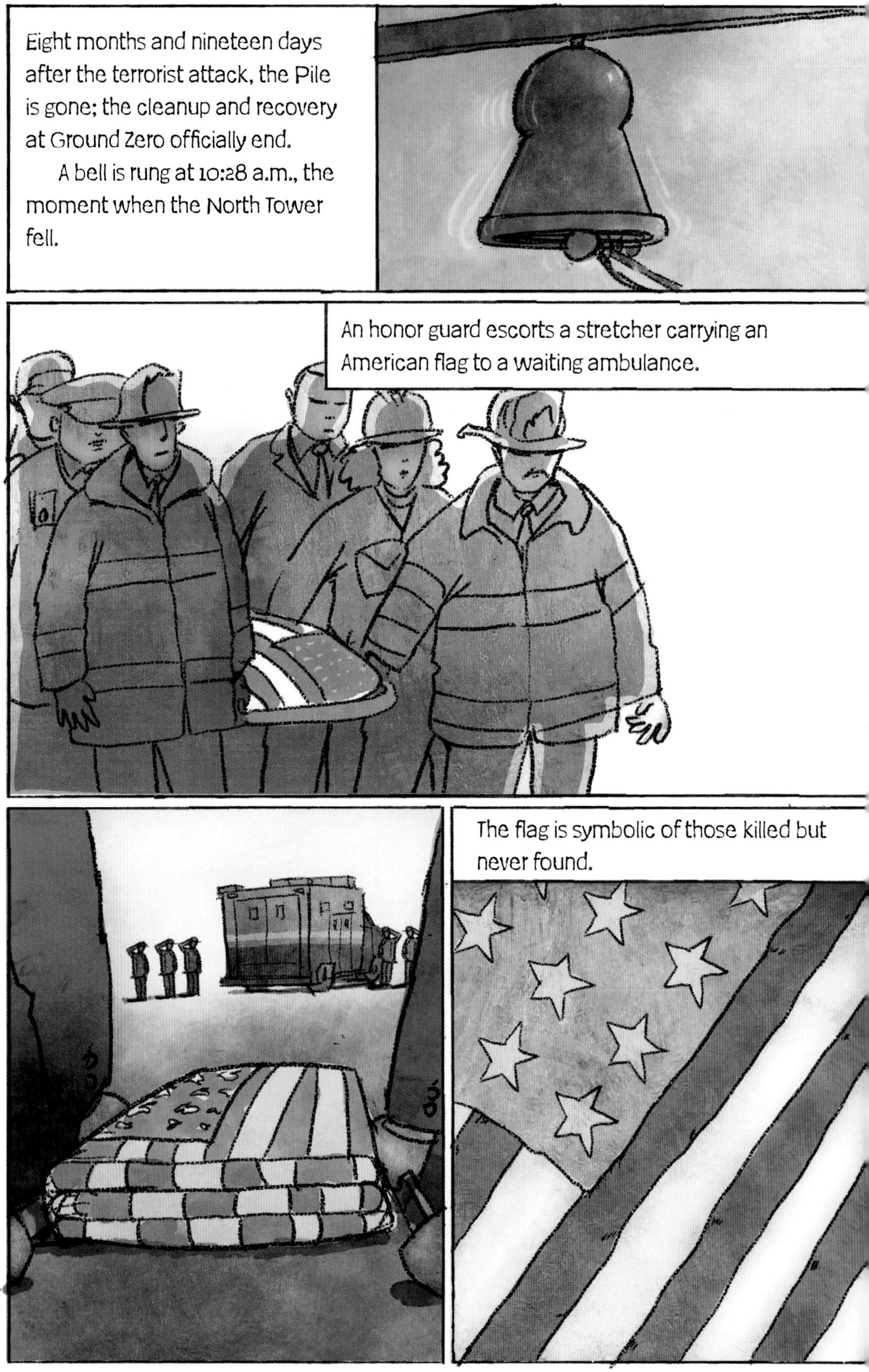
Eight months and nineteen days after the terrorist attack, the Pile is gone; the cleanup and recovery at Ground Zero officially end.
A bell is rung at 10:28 a.m., the moment when the North Tower fell.
An honor guard escorts a stretcher carrying an American flag to a waiting ambulance.
The flag is symbolic of those killed but never found.

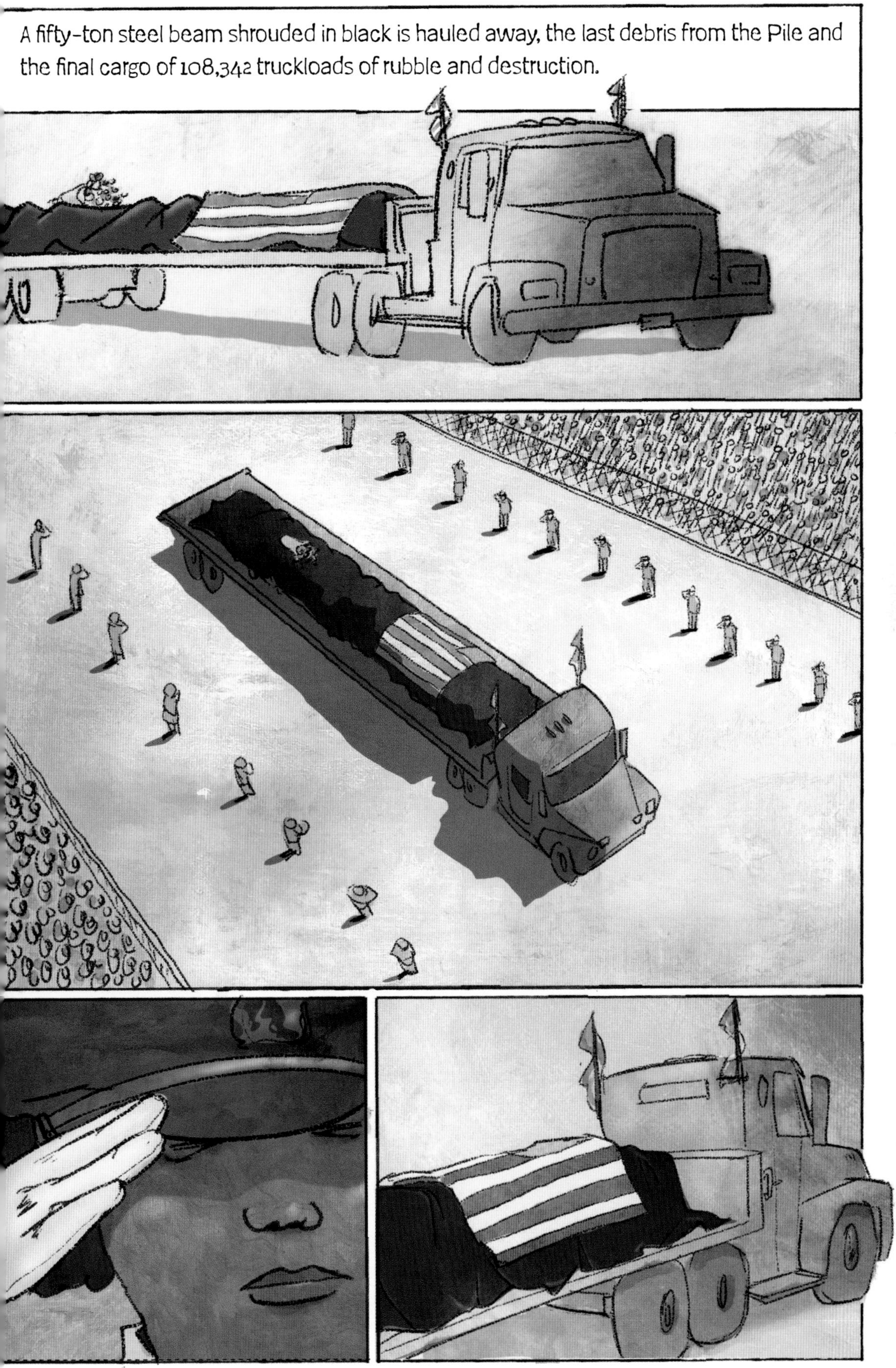
A fifty-ton steel beam shrouded in black is hauled away, the last debris from the Pile and the final cargo of 108,342 truckloads of rubble and destruction.

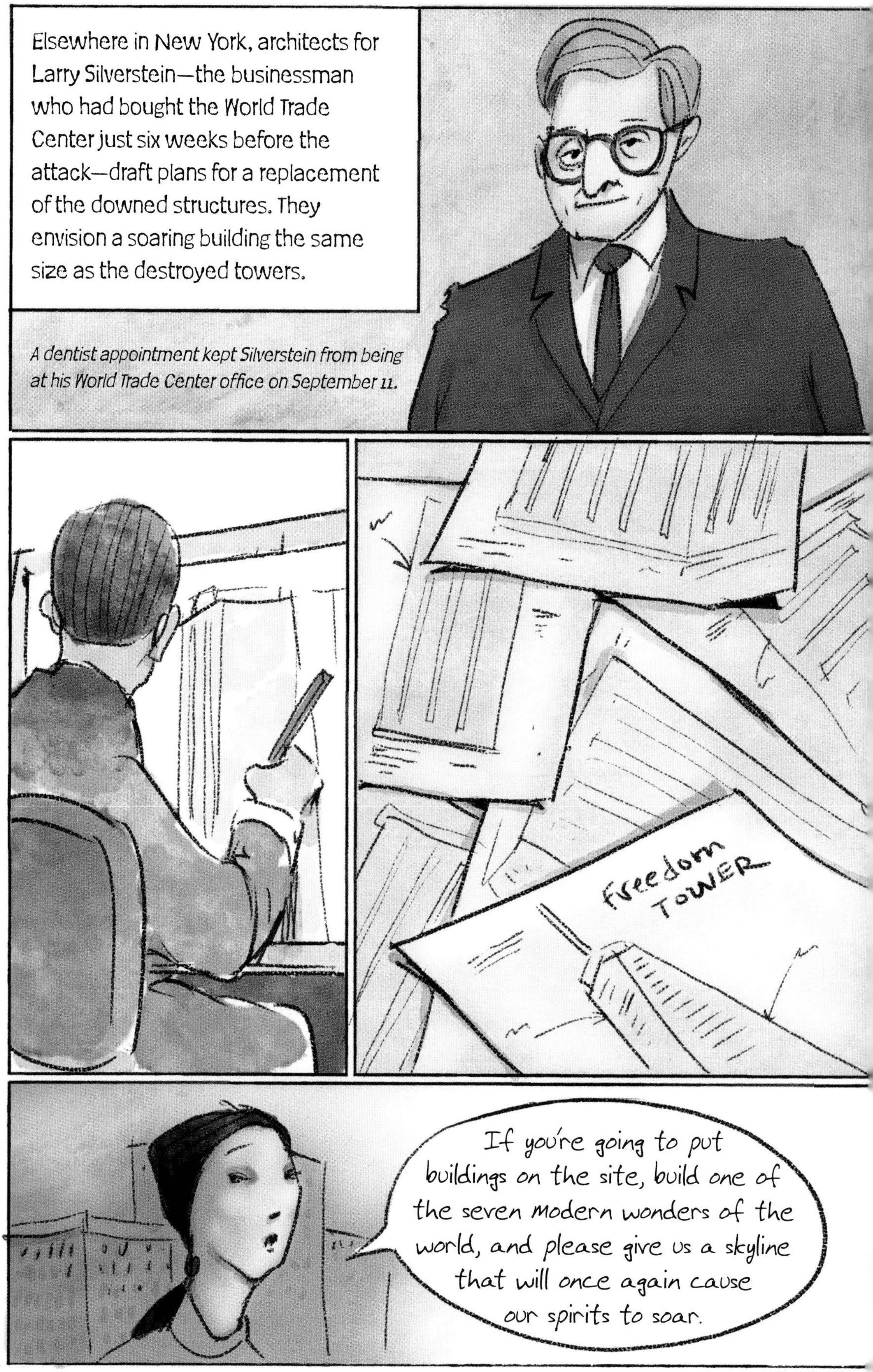
Elsewhere in New York, architects for Larry Silverstein—the businessman who had bought the World Trade Center just six weeks before the attack—draft plans for a replacement of the downed structures. They envision a soaring building the same size as the destroyed towers.
A dentist appointment kept Silverstein from being at his World Trade Center office on September 11.
Freedom TOWER
If you're going to put buildings on the site, build one of the seven modern wonders of the world, and please give us a skyline that will once again cause our spirits to soar.

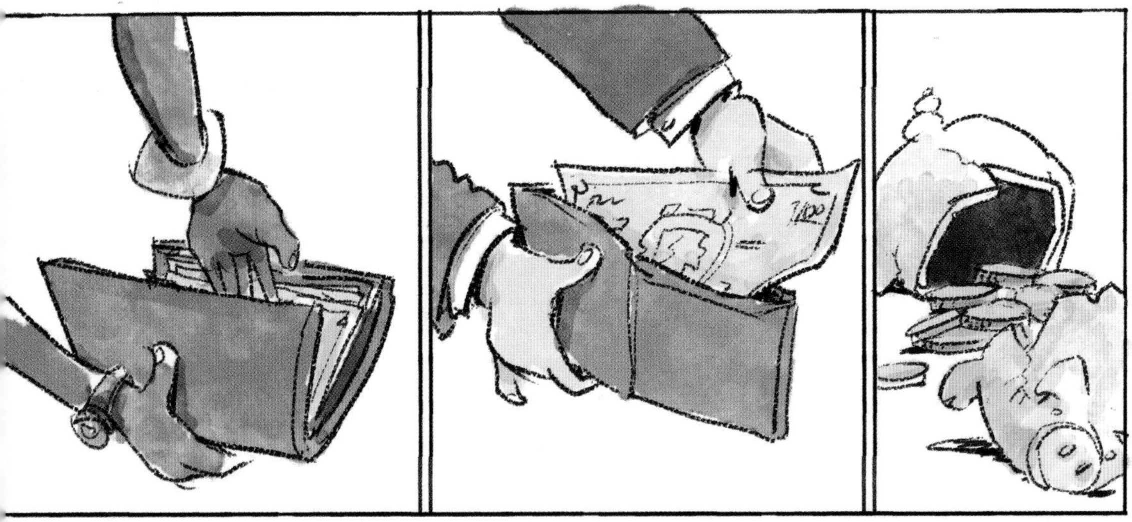

Americans unable to lend a physical hand to the cleanup and recovery open their wallets and donate to charities for survivors and their families.

In Afghanistan, a new American-supported government takes control. The U.S. Congress votes to give them $38 billion in aid.

Still, a stubborn Taliban keeps up the fight.

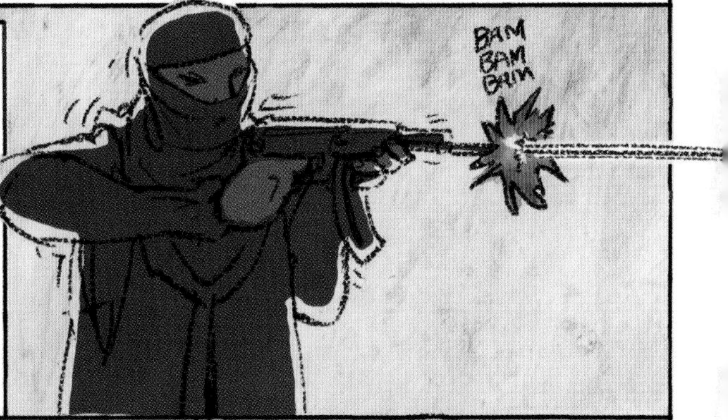
BAM
BAM
BAM

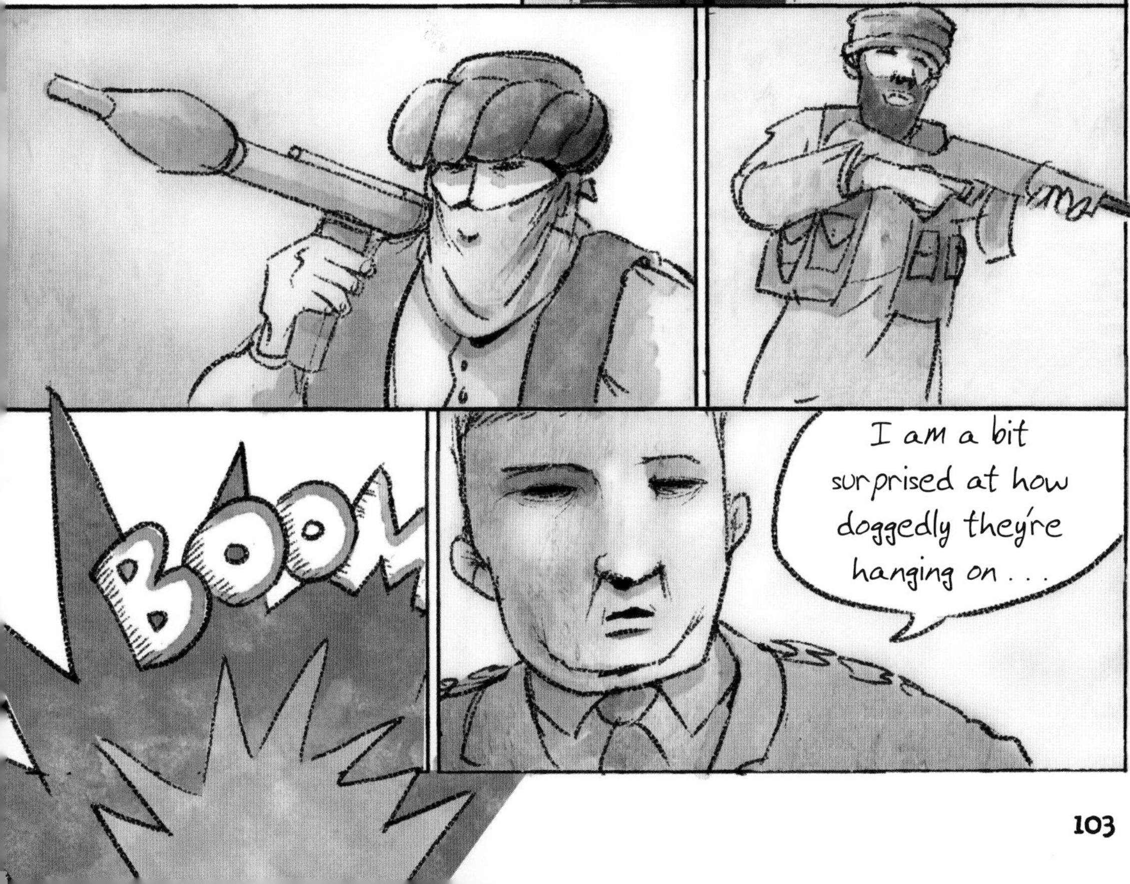
BOOM
I am a bit surprised at how doggedly they're hanging on . . .

On September 11, 2002, America marks the one-year anniversary of the attack. President Bush takes part in ceremonies at the Pentagon and Shanksville, Pennsylvania, and then travels to New York City.

There, in the dirt that had once been the foundation of the World Trade Center, a rough ring is constructed. In it, mourners place flowers, photographs, and American flags.

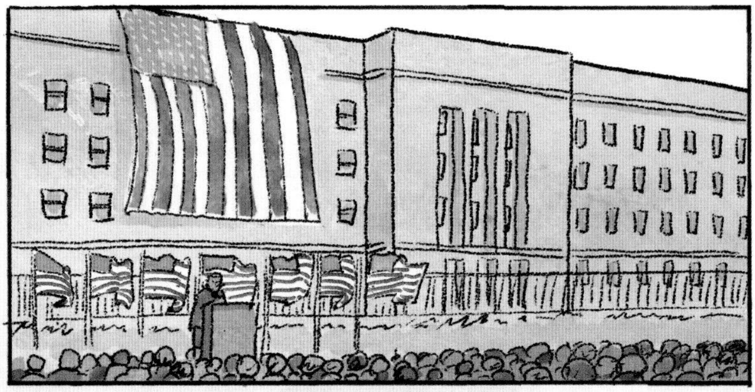

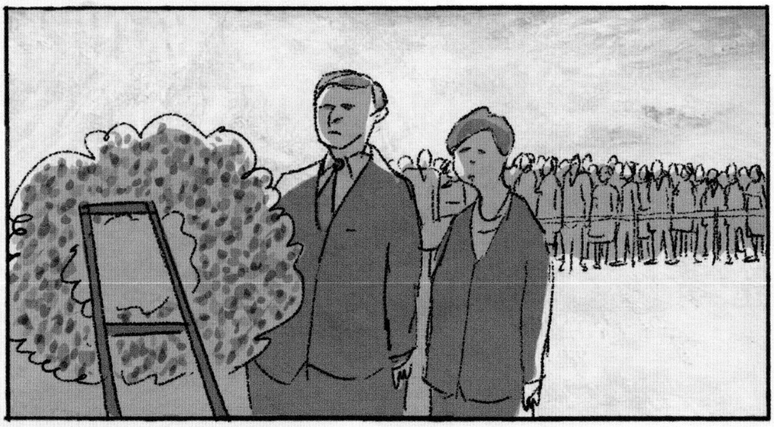

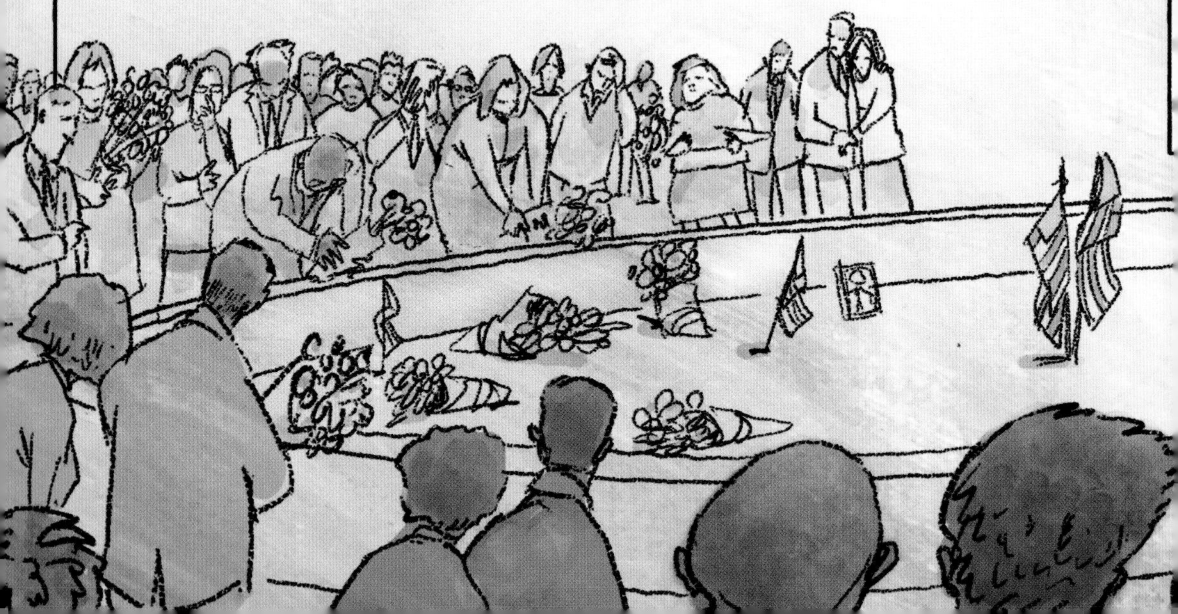

At 8:46 a.m., the moment the first jet had struck the North Tower, silence is called for. Then the names of the victims are read, pausing only for the ringing of bells at 9:03 a.m., the moment the South Tower was struck, and at 9:59 a.m. and 10:28 a.m., when the South and then the North Towers fell.

One by one, the names of 2,726 people—fathers, mothers, brothers, sisters, husbands, wives, children, relatives, friends, colleagues, and lovers—are read and carried away on the breeze.

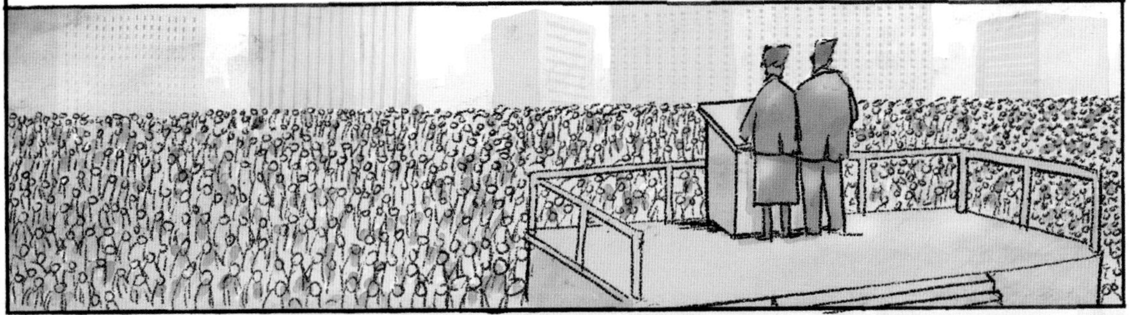

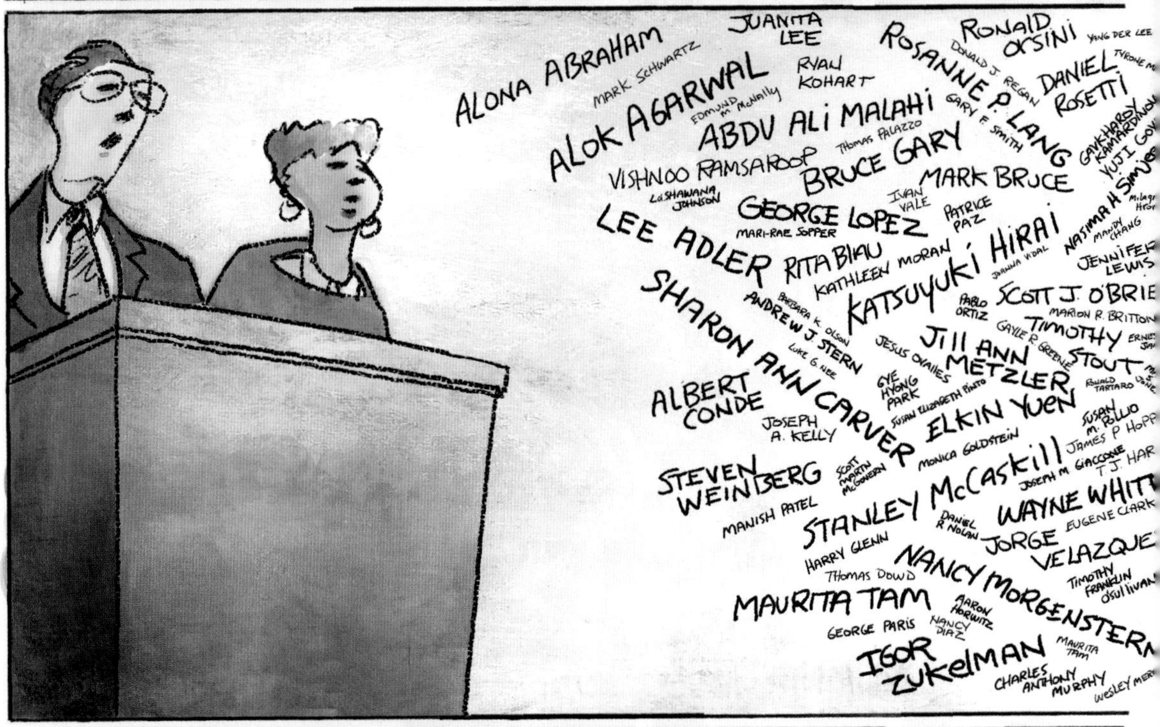

ALONA ABRAHAM
JUANITA LEE
ROSANNE P. LANG
RONALD ORSINI
YANG DER LEE
MARK SCHWARTZ
RYAN KOHART
DONALD J. REGAN
DANIEL ROSETTI
ALOK AGARWAL
EDMUND M. McNally
ABDU ALI MALAHI
GARY F. SMITH
Thomas PALAZZO
BRUCE GARY
VISHNOO RAMSAROOP
MARK BRUCE
LASHAWANA JOHNSON
IVAN VALE
GEORGE LOPEZ
PATRICE PAZ
MARI-RAE SOPPER
LEE ADLER
RITA BLAU
KATHLEEN MORAN
KATSUYUKI HIRAI
JOANNA VIDAL
MANDY CHANG
JENNIFER LEWIS
SHARON ANN CARVER
BARBARA K. OLSON
ANDREW J. STERN
PABLO ORTIZ
MARION R. BRITTON
TIMOTHY STOUT
GAYLE R. GREENE
JESUS OVALLES
JILL ANN METZLER
LUKE G. NEE
GYE HYONG PARK
SUSAN ELIZABETH PINTO
RONALD TARTARO
ALBERT CONDE
ELKIN YUEN
SUSAN M. POLLIO
JOSEPH A. KELLY
MONICA GOLDSTEIN
STANLEY McCASKILL
JOSEPH M GIACCONE
STEVEN WEINBERG
SCOTT MARTIN McGOVERN
MANISH PATEL
DANIEL R NOLAN
EUGENE CLARK
JORGE
HARRY GLENN
THOMAS DOWD
TIMOTHY FRANKLIN O'SULLIVAN
MAURITA TAM
AARON HORWITZ
GEORGE PARIS
NANCY DIAZ
IGOR ZUKELMAN
CHARLES ANTHONY MURPHY

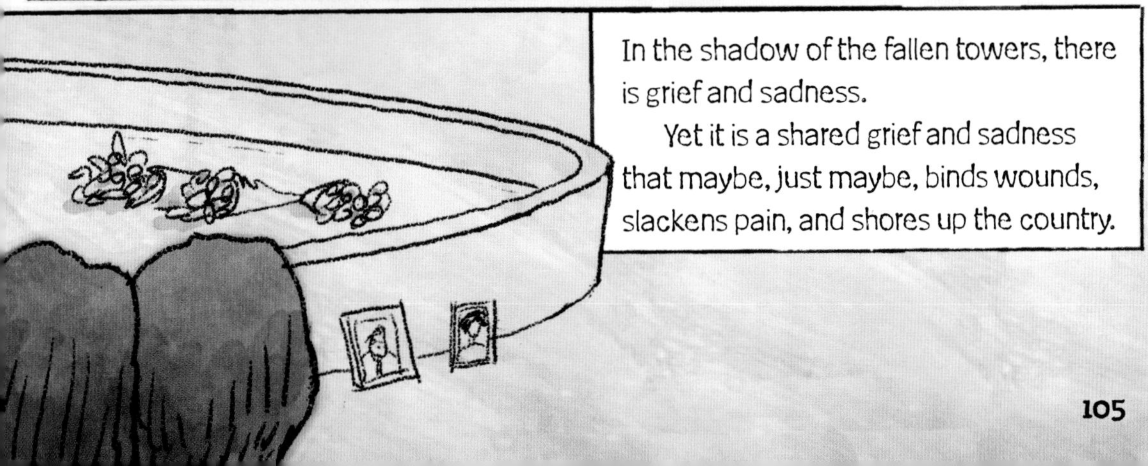

In the shadow of the fallen towers, there is grief and sadness.

Yet it is a shared grief and sadness that maybe, just maybe, binds wounds, slackens pain, and shores up the country.

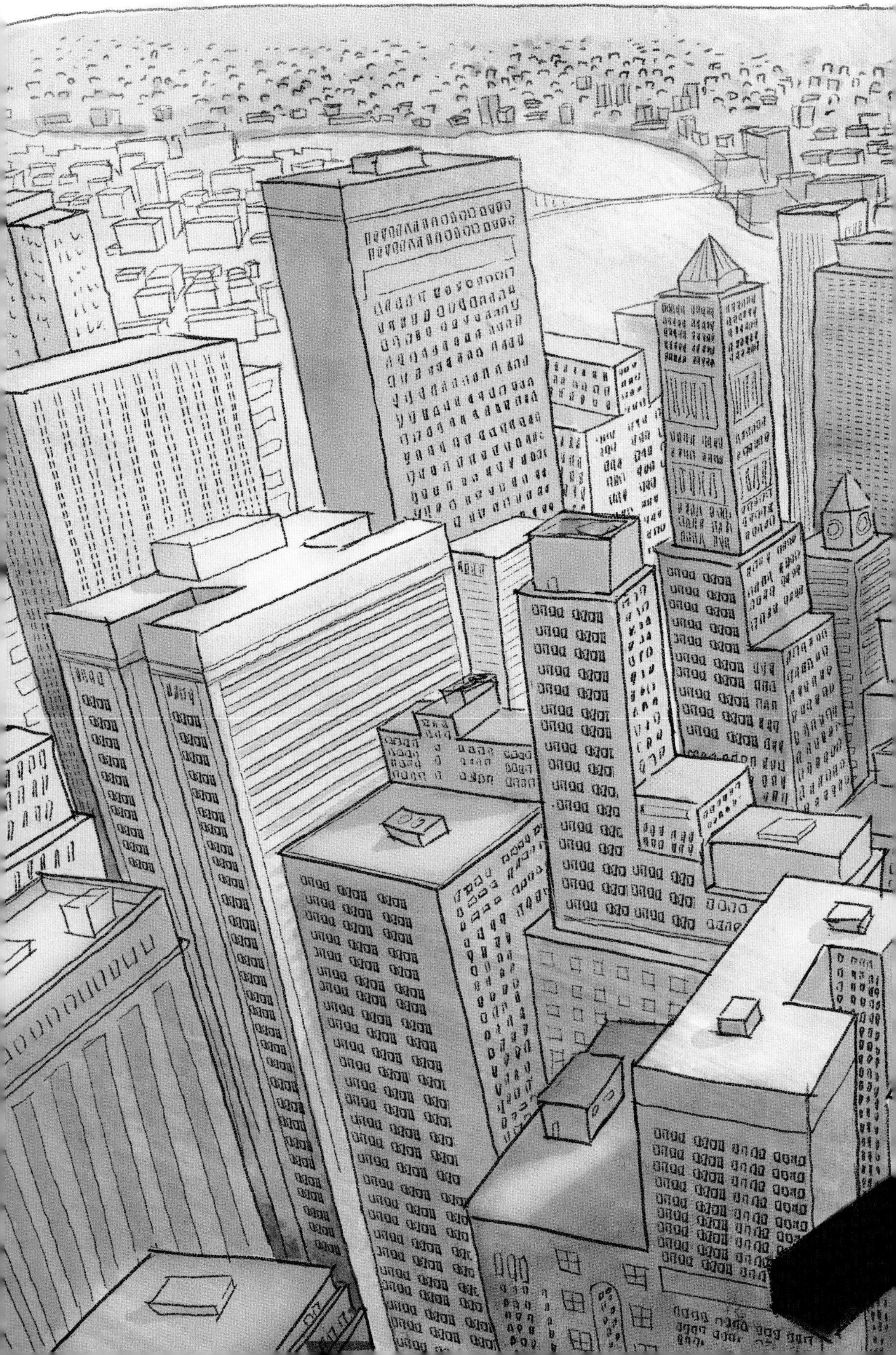

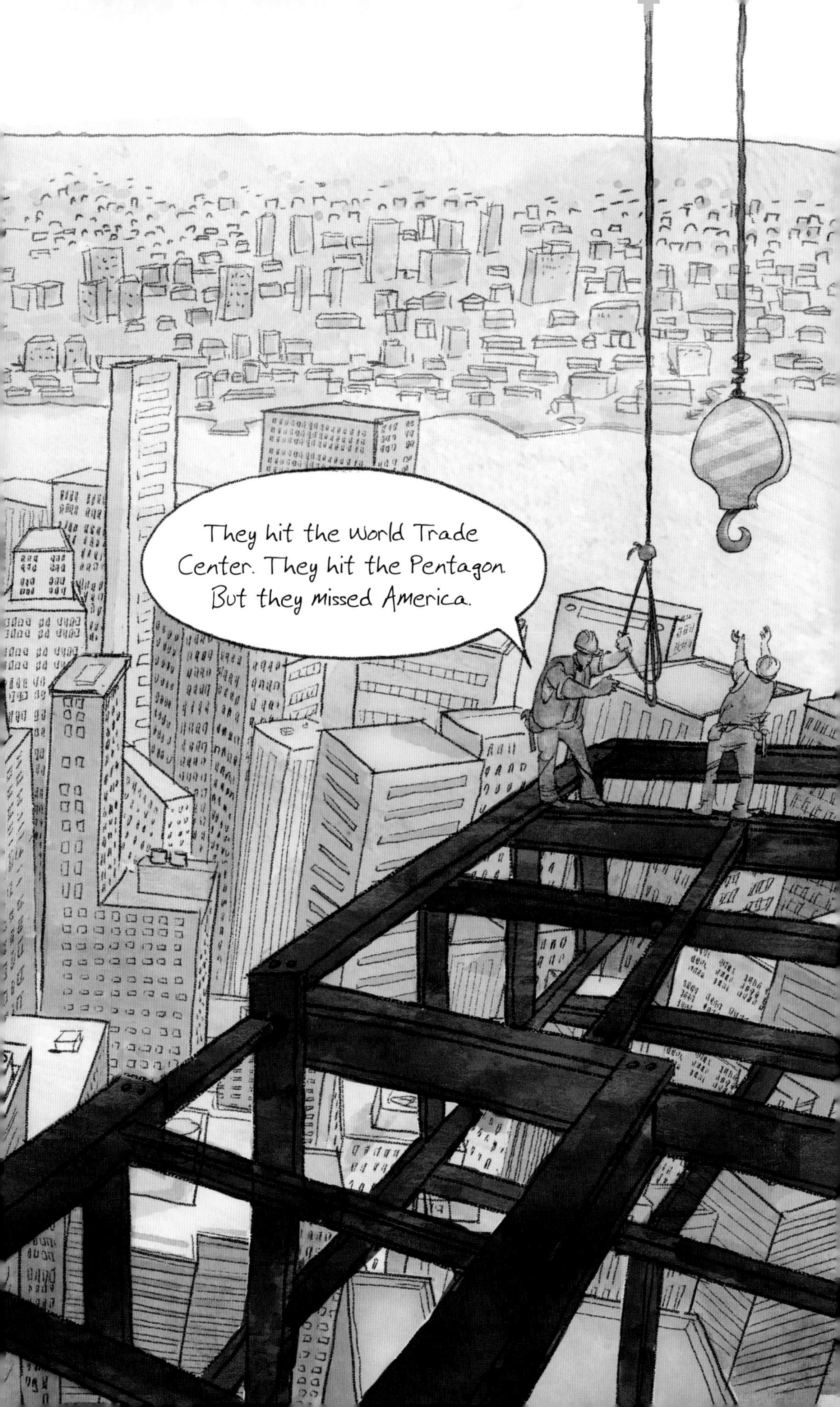
They hit the World Trade Center. They hit the Pentagon. But they missed America.

AFTERWORD

The war in Afghanistan becomes America's longest war. Scores of countries join America. Many suffer casualties, including the U.K., France, Germany, Australia, Canada, Poland, Denmark, the Netherlands, Georgia, Romania, Italy, and Spain. Stubborn Taliban resistance brings the United States to the negotiating table. But as of early 2021, the fighting goes on; American soldiers still die: about twenty-four hundred to date. The financial cost of the war will be in the trillions.

While fighting the Taliban in Afghanistan, President George Bush launches a war against Iraq in March 2003. He suggests Iraq has weapons of mass destruction and had contact with the 9/11 terrorists. No evidence has proven either claim correct. As of early 2021, American troops remain in Iraq.

As of early 2021, the military prison in the Guantánamo Bay detention camp houses forty prisoners deemed by the U.S. government as too dangerous to be released. Among them is Abu Zubaydah. Since his "enhanced interrogation," the American government has admitted that he had no connection to the September 11 attacks or played any part in al-Qaeda's terrorism.

Jules Naudet survived September 11, as did his brother and partner filmmaker, Gédéon, also on the scene of the twin towers' collapse. Their combined video of the unfolding tragedy is raw, chilling, and distressingly honest, a haunting, heartbreaking memorialization.

As of early 2021, the average age of a New York City 9/11 first responder is roughly fifty-six years old, putting them close to or at retirement. Chief Joe Pfeifer—one of the sixteen people who miraculously survived the collapse of the North Tower—retired in 2018. He was the first chief through the doors at the World Trade Center on September 11 and the last 9/11 chief to retire. His firefighter brother, Lieutenant Kevin Pfeifer, did not survive the collapse of the towers.

About twenty thousand first responders at the World Trade Center have been sickened from their exposure to toxic materials. Two thousand have died. It is only a matter of time before the number of people killed from the aftermath of the attack will exceed the number who died in the attack itself.

After the attack, the September 11th Victim Compensation Fund was established by the government to help victims of the September 11 attacks and their families. The fund awarded about $7 billion to 5,560 claimants. It closed in 2003 but reopened in 2011 to address the health issues incurred by first responders at the toxic crash site. About $5 billion has been paid out.

Assaults against Muslims in America spiked after the 9/11 attack, then dropped off, but they remain at levels higher than before 2001. The number of anti-Muslim hate crimes began to rise and in 2016 exceeded those in 2001.

On May 2, 2011, President Barack Obama ordered a raid into Pakistan, where Navy SEALs, elite fighters, surprised and killed Osama bin Laden.

On November 3, 2014, One World Trade Center opened near the site of the former twin towers. The building and observation deck are 1,368 feet tall, the height of the former North Tower.

STATISTICS

The Office of the Chief Medical Examiner of the City of New York recorded death certificates for the victims of the World Trade Center attack as homicides. Death certificates for the ten terrorists on the two airplanes have not been issued; these deaths might be classified as suicides.

As of August 16, 2002, a total of 2,726* death certificates related to the World Trade Center attacks have been filed. All but thirteen persons died on September 11.

Of the 2,726:

- Remains for roughly half have never been found.

- 2,103 (77 percent) were males.

- 623 (23 percent) were females.

- The median age for these decedents was thirty-nine years (range: two to eighty-five years); the median age was thirty-eight years for females (range: two to eighty-one years) and thirty-nine years for males (range: three to eighty-five years).

- 3 persons were younger than five years old, and 3 were over eighty years old.

- 1,659 (61 percent) were non-Hispanic white males.

- 407 (15 percent) were non-Hispanic white females.

- 177 (6 percent) were Hispanic males.

- 81 (3 percent) were Hispanic females.

- 136 (5 percent) were non-Hispanic black males.

- 79 (3 percent) were non-Hispanic black females.

- 122 (4 percent) were Asian/Pacific Islander (API) males.

- 54 (2 percent) were API females.

- 2,158 (79 percent) were born in the fifty U.S. states, compared with 59 percent of the NYC population.

- 568 (21 percent) were born outside the fifty states, including the United Kingdom (56), India (36), Puerto Rico (34), the Dominican Republic (26), and Japan (25).

- 1,169 (43 percent) were residents of New York City.

- 593 (22 percent) were residents elsewhere in New York State.

- 674 (25 percent) were residents of New Jersey.

- 27 (1 percent) were residents of foreign countries.

- A total of 90 decedents were residents of Massachusetts, the origin of the two airplanes that struck the World Trade Center, and 29 were residents of California, the destination of the flights.

- 343 firefighters and paramedics, 23 New York City police officers, and 37 Port Authority officers died.

At the Pentagon, 189 people were killed, including 64 on American Airlines Flight 77, the airliner that struck the building.

Forty-four people died when United Airlines Flight 93 crashed in Shanksville, Pennsylvania.

*"The findings in this report are subject to at least two limitations. First, the data are preliminary because some families have not yet requested death certificates, and investigations into certain requests for certificates are ongoing. Second, demographic information was collected from family members through special affidavits; this information is being revised as corrections are made by family members."
— *The New York City Department of Health and Mental Hygiene Report,* NYC Department of Health and Mental Hygiene

SOURCE NOTES

6 *"I didn't even have time to think"*: Friends, "Bond of Brothers."

8 *"Anyone out there?"*: Halasy, "The Earth Fell," 17.

11 *"It was coming in"*: Leung, "Last Man Out."

13 *"Don't breathe the air"*: Kleinfield, "U.S. Attacked," A1.

14 *"Oh my God"*: Ibid.

   "Any company on the scene": Hagen, *Women at Ground Zero*, 16.

17 *"I'm trapped and hurt bad"*: Fishman, "The Miracle Survivors."

   "We couldn't go down": World Trade Center Task Force Interview (WTCTFI): McGlynn.

   "Tell my wife and kids": Fishman, "The Miracle Survivors."

   "We're in the North Tower": WTCTFI: McGlynn, 23–24.

   "Where is the North Tower?": Ibid.

   "What do you mean": Ibid.

18 *"Guys, I see sunshine"*: Jonas, "Ladder 6."

19 *"It was just mind-boggling"*: WTCTFI: McGlynn.

20 *"We're all going to walk"*: WTCTFI: Cachia.

21 *"We did that for some time"*: Ibid.

25 *"Out of nowhere"*: Eyepop Productions, *Boatlift*.

   "It's extraordinarily unsettling": Barry, "A Day of Terror," A9.

27 *"I remember several guys"*: WTCTFI: Cachia.

30 *"I just opened my eyes"*: Joseph, "'The Birth of My Daughter.'"

31 *"Help!"*: Fishman, "The Miracle Survivors."

   "We have a civilian": Ibid.

   "He looked like he was in a castle": Joseph, "'The Birth of My Daughter.'"

32 *"There were dead and gravely"*: Lone Wolf Documentary Group, *9/11 Inside the Pentagon*.

34 *"You could not see your hand"*: Ibid.

35 *"We started kicking"*: Ibid.

37 *"These were plumbers"*: Ibid.

38 *"Evacuate five hundred yards"*: Ibid.

42 *"[Air Force One] took off like a rocket"*: Graff, "We're the Only Plane."

   "[The pilot] stood that thing on its tail": Ibid.

43 *"He fought with us tooth and nail"*: Ibid.

   "Who did this?": Ibid.

46 *"It was like casserole city"*: Lackey, "An Oasis of Kindness."

   "We ran out of underwear": Schulman, "Stuck in Gander."

47 *"It was like the apocalypse"*: Derrig, interview.

51 *"If you can hear us"*: Liss, "An Unlikely Hero."

   "I think I hear something": Ibid.

52 *"We're over here!"*: Ibid.

54 *"[One of] two things are gonna happen"*: Dwyer, "A Nation Challenged: Objects; Beneath the Rubble."

   "I decided my life was not worth": Ibid.

56 *"[My injuries were] so severe"*: Leung, "Last Man Out."

57 *"I've got you"*: Langewieche, *American Ground*, 106.

58 *"It's like pickup sticks"*: Ibid.

60 *"You keep hitting it"*: Ibid.

62 *"A true search-and-rescue dog"*: Ibid.

63 *"Some of our customers worked"*: Allen, "Clock Ticking for Stranded Pets," 25.

65 *"Lloro y lloro y lloro"*: Waldman, "After the Attacks: The Memorials."

66 *"I can't hear you"*: Walsh, "George W. Bush's 'Bullhorn' Moment."

"I can hear you": Ibid.

71 *"I feel like after that day"*: Desmond-Harris, "9 Devastating, Revealing Stories."

"I'll kill you!": Crowley, "Muslim Mom Chased," 22.

"The face of terror": Bush, "Islam Is Peace."

72–73 *"Americans are asking"*: "Presidential Address: Bush Issues Ultimatum to Taliban."

78 *"[The team should] exert all efforts"*: Stanton, *Horse Soldiers*, 37–38.

79 *". . . flying when you can't see"*: Collins, "First to Go."

80 *"Here's how you make this thing go"*: Stanton, *Horse Soldiers*, 125.

"Now, if your horse runs off": Ibid.

81 *"It was like riding a bobcat"*: Quade, "Monument Honors U.S. 'Horse Soldiers.'"

"You look down": Ibid.

84 *"It represents the person"*: Langewieche, *American Ground*, 13.

88 *"There was a pervasive sadness"*: History Channel, "Volunteers."

89 *"The city may be ready"*: Langewieche, *American Ground*, 150.

91 *"Excavation, remains, recovery"*: Ibid.

93 *"These are very, very dangerous"*: CNN, "Shackled Detainees Arrive."

97 *"This is one of the bigger fish"*: Washington Post and Associated Press, "Anti-Terror Raids Yield Bonanza."

"Reports to that effect are wrong": Stout, "Rumsfeld Says Captured Qaeda Leader Won't Be Tortured."

102 *"If you're going to put buildings"*: Wyatt, "At Hearing, a Resolve to Rebuild," 33.

103 *"I am a bit surprised"*: Gordon, "A Nation Challenged: The Strategy."

107 *"They hit the World Trade Center"*: Leduff, "After the Attacks: The Disposal," A1.

BIBLIOGRAPHY

Abed, Fahim. "2 U.S. Soldiers Killed in Fierce Firefight in Afghanistan." *New York Times,* June 26, 2019. (www.nytimes.com/2019/06/26/world/asia/afghanistan-american-soldiers-killed.html; accessed June 26, 2019)

Ackman, Dan. "Larry Silverstein's $3.5B Definition." *Forbes,* July 23, 2003. (www.forbes.com/2003/07/23/cx_da_0723topnews.html#6f0e72237675; accessed February 14, 2019)

Allen, Angela C., and Kirsten Danis. "Clock Ticking for Stranded Pets." *New York Post,* September 15, 2001. (link.galegroup.com/apps/doc/A78337213/SPN.SP02?u=mklopacplus&sid=SPN.SP02&xid=0e1b44ee; accessed February 6, 2019)

Barry, Dan. "A Day of Terror: Hospitals; Pictures of Medical Readiness, Waiting and Hoping for Survivors to Fill Their Wards." *New York Times,* September 12, 2001. (www.nytimes.com/2001/09/12/us/day-terror-hospitals-pictures-medical-readiness-waiting-hoping-for-survivors.html; accessed February 6, 2019)

BBC News. "Bring Me the Head of bin Laden" May 4, 2005. (news.bbc.co.uk/2/hi/americas/4511943.stm; accessed February 5, 2019)

Britzky, Haley. "Afghanistan Is by Far America's Longest War."*Axios,* October 8, 2018. (www.axios.com/longest-us-wars-afghanistan-iraq-vietnam-da95c63d-6cec-4708-930c-632f931aaf8b.html; accessed June 26, 2019)

Burns, John F. "A Nation Challenged: The Fugitives; In Pakistan's Interior, a Troubling Victory in Hunt for Al Qaeda." *New York Times,* April 14, 2002. (www.nytimes.com/2002/04/14/world/nation-challenged-fugitives-pakistan-s-interior-troubling-victory-hunt-for-al.html; accessed February 7, 2019)

Bush, President George W. "Islam Is Peace, Says President." The White House Archives. September 17, 2001. (georgewbush-whitehouse.archives.gov/news/releases/2001/09/20010917-11.html; accessed October 19, 2019)

Bybee, Jay S. "Memorandum for John Rizzo, Acting General Counsel of the Central Intelligence Agency." Office of the Assistant Attorney General, Justice Department, United States of America. August, 1, 2002. (www.justice.gov/sites/default/files/olc/legacy/2010/08/05/memo-bybee2002.pdf; accessed February 7, 2019)

Carter, Bill, and Felicity Barringer. "A Nation Challenged: The Coverage; Networks Agree to U.S. Request to Edit Future bin Laden Tapes." *New York Times,* October 11, 2001. (www.nytimes.com/2001/10/11/us/nation-challenged-coverage-networks-agree-us-request-edit-future-bin-laden-tapes.html; accessed January 30, 2019)

Case of Al Nashiri v. Romania. European Court of Human Rights. Strasbourg, May 31, 2018. (hudoc.echr.coe.int/eng#_Toc515297759; accessed February 7, 2019)

CBS News. "McCain: Japanese Hanged for Waterboarding." November 29, 2007. (www.cbsnews.com/news/mccain-japanese-hanged-for-waterboarding; accessed June 28, 2019)

Centers for Disease Control and Prevention. "Deaths in World Trade Center Terrorist Attacks—New York City, 2001." *Morbidity and Mortality Weekly Report,* September 11, 2002. (www.cdc.gov/mmwr/preview/mmwrhtml/mm51SPa6.htm; accessed June 10, 2019)

CNN. "Bush Delivers Ultimatum." September 21, 2001. (edition.cnn.com/2001/WORLD/asiapcf/central/09/20/ret.afghan.bush; accessed May 9, 2019)

———. "Ceremony Closes 'Ground Zero' Cleanup." May 30, 2002. (edition.cnn.com/2002/US/05/30/rec.wtc.cleanup; accessed May 9, 2019)

———. "CIA Torture Report Fast Facts." September 26, 2019. (www.cnn.com/2015/01/29/us/cia-torture-report-fast-facts/index.html; accessed February 11, 2019)

———. "Death of Osama bin Laden Fast Facts." CNN Library. April 18, 2019. (www.cnn.com/2013/09/09/world/death-of-osama-bin-laden-fast-facts/index.html; accessed June 26, 2019)

———. "Hate Crimes Reports Up in Wake of Terrorist Attacks." September 17, 2001. (web.archive.org/web/20100620204632/archives.cnn.com/2001/US/09/16/gen.hate.crimes; accessed February 5, 2019)

———. "New York Marks Anniversary of Tragedy: Painful Memories Linger as Families, Officials Honor Victims." September 11, 2002. (edition.cnn.com/2002/US/09/11/ar911.memorial.newyork/index.html; accessed August 5, 2019)

———. "One World Trade Center Fast Facts." July 24, 2018. (www.cnn.com/2013/11/22/us/one-world-trade-center-fast-facts/index.html; accessed June 26, 2019)

———. "September 11th Victim Aid and Compensation Fast Facts." June 12, 2019. (www.cnn.com/2013/07/27/us/september-11th-victim-aid-and-compensation-fast-facts/index.html; accessed June 27, 2019)

———. "Shackled Detainees Arrive in Guantanamo." January 11, 2002. (edition.cnn.com/2002/WORLD/asiapcf/central/01/11/ret.detainee.transfer/index.html; accessed May 14, 2019)

———. "Taliban Fast Facts." January 31, 2019. (www.cnn.com/2013/09/20/world/taliban-fast-facts/index.html; accessed February 14, 2019)

Collins, Elizabeth M. "First to Go: Green Berets Remember Earliest Mission in Afghanistan." U.S. Army. January 30, 2017. (www.army.mil/article/181582/first_to_go_green_berets_remember_earliest_mission_in_afghanistan; accessed February 1, 2019)

Council on Foreign Relations. "The U.S. War in Afghanistan." (www.cfr.org/timeline/us-war-afghanistan; accessed May 10, 2019)

Cowell, Alan, and Charlie Savage. "Lithuania and Romania Complicit in C.I.A. Prisons, European Court Says." *New York Times,* May 18, 2018. (www.nytimes.com/2018/05/31/world/europe/lithuania-romania-cia-torture.html; accessed February 7, 2019)

Cronin, Ann. "After the Attacks: The Voices; A Black Cloud. A Shower of Glass. A Glimpse of Hell."

New York Times, September 16, 2001. (www.nytimes.com/2001/09/16/us/after-attacks-voices-black-cloud-shower-glass-glimpse-hell-run.html; accessed February 6, 2019)

Crowley, Kieran. "Muslim Mom Chased; Cops: L.I. Man Aimed Car at Her." *New York Post,* September 14, 2001. (link.galegroup.com/apps/doc/A78260308/SPN.SP02?u=mklopacplus&sid=SPN.SP02&xid=f9c0d855; accessed February 6, 2019)

Cutler, Nancy. "Deaths from 9/11 Diseases Will Soon Outnumber Those Lost on That Fateful Day." *Rockland/Westchester Journal News,* September 6, 2018 (www.lohud.com/story/opinion/perspective/2018/09/06/deaths-9-11-aftermath-soon-outpace-number-killed-sept-11/1137572002; accessed May 13, 2019)

Derrig, Rob. New York City Fire Department. Interview, June 11, 2019.

Desmond-Harris, Jenee. "9 Devastating, Revealing Stories of Being Muslim in Post-9/11 America." Vox.com. September 11, 2016. (www.vox.com/2016/9/11/12868452/muslim-americans-islamophobia-9-11; accessed May 10, 2019)

Duke, Lynne. "The Hidden Hero of 9/11." *Washington Post,* August 11, 2003. (www.washingtonpost.com/archive/lifestyle/2003/08/11/the-hidden-hero-of-911/e98f74c6-26c5-4cef-9b0f-d543dcb2a6db/?utm_term=.65cb415489fa; accessed Februrary 11, 2019)

Dwyer, Jim. "The Last 9/11 Fire Chief Bows Out." *New York Times,* July 10, 2018. (www.nytimes.com/2018/07/10/nyregion/joseph-pfeifer-fire-chief-retires.html; accessed June 26, 2019)

———. "A Nation Challenged: Objects; Beneath the Rubble, the Only Tool Was a Pair of Cuffs." *New York Times,* October 30, 2001. (www.nytimes.com/2001/10/30/nyregion/a-nation-challenged-objects-beneath-the-rubble-the-only-tool-was-a-pair-of-cuffs.html; accessed July 4, 2019)

———. "A Nation Challenged: Objects; Medic, Out of the Rubble, Finds an Identity Restored." *New York Times,* November 6, 2001. (www.nytimes.com/2001/11/06/nyregion/a-nation-challenged-objects-medic-out-of-the-rubble-finds-an-identity-restored.html; accessed February 5, 2019)

———. "Real World Doesn't Give Even an Inch in Real Estate." *New York Times,* April 23, 2008. (www.nytimes.com/2008/04/23/nyregion/23about.html?rref=collection/byline/jim-dwyer&action=click&contentCollection=undefined&region=stream&module=stream_unit&version=search&contentPlacement=1&pgtype=collection; accessed June 26, 2019)

Eyepop Productions. *Boatlift, An Untold Tale of 9/11 Resilience.* (www.youtube.com/watch?v=MDOrzF7B2Kg; accessed March 19, 2020)

Fishman, Steve. "The Miracle Survivors." *New York Magazine,* September 11, 2003. (nymag.com/nymetro/news/sept11/2003/n_9189; accessed February 12, 2019)

Friends, David. "Bond of Brothers." *Vanity Fair,* March 2002. (archive.vanityfair.com/article/2002/3/bond-of-brothers; accessed July 1, 2019)

Goldberg, Jonah. "Canines to the Rescue." *National Review,* November 12, 2001. (www.nationalreview.com/2001/11/canines-rescue-jonah-goldberg; accessed May 10, 2019)

Goldstein, Laurie. "A Day of Terror: The Ties; In U.S., Echoes of Rift of Muslims and Jews." *New York*

Times, September 12, 2001. (www.nytimes.com/2001/09/12/us/a-day-of-terror-the-ties-in-us-echoes-of-rift-of-muslims-and-jews.html; accessed February 6, 2019)

Goodman, Dr. Barry. Interview, June 29, 2019.

Gordon, Michael R. "A Nation Challenged: The Bombing; U.S. Bombs Taliban's Forces on Front Lines Near Kabul; Powell Sees Rebel Advance." *New York Times,* October 22, 2001. (www.nytimes.com/2001/10/22/world/nation-challenged-bombing-us-bombs-taliban-s-forces-front-lines-near-kabul.html; accessed February 4, 2019)

———. "A Nation Challenged: The Strategy; Allies Preparing for a Long Fight as Taliban Digs In." *New York Times,* October 28, 2001. (www.nytimes.com/2001/10/28/world/nation-challenged-strategy-allies-preparing-for-long-fight-taliban-dig.html; accessed February 4, 2019)

Graff, Garret M. "We're the Only Plane in the Sky." *Politico Magazine,* September 9, 2016. (www.politico.com/magazine/story/2016/09/were-the-only-plane-in-the-sky-214230; accessed February 12, 2019)

Guardian. "US Detains Children at Guantanamo Bay." April 23, 2003. (www.theguardian.com/world/2003/apr/23/usa; accessed June 10, 2019)

Guttman, Ed. Interview, September 19, 2019.

Haberman, Clyde. "An Overview: October 7, 2001; A Mission Begun, a Defiant bin Laden and Another Crisp, Clear Day." *New York Times,* October 8, 2001. (www.nytimes.com/2001/10/08/world/overview-oct-7-2001-mission-begun-defiant-bin-laden-another-crisp-clear-day.html; accessed January 30, 2019)

Hagen, Susan, and Mary Carouba. *Women at Ground Zero.* Indianapolis: Alpha Books, 2002.

Halasy, Don. "The Earth Fell on Top of Me: Post Fotog Tells of His Near-Death." *New York Post,* September 12, 2001. (link.galegroup.com/apps/doc/A78171111/STND?u=mklopacplus&sid=STND&xid=f08dced4; accessed February 6, 2019)

Hassan, Sharif, and William Branigin. "Two U.S. Service Members Killed in Afghanistan, Military Says." *Washington Post,* June 26, 2019. (www.washingtonpost.com/world/asia_pacific/two-us-service-members-killed-in-afghanistan-military-says/2019/06/26/8da23f82-97f9-11e9-830a-21b9b36b64ad_story.html?utm_term=.6dbb35e8d1ec; accessed June 27, 2019)

History Channel. "Cleanup and Recovery." (www.history.com/topics/21st-century/cleanup-and-recovery-video; accessed February 5, 2019)

———. "Volunteers." (www.history.com/topics/21st-century/volunteers-video; accessed February 5, 2019)

Italiano, Laura, and Kate Sheehy. "They Dig with Their Fingers." *New York Post,* September 14, 2001. (link.galegroup.com/apps/doc/A78260361/SPN.SP02?u=mklopacplus&sid=SPN.SP02&xid=b46c3ba2; accessed February 6, 2019)

Jehl, Douglas. "A Nation Challenged: The Navy; Tension and Secrecy on Warships as the Jets and

Missiles Roar Off." *New York Times,* October 8, 2001. (www.nytimes.com/2001/10/08/world/nation-challenged-navy-tension-secrecy-warships-jets-missiles-roar-off.html; accessed February 1, 2019)

Jonas, John A. "Ladder 6: Rescue of the Rescuers." *Fire Engineering,* September 1, 2002. (www.fireengineering.com/articles/print/volume-155/issue-9/world-trade-center-disaster/volume-i-initial-response/ladder-6-rescue-of-the-rescuers.html; accessed July 9, 2019)

Jones, Ilaina. "WTC Developer Silverstein Soldiers On Post-Sept 11." Reuters, September 9, 2011. (www.reuters.com/article/us-sept11-people-silverstein/wtc-developer-silverstein-soldiers-on-post-sept-11-idUSTRE78876020110909; accessed February 14, 2019)

Joseph, Claudia. "'The Birth of My Daughter Allowed Me to Lose My Feelings of Guilt': Man Who Survived 9/11 by 'Surfing' Collapsing Tower Reveals How His Children Have Helped Him Rebuild His Life." *Daily Mail,* September 5, 2012. (www.dailymail.co.uk/news/article-2198838/9-11-Survivors-Pasquale-Buzzelli-survived-surfing-wave-falling-debris-speaks-miracle.html; accessed May 8, 2019)

Katersky, Aaron. "The 9/11 Toll Still Grows: More Than 16,000 Ground Zero Responders Who Got Sick Found Eligible for Awards." ABC News, September 10, 2018. (abcnews.go.com/US/911-toll-growsl-16000-ground-responders-sick-found/story?id=57669657; accessed June 25, 2019)

Kessler, Glen. "Was Khalid Sheikh Mohammed 'Waterboarded' 183 Times?" *Washington Post,* February 6, 2017. (www.washingtonpost.com/news/fact-checker/wp/2017/02/06/was-khalid-sheikh-mohammed-waterboarded-183-times/?utm_term=.f06fe1f9960e; accessed February 7, 2019)

Kifner, John, and Susan Saulny. "After the Attacks: The Families; Posting Handbills as Votive Offerings, in Hope of Finding Missing Loved Ones." *New York Times,* September 14, 2001. (www.nytimes.com/2001/09/14/us/after-attacks-families-posting-handbills-votive-offerings-hope-finding-missing.html; accessed February 5, 2019)

Kishi, Katayoun. "Assaults Against Muslims in U.S. Surpass 2001 Level." Pew Research Center, November 15, 2017. (www.pewresearch.org/fact-tank/2017/11/15/assaults-against-muslims-in-u-s-surpass-2001-level; accessed June 28, 2019)

Kleinfield, N.R. "A Nation Challenged: The Scent; 20 Days Later, an Invisible Reminder Lingers." *New York Times,* October 20, 2001. (www.nytimes.com/2001/10/01/nyregion/a-nation-challenged-the-scent-20-days-later-an-invisible-reminder-lingers.html; accessed January 31, 2019)

————. "U.S. Attacked; Hijacked Jets Destroy Twin Towers and Hit Pentagon in Day of Terror." *New York Times,* September 12, 2001. (www.nytimes.com/2001/09/12/us/us-attacked-hijacked-jets-destroy-twin-towers-and-hit-pentagon-in-day-of-terror.html; accessed February 6, 2019)

Lackey, Katherine. "An Oasis of Kindness on 9/11: This Town Welcomed 6,700 Strangers Amid Terror Attacks." *USA Today,* September 8, 2017. (www.usatoday.com/story/news/nation/2017/09/08/gander-newfoundland-september-11-terror-attacks-kindess-come-from-away/631329001; accessed February 6, 2019)

Langewieche, William. *American Ground: Unbuilding the World Trade Center.* New York: North Point Press, 2003.

Leduff. Charles. "After the Attacks: The Disposal; Hauling the Debris, and Darker Burdens." *New York Times,* September 17, 2001. (www.nytimes.com/2001/09/17/nyregion/after-the-attacks-the-disposal-hauling-the-debris-and-darker-burdens.html; accessed February 7, 2019)

Leung, Rebecca. "Last Man Out." *60 Minutes,* CBS News, November 23, 2004. (www.cbsnews.com/news/last-man-out; accessed May 8, 2019)

Lipton, Eric, and Andrew C. Revkin. "A Nation Challenged: The Firefighters; With Water and Sweat, Fighting the Most Stubborn Fire." *New York Times,* November 19, 2001. (www.nytimes.com/2001/11/19/nyregion/nation-challenged-firefighters-with-water-sweat-fighting-most-stubborn-fire.html; accessed February 4, 2019)

Liss, Rebecca. "Oliver Stone's World Trade Center Fiction." *Slate,* August 6, 2006. (slate.com/news-and-politics/2006/08/how-the-9-11-rescue-really-happened.html; accessed February 5, 2019)

———. "An Unlikely Hero." *Slate,* September 11, 2015. (slate.com/news-and-politics/2015/09/the-marine-who-found-two-wtc-survivors.html; accessed February 5, 2019)

Lone Wolf Documentary Group. *9/11 Inside the Pentagon.* PBS, September 6, 2016.

Margulies, Joseph. "The Innocence of Abu Zubaydah." *New York Review of Books,* September 28, 2018. (www.nybooks.com/daily/2018/09/28/the-innocence-of-abu-zubaydah; accessed June 26, 2019)

Montero, Douglas. "Ground Where Towers Stood Is Now Littered with Sadness." *New York Post,* September 12, 2001. (link.galegroup.com/apps/doc/A78171074/STND?u=mklopacplus&sid=STND&xid=43c830a0; accessed February 6, 2019)

Murphy, Dean. "A Day of Terror: The Hopes; Survivors Are Found in the Rubble." *New York Times,* September 12, 2001. (www.nytimes.com/2001/09/12/us/a-day-of-terror-the-hopes-survivors-are-found-in-the-rubble.html; accessed February 6, 2019)

National Geographic. "Inside 9/11." YouTube. (www.youtube.com/watch?v=z1gpJyFHETw; accessed February 12, 2019)

National Public Radio. "Jawbreaker: The Hunt for Bin Laden." *Morning Edition,* January 19, 2006. (www.npr.org/templates/story/story.php?storyId=5162925; accessed February 1, 2019)

Naudet, Jules and Gédéon. *9/11.* CBS, Goldfish Pictures, Reveille Productions, and Silverstar Productions, 2002. (www.youtube.com/watch?v=MJgoDYeP0J; accessed February 11, 2019)

New York Times. "The Guantánamo Docket." May 2, 2018. (www.nytimes.com/interactive/projects/guantanamo; accessed June 26, 2019)

O'Brian, Mike. "The Miraculous Escape of the 16 People Trapped in the North Tower's Stairwell B . . . And the Nightmare Years That Followed." *Daily Mail,* September 10, 2011. (www.dailymail.co.uk/news/article-2035963/9-11-Anniversary-Miraculous-escape-16-trapped-North-Towers-Stairwell-B.html; accessed May 7, 2019)

"Presidential Address: Bush Issues Ultimatum to Taliban, Calls Upon Nation and World to Unite and Destroy Terrorism." *CQ Almanac,* 2001. (library.cqpress.com/cqalmanac/document.php?id=cqal01-106-6369-328092; accessed May 9, 2019)

Quade, Alex. "Monument Honors U.S. 'Horse Soldiers' Who Invaded Afghanistan." CNN, October 6, 2011. (www.cnn.com/2011/10/06/us/afghanistan-horse-soldiers-memorial/index.html; accessed July 29, 2019)

"Reading of the Names at Ground Zero—September 11, 2002." YouTube. (www.youtube.com/watch?v=bkfes3vq9_c; accessed August 5, 2019)

Sahadi, Jeanne. "The Financial Cost of 16 Years in Afghanistan." CNN, August 22, 2017. (money.cnn.com/2017/08/21/news/economy/war-costs-afghanistan/index.html; accessed June 27, 2019)

Sanger, David E. "A Nation Challenged: The President; Bin Laden Is Wanted in Attacks, 'Dead or Alive,' President Says." *New York Times*, September 18, 2001. (www.nytimes.com/2001/09/18/us/nation-challenged-president-bin-laden-wanted-attacks-dead-alive-president-says.html; accessed February 7, 2019)

Schroen, Gary. *First In: An Insider's Account of How the CIA Spearheaded the War on Terror in Afghanistan.* New York: Ballantine Books, 2005.

Schulman, Michael. "Stuck in Gander, Newfoundland." *New Yorker*, March 27, 2017. (www.newyorker.com/magazine/2017/03/27/stuck-in-gander-newfoundland; accessed February 7, 2019)

Sengupta, Somini. "A Day of Terror: The Rivers; A Battered Retreat on Bridges to the East." *New York Times*, September 12, 2001. (www.nytimes.com/2001/09/12/us/a-day-of-terror-the-rivers-a-battered-retreat-on-bridges-to-the-east.html; accessed February 12, 2019)

Shane, Scott. "Abu Zubaydah, Tortured Guantánamo Detainee, Makes Case for Release." *New York Times*, August 23, 2016. (www.nytimes.com/2016/08/24/us/abu-zubaydah-torture-guantanamo-bay.html; accessed June 26, 2019)

Stanton, Doug. *Horse Soldiers: The Extraordinary Story of a Band of U.S. Soldiers Who Rode to Victory in Afghanistan.* New York: Simon & Schuster, 2005.

St. George, Donna, and Avram Goldstein. "Sleepless Nights, Shattered Psyches." *Washington Post*, September 23, 2001. (www.washingtonpost.com/archive/politics/2001/09/23/sleepless-nights-shattered-psyches/c1f75926-4c72-443a-a60a-051d61121e5e/?utm_term=.6db95571626a; accessed February 14, 2019)

Stockton, Dale. "Buried Alive: 10 Years Later." *Law Officer*, August 2, 2011. (lawofficer.com/911/buried-alive-10-years-later; accessed July 4, 2019)

Stout, David. "Rumsfeld Says Captured Qaeda Leader Won't Be Tortured." *New York Times*, April 3, 2002. (www.nytimes.com/2002/04/03/international/rumsfeld-says-captured-qaeda-leader-wont-be-tortured.html; accessed February 7, 2019)

Szabo, Julia. "Fast-Acting Workers Save Brave K9." *New York Post*, September 14, 2001. (link.galegroup.com/apps/doc/A78260360/SPN.SP02?u=mklopacplus&sid=SPN.SP02&xid=cf6da962; accessed February 6, 2019)

Taylor, Adam. "Do U.S. Troops Have a Future in Iraq?" *Washington Post*, February 7, 2019. (www.washingtonpost.com/world/2019/02/07/do-us-troops-have-a-future-iraq/?utm_term=.d95445666f18; accessed June 26, 2019)

Telegraph. "Bush Gives Taliban Ultimatum." September 21, 2001. (www.telegraph.co.uk/news/1341196/Bush-gives-Taliban-ultimatum.html; accessed May 9, 2019)

Tyler, Patrick. "A Nation Challenged: The Attack; U.S. and Britain Strike Afghanistan, Aiming at Bases and Terrorist Camps; Bush Warns 'Taliban Will Pay a Price,'" *New York Times,* October 8, 2001. (www.nytimes.com/2001/10/08/world/nation-challenged-attack-us-britain-strike-afghanistan-aiming-bases-terrorist.html; accessed February 1, 2019)

United States Department of Justice. "Justice Department 2002 Pages 3 and 4 Memos on CIA Interrogation Program." SCRIBD. Uploaded by Glenn Kessler, Washington Post. (www.scribd.com/document/338493938/Justice-Department-2002-Pages-3-and-4-Memos-on-CIA-Interrogation-Program; accessed February 7, 2019)

United States Senate. *Report of the Senate Select Committee on Intelligence: Committee Study of the Central Intelligence Agency's Detention and Interrogation Program.* December 9, 2014. (www.intelligence.senate.gov/sites/default/files/publications/CRPT-113srpt288.pdf; accessed May 14, 2019)

Van Natta, Don, and Lizette Alvarez. "A Day of Terror: Attack on Military; A Hijacked Boeing 757 Slams into the Pentagon, Halting the Government." *New York Times,* September 12, 2001. (www.nytimes.com/2001/09/12/us/day-terror-attack-military-hijacked-boeing-757-slams-into-pentagon-halting.html; accessed February 6, 2019)

Waldman, Amy. "After the Attacks: The Memorials; Grief Is Lessened by Sharing and Solace from Strangers." *New York Times,* September 14, 2001. (www.nytimes.com/2001/09/14/us/after-attacks-memorials-grief-lessened-sharing-solace-strangers.html; accessed February 5, 2019)

Walsh, Kenneth T. "George W. Bush's 'Bullhorn' Moment." *U.S. News & World Report,* April 25, 2013. (www.usnews.com/news/blogs/ken-walshs-washington/2013/04/25/george-w-bushs-bullhorn-moment; accessed February 14, 2019)

Washington Post and Associated Press. "Anti-Terror Raids Yield Bonanza for U.S. Intelligence." *Seattle Times,* April 3, 2002. (community.seattletimes.nwsource.com/archive/?date=20020403&slug=zub03; accessed February 7, 2019)

Wong, Edward. "Overview: The Iraq War." *New York Times,* February 15, 2008. (archive.nytimes.com/www.nytimes.com/ref/timestopics/topics_iraq.html?scp=8&sq=the%2525; accessed June 26, 2019)

World Trade Center Task Force Interview (WTCTFI): Firefighter Edward Cachia. *New York Times* Archive, December 6, 2001. (static01.nyt.com/packages/pdf/nyregion/20050812_WTC_GRAPHIC/9110251.PDF; accessed May 8, 2019)

World Trade Center Task Force Interview (WTCTFI): Lieutenant James McGlynn. *New York Times* Archive, January 2, 2002. (static01.nyt.com/packages/pdf/nyregion/20050812_WTC_GRAPHIC/9110447.PDF; accessed May 8, 2019)

"WTC Bathtub 9/11 Analyzed by Dr. Wood." YouTube. (www.youtube.com/watch?v=h_z6NBjaYCk; accessed February 11, 2019)

Wyatt, Edward. "At Hearing, a Resolve to Rebuild Twin Towers." *New York Times,* May 26, 2002.

Yuan, Jada. "Let's Roll." *New York Magazine,* August 27, 2011. (nymag.com/news/9-11/10th-anniversary/lets-roll; accessed February 14, 2019)

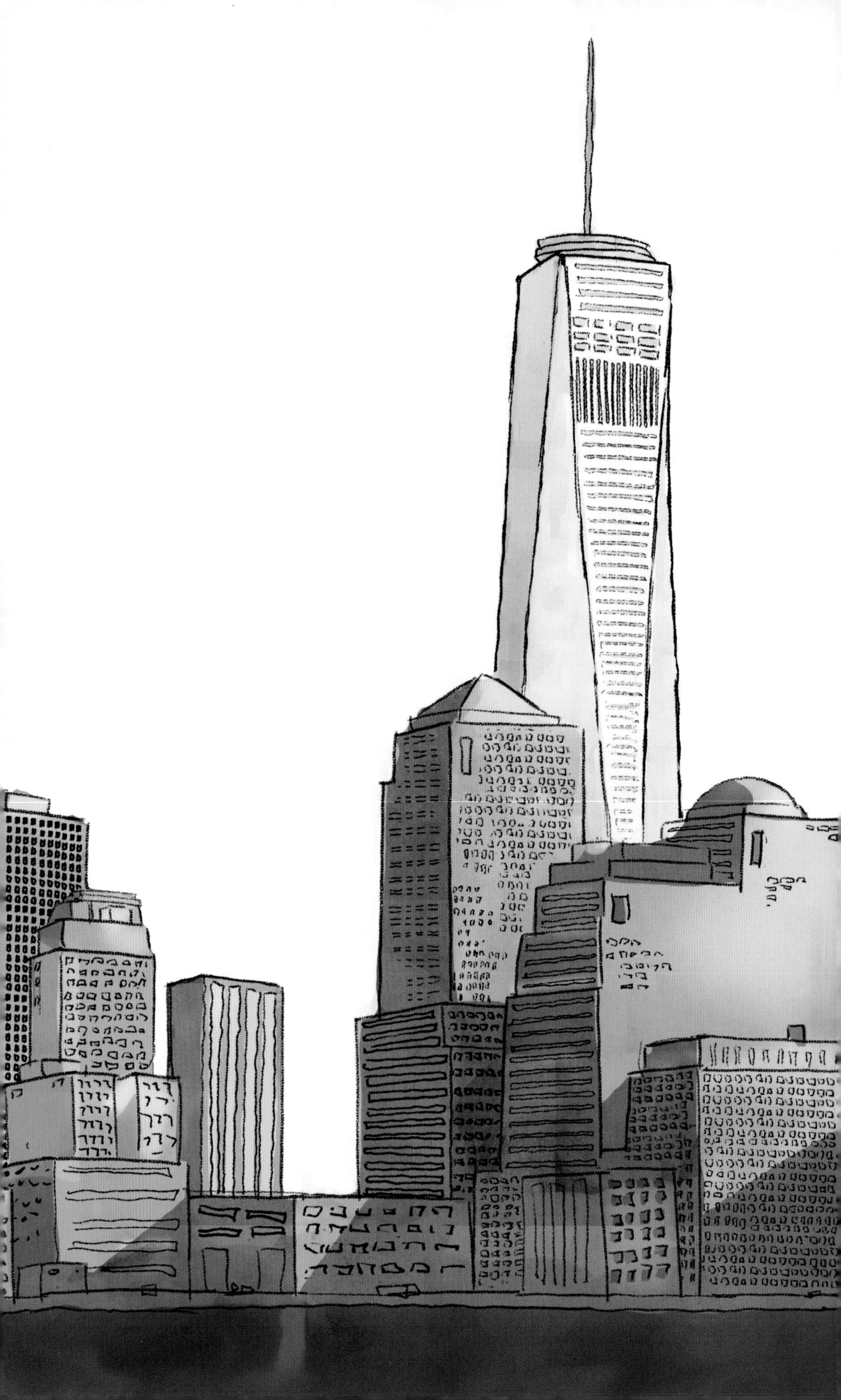